THE PURSUIT OF
PIZZA

TONY GEMIGNANI, LAURA MEYER, NICK BOGACZ & MIKE BAUSCH

THE PURSUIT OF
PIZZA

RECIPES FROM THE WORLD PIZZA CHAMPIONS

A COLLECTION OF PIZZA RECIPES BY SOME OF THE
WORLD'S FINEST, MOST AWARD-WINNING PIZZAIOLI

PHOTOGRAPHY BY Valerie Wei-Haas

WINDERMERE
PRESS

CONTENTS

HOW IT ALL BEGAN ...

BY TONY GEMIGNANI

GEMIGNANI RESTAURANT GROUP
WORLD PIZZA CHAMPIONS FOUNDER 2004

If you'd told me in 2004, when World Pizza Champions (WPC) was formed, that we would now have more than 50 members, countless accolades, and a curated cookbook, I would've said your brain was foggy from eating too many slices. But even if I could not imagine the path I paved would eventually bring us here, all in the pursuit of pizza. I did always know this group had the potential to be much more than the sum of its parts (which is already quite a bit). That was always part of my plan.

When I was getting started, I participated in dough-tossing competitions in Italy. I often saw teams of pizza makers, many from the same town, who helped each other. They were better pizzaioli when they worked together. I wanted to make that happen with a group of pizza makers I knew. I thought, what if we could help each other win competitions—and improve our businesses, give a leg up to other up-and-coming pizza makers, and even build community in our respective towns.

So in 2004, I shared my idea with the pizza makers I knew and trusted the most: Siler Chapman, Michael Shepherd, Joe Carlucci, and Ken Bryant, four talented guys I knew well from competing alongside them. They were passionate about the craft. They enjoyed the competition and, more importantly, the work it took to get better.

WPC gave us a way to sharpen our blades for pizza-making battles but, throughout, has also asked us to give in turn. We share ourselves, our minds and our businesses. It's what we do and who we are. (That is why we are sharing our best recipes with you!) These two philosophies—competition and selfless giving—are not in opposition. Rather, their marriage defines our group.

In addition to winning pizza competitions, our fledgling team set out to support other independent operators. We created training videos for pizzeria owners—the types you see now on Youtube, but before Youtube existed. We fought to get bulk pricing, the type the big chains get, but for individual shops. Every decision revolved around the question, "How does this make us all stronger?" By being closer to other pizza people, we could help solve each other's business problems with the support and encouragement we weren't finding elsewhere.

Along the way, we attracted attention: Winning competitions and building community are both magnets for the press. Our next step was a big one. We developed the International Pizza Challenge with Pizza Expo. With the help of our first new member Sean Brauser, we defined what an organized and fair pizza-baking contest should look like. What we created is now the gold standard. Not long after, we began leading most of the seminars at the Pizza Expo. It didn't take long for us to fill those rooms with "indie ops" like us who needed information to survive and thrive. Instead of restaurant consultants and motivational speakers trained on the speaker circuit, our team were the ones helping attendees improve their businesses and elevate the standard of pizza in America.

I'm often asked how teammates are chosen to be a World Pizza Champion. The short and boring answer is there's no scientific strategy involved, but I do lean on the words of my father, Frank Gemignani, who coached soccer and built winning teams for more than 40 years. "To win, you must have a great all-around team. It's about all the players, not the player."

So, I look beyond the surface and to the core of the pizza maker to see the potential in each teammate. At each person's core is what unites us all: passion without ego. I study people's drive to learn more about the craft, their professionalism in public and among their peers, and their humility and dedication to the team and its members.

Sometimes I've chosen veterans with tons of existing accolades. Other times I choose young upstarts with the chops to get to the top of the industry (which can happen with a network of champions around them who believe in them). That makes for an increasingly diverse collection of men and women of varied ages from the United States and abroad. Today, we not only have restaurateurs and chefs but also teachers, writers, educators, philanthropists, consultants and speakers in the pizza industry. Through our different backgrounds, unique knowledge and skill sets, we all gain strength.

I get asked repeatedly, "Why do you tell all your secrets?" I'm always blown away by the surprise behind that question. If we share what we know, the industry gets better. I'm all for that and so is the team. We all have been taught and given so much that it drives us to be teachers and givers in turn. I believe the generosity I've witnessed in the pizza industry—to customers and charitable causes—is unmatched by any other group in the restaurant industry. The World Pizza Champions embody that philosophy.

That is why I wrote *The Pizza Bible* in 2014: to blow the lid off the secrets of this edible artform and make it accessible to all. It's a DIY book to make every style of pizza and all the techniques needed to get your start or magnify your pizza-making journey whether you're a pro or a home enthusiast. This book does the same but from many people's perspectives. These people don't do it for the payday or limelight, but because that is who they are.

Since 2004, we've grown from the five of us to more than 50 members. I'm proud of that. When I started the team, we were kids touring the world in dough-tossing competitions. Still, I had a vision that we would grow and go in different directions and I handpicked most of the members in order to achieve that dream. My vision for this team has come true.

Still I can say this for sure that in 2004, we could not have imagined we'd eventually collaborate on a book like this. Forty pizza makers from across the world, all making their pizza their way, no other chef doing their recipe, all hands on deck with 40 authors, every one of them a pizzeria all-star, showing you their exact techniques, styles and secrets to some of their most famous pizzas.

It falls entirely in line with our mission: another tool put in the hands of anyone interested in making, eating, and sharing great pizza. It is a sort of Pizza University Cliff's Notes-like book written by 40 world-champion professors. So go to town on this book. Underline it, highlight it all you want, and put sticky notes everywhere you like. If I meet you somewhere and you show me your copy of this book, and it looks like that, and you also tell me the recipes made people in your family or community happy, our mission will have been accomplished.

TONY GEMIGNANI

THE WORLD PIZZA CHAMPIONS

Why We Exist and What We Do

MIKE BAUSCH

ANDOLINI'S WORLDWIDE RESTAURANT GROUP
WORLD PIZZA CHAMPIONS PRESIDENT

The genesis of the World Pizza Champions is humble: Five guys realizing they could help each other become better pizzaioli by working as a team. Two decades and 50-plus members later, our core aims have evolved: Help other independent pizza makers succeed operationally, impact the pizza industry positively as a whole and benefit the communities in which we work.

When the original five started in 2004, dough-tossing acrobatics gained them valuable exposure that benefited their businesses immensely. But at their core, they were all bakers—pizza makers committed to their craft. When spotting similarly passionate pizza makers around the globe, the WPC's ranks grew steadily. Tony Gemiginani sought people who were able to teach and willing to learn. This thirst for knowledge and a passion to lead were defining characteristics of what the team would become.

During those early years, many of our members were like me: young, inexperienced, and struggling to run one or two pizza shops while simultaneously pushing to be more than that. As the team grew, our support network broadened and deepened. There was no question any could ask of the group that another couldn't answer. That's incredibly valuable when you're a small business owner trying to survive in the most competitive and saturated restaurant field, pizza. We made each other better, and as a result, our restaurants got

better. What would be an otherwise lonely endeavor, owning a small business, turned into a camaraderie when we realized there were others out there, just like us, dorks for pizza, people with no ego seeking to make it the best way possible.

As our influence in the industry grew, the owners of the industry's largest trade show, Pizza Expo, asked us to give its long-running pizza competition a complete makeover. It needed to be run by and judged by pizza professionals. The contest now attracts pizza makers from all over the globe and is viewed as the gold standard of pizza competitions. Many of our WPC members have also become writers and contributors to Pizza Today, the industry's leading trade magazine.

In 2018 we took this to another level by becoming an official non-profit charity-driven organization governed by a board of directors and mission-minded to teach and help as many people as possible through what we know and love: pizza.

Aside from what the WPC does, each one of our members fields, on average, about 100 requests a month for charitable donations from their stores. Why us? Because our members—and many thousands of other pizza operators like us—are known for their generosity. Think about how many charitable events you attend where someone's handing out donated pizza. It's practically expected at this point. That is what this industry is: entrepreneurs with minimal profit margins, still seeking to give more than they take.

As you'll read in this book, the WPC's biggest-ever charitable endeavor was setting a Guinness World Record for the largest pizza party on January 21, 2023. (Read all about it on page 273.) We raised more than $40,000 for the Make-A-Wish Foundation by utilizing the team's acumen to surpass the world's largest previous record. The most inspiring detail is that most of our members flew cross-country or drove long hours, even flying from Europe and Canada, to make this happen. These

people took days away from their demanding businesses to travel to my city, Tulsa, Okla., to accomplish this unprecedented record and fulfill several children's wishes.

In 2024, our ranks include some of the world's most skilled, knowledgeable, and inspiring pizza makers. Some operate outside the spotlight, while others have been featured on Food Network and network television. Some live in huge media markets, while others operate in smaller towns off the beaten path. Some own smaller dine-in, craft-forward shops, while others operate the highest-revenue-grossing pizzerias in the country. Some of those are slice-and-gelato joints; others are full-blown Italian restaurants with deep wine lists and craft cocktail bars. Some on our team have left restaurant operations to become teachers and consultants who instruct pizza making at an elite level. Many of us have authored books on pizza making and running pizzerias. Regardless of our backgrounds, businesses, or locations, this team is composed of the best, the absolute cream of the crop, which brings me to this book you have in your hands.

The following pages contain the most diverse amalgamation of pizza recipes ever put into a single book. Every photograph is of the people who created each recipe as they physically made it. It's an unheard-of accomplishment to have 39 active recipe contributors demonstrating in-depth—with video accompaniments—how to do this. Also included are profile stories of each team member.

If you're a pizza professional, this book is made for you. If you're an aspirational home cook, this book is also made for you. Many of these recipes are written precisely for amateurs eager to up their pizza game. Yet all can be scaled to restaurant-size batches. Some recipes work ideally in professional-grade, high-temperature ovens, but we also give tips for making adjustments using home ovens if you're eager to tweak them.

These are my professional peers, my personal friends, and the people who inspire me to improve in every facet of my operation. Having them all here, shooting this at my Tulsa pizzeria, was a gift I'll never let myself forget. It was an extraordinary endeavor that came out better than all my combined hopes.

I'm very proud of this book. We all are. And we're excited to share our passion for the craft with each and every one of you.

MIKE BAUSCH

HOW TO USE THIS COOKBOOK

Eight Steps to Pizza Success!

Dear Reader:

We're excited that you're reading *The Pursuit of Pizza*, because we promise you're in for an adventure. We believe this is the only pizza book of its kind, a hands-on user manual—complete with QR-coded video references—for making pizza from recipes created by pizza experts.

If you're intimidated by the word "experts," relax. No one starts off at that level, including us. Everyone makes that first pizza—which probably wasn't that great—and then makes another, and another and another, sometimes improving, other times getting frustrated enough to ask for help. Where pros like us differ from most people is we just keep making more and more of them until we get good enough to warrant a paycheck from it or win a contest using it or, ultimately, open our own pizzeria and charge people for it.

Maybe you're looking to improve your date-night game. Or possibly you hope to one day own your own pie shop—maybe you already do! Whatever the case, practice does lead to mastery. Fortunately, with this book, you can skip ahead several levels. We've already done most of the hard work for you. One of our biggest goals here is to free you from feeling intimidated.

This book is a collection of pizza-making formulas and guidelines written by masters of the craft, women and men who've channeled

their knowledge into steps and tips for home cooks and professionals. We took recipes for 100, 200 or more servings and scaled them down smartly to amounts for two to four people. We tested them and they worked, so we know they'll work for you . . .

If you follow them. That's the key: Follow these recipes closely to execute them correctly. In doing that, you'll also naturally learn core techniques. Plus, mastering a recipe as prescribed will later give you the confidence to tweak it to your liking. Now, before you dive in, here are the eight most important pieces of advice we believe will set you up for success.

STEP 1 TO PIZZA SUCCESS: Read the whole recipe before starting and block out ample time to make it. Rushing into a new recipe rarely produces good results and spoils the fun. But planning helps ensure an accurate shopping list, gets you organized before you start and leaves you unsurprised by any step in the process. * Most importantly, since every recipe here is made from scratch, expect to make dough that needs to ferment one to three days.

STEP 2 TO PIZZA SUCCESS: Always buy quality ingredients. In many recipes here, pizza makers specify ingredient brands they prefer. Use those if you can get them. If you're a confident-enough cook to pick something analogous, do that or ask advice from a pizza pro or another veteran. In every case, better ingredients yield better results.

STEP 3 TO PIZZA SUCCESS: Gather the right tools for the job. Pizza steels aren't cheap, but they produce excellent results—often better than pizza stones. A roller cutter is the slicing standard for most, but not all, pizzas. Sometimes you need pizza shears, while other times a rocker knife is best. You'll see those and others explained in detail on our Tools page, and every recipe specifies which is best.

4 **STEP 4 TO PIZZA SUCCESS:** You'll see the term "Pro Tip" used often. Here's another Pro Tip: Practice, practice, practice what we preach here. If all you did was buy 10 pounds of flour, some yeast and salt, then bake your heart out in order to master one dough recipe, you'd spend about $20. If you topped all those experiments with mere sauce and cheese, you'd only double your cost. But, if you fed all those experiments to your family and friends rather than take them out to eat, think of all the money you'd save and the experience you'd gain!

Another Pro Tip: When learning a new recipe, consider buying double the ingredients required. Why? If you mess up, you can just start over. And if you succeed, you'll be so excited that you'll make it again and share it with friends.

5 **STEP 5 TO PIZZA SUCCESS:** Enjoy the process. Most of the pizzaioli in this book will tell you that—*even if they learned pizza making quickly—* it took time to master it. Many also will tell you that they love the process . . . that dough making is enjoyable and relaxing . . . that tweaking recipes to your taste is part of true mastery . . . and that feeding great pizza to people is a joy.

6 **STEP 6 TO PIZZA SUCCESS:** Use the QR-coded videos to watch our masters at work. Many feature dough-making and dough stretching tips, while others show how to make some of the more bespoke ingredients. All these videos reveal nuances sometimes hard to verbalize in printed recipes.

7 **STEP 7 TO PIZZA SUCCESS:** Any professional cook, chef or baker will benefit immensely from this book, especially when it comes to dough. The more advanced recipes in these pages, and even the novice recipes, demonstrate how to make legendary pizza styles you might want on your menu. In fact, every recipe in this book was taken from a pizzeria menu somewhere.

8 **STEP 8 TO PIZZA SUCCESS:** Use this book as if you'll never give it away. Highlight text, write notes in margins, use a hundred sticky notes to mark pages and make apologies to no one for any of it. This is a user manual, so if you spill sauce on it, wipe it off and keep going. Or, if you truly ruin it, trust us, we'll print another.

TOOLS FOR EVERY TASK

First, a tribute to our sponsors . . .

"Pizza tools" is a short term for a long list of devices required to run a pizzeria, many of which are also helpful to the home chef. Some are small and handheld, others are machines whose weights are measured in tons. Whether large or small, the co-authors of this book can't do business without them, and we cannot have created The Pursuit of Pizza without the help of those who make those tools.

A glance at our pizzerias' accounting journals would show those companies listed as vendors. But we consider those manufacturers and suppliers our partners. They know our pizzerias and our products, so they know what we need. Often, they see operational problems before we do, and they suggest—sometimes even customize—solutions to those challenges. When we succeed, they do also, and naturally, we all become friends.

This book is dedicated to their support of the World Pizza Champions and the pages before you. It's a reminder of how, when businesses work together, great things happen.

Simplifying pizza making begins with the right tools. Some tools deliver precision (digital scale, thermometer), some provide ease (stand mixer, bowl scraper, immersion blender), some are essential (pizza pans, stones and steels) and others are great for storage (dough boxes, sheet pans, wide plastic wrap).

Outside of a sturdy stand mixer and a pizza oven, all else listed below costs somewhere between just a few dollars (plastic bowl scraper) to $125 (pizza steel). Here's a quick rundown of the essentials and what they do. As you read through the book, you'll find suggestions for additional tools, but in most cases, this is a fairly comprehensive start.

BOWLS: Use for mixing and proofing dough before cutting and cold fermenting. You can use plastic bowls, but heavy aluminum bowls are more durable and easier to clean.

BOXES: This listing is mostly for professionals who offer carryout and delivery. In terms of technology, cardboard pizza boxes remain the standard. But improvements have been made in liners placed below the pizza. Liners eliminate unwanted flavor transfer from the box to the pizza, they absorb grease and they allow moisture to escape the crust instead of trapping it in the pizza, which softens the crisp dough. You'll see the brand, **Perfect Crust Pizza Liner**, mentioned in some of our recipes.

BRUSHES (2 TYPES): The first is a large, heat-resistant brush to clean off pizza steels and stones when flour accumulates during baking. The second type is a pastry brush that's also heat resistant. Use this for brushing oil or sauce onto baked dough or other toppings.

CHEESE GRATERS AND GRINDERS: A handheld "box" cheese grater will do the trick for any home cook needing freshly grated cheese (which we recommend). But for professionals who need fast production, labor reduction and a *lot of cheese* all at once, an electric cheese grinder is a great investment. Those can be grinding attachments to a large mixer, or they can be high speed, high-volume machines such

as **The Palazzolo Cheese Hog**, which grinds 100 pounds of cheese in about 3 minutes.

DIGITAL SCALE: One of our favorite tools! Weighing ingredients—rather using than liquid or cup measures—is accurate every time. We're fans of precision baking for ideal results. An **Ooni Double Platform Scale** is worth its $50 cost, but there are less expensive options.

DOUGH BOX: This is a heavy plastic box-and-lid combo that keeps your dough safe and protected. Plus, they're stackable. Half size boxes (17 × 13 × 3.5 inches) fit easily into most home refrigerators. If you really dive into pizza making, you'll want and love these.

DOUGH CUTTER/BENCH SCRAPER: This is a metal or heavy plastic square-blade cutter with a thick plastic handle that cuts dough cleanly and easily for portioning. It also doubles as a nifty clean-up tool to "scrape" flour and other dry matter from your workspace.

DOUGH DOCKER: A must-have for thin-crust pizzas. This allows your dough to degas in the oven and stay thin and crispy.

GLAD AND TUPPERWARE SEALABLE CONTAINERS: No room for a dough box? No problem. Use these to store and stack individual dough balls. When your dough is ready to bake, just flour a work surface, invert the container onto the flour and let gravity do the rest.

IMMERSION BLENDER/STICK BLENDER: These are super handy for making sauce directly in a pot or pureeing anything soft to a spreadable consistency.

INSTANT-READ THERMOMETER: Affordable and accurate, these are essential tools for quick temperature checks on doughs.

MEASURING SPOONS: These are helpful if your gram scale isn't sensitive to 5 grams or less.

OVENS: Run-of-the-mill home ovens have long been reliable for baking pizzas, but with temperatures maxing out at 550°F, they can't easily replicate certain pizza styles. In recent years, products like **Ooni Pizza Ovens** (outdoor wood and gas fired) can heat up to 900°F and help home cooks make true Neapolitan-style pizza. Affordable and portable, these are ovens WPC team members use often. For professional pizzaioli reading this, a name you'll see regularly in this book is **PizzaMaster Electric Pizza Ovens**. These are great, all-around ovens that will allow the baker to create several styles of pizza.

PIZZA CUTTERS: Any way you slice it, you'll need something to cut your pizza. A classic pizza wheel, an equalizer by Lloyd Pans, a rocker knife or pizza shears will ensure a straight cut and even slices all around. **Gi.Metal** and **Lloyd Pans** have great options depending on pizza style and preference.

PIZZA PEELS: This is the large, flat, long-handled tool bakers use to move a pizza into and out of an oven. Like any handheld tool for this task, there are many types and brands. In this book, you'll see several unique peels made by **Gi.Metal**.

A wood peel is best for assembling your pizza before sliding it onto a stone or steel, but a thinner stamped aluminum peel is best for maneuvering the pizza within the oven, though either will get the job done. But while the perforations are excellent for allowing excess flour to fall onto the work surface rather than in the oven, dough that sits too long on such a peel can stick more easily—and disastrously—to the perforations. To use this effectively, one must work fast.

PIZZA PANS: These vary from lightweight aluminum discs to heavy stamped steel pans for specific styles such as Detroit and Grandma pizzas. Each recipe here comes with its own recommended pan type. While we prefer professional grade pans manufactured by **Lloyd Pans**, you can find less-expensive alternatives. Still, better pans often make better pizza!

PIZZA PAN GRABBERS: These are excellent tools for handling heavy steel pans safely. Sure, pot holders and clean, dry towels will work also. But for safety and ease, a **Gi.Metal** pan grabber is hard to beat.

PIZZA STEEL: These stamped steel squares

are commonly 15 × 15 inches and ¼ to ½-inch thick. When preheated, the steel holds heat equal to the oven's temperature. When the dough hits that steel, the result is a crispy crust bottom. It also recovers that shared heat quickly for the next pizza.

PIZZA STONE: Natural stone mimics the heat holding properties of a deck oven and crisps the bottom of your pizza. Tried and true, and about half the cost of a pizza steel, these have done the job well for a long time. But unlike pizza steels, they can break and are more challenging to clean.

PLASTIC WRAP: This is essential for storing dough on sheet pans (Pro Tip: Wrap the whole pan with it), or just prepping ingredients ahead of time. Big-box stores typically sell large 12-inch by 3,000-square-foot rolls, which we strongly recommend for cost, stickiness and ease of use.

ROUND-EDGED BOWL SCRAPER: This flexible plastic tool is great for releasing sticky dough from a bowl and then scraping that same bowl clean. This cheapest tool on the list will become a favorite.

RUBBER SPATULA, FLEXIBLE-SCOOPED AND HEATPROOF: Great for scraping the bottom of a pot when heating sauce, and it's a good spreader of sauce onto a pizza. They're also unmatched at getting everything out of a bowl cleanly. Heatproof versions are a little more expensive, but they'll last for years.

SHEET PAN: A rectangular aluminum baking tray, this tool is used most often in this book as a storage device but most operators use a cooling rack inside a baking tray to keep a pizza crispy while serving. Aluminum versions are preferable because they are durable, don't rust, and are stackable.

STAND MIXER: An invaluable tool for dough making. Several recipes mention KitchenAid mixers, which are legendary in this role. Still, we encourage you to shop other options for features like bowl capacity, power and durability, as these are all matters of high importance when mixing high-gluten flour.

TIMER: A dedicated timer is not only helpful for dough making, especially one with large numbers you can read easily from a distance. (Some also come with temperature probes if you require that feature.) Using one of these will ensure your smartphone doesn't get filthy in the role of a timer.

WHISK: The handiest of tools for mixing food and liquid. We recommend metal whisks because they're heat proof and durable.

MASTER PIZZA DOUGHS

For every pizza maker featured in this book, you'll find a unique dough recipe. Sure, they may fall under the same heading as New York-style or Detroit-style or Neapolitan. But each and every one of them is tweaked uniquely to that pizza maker's taste preference, fermentation technique and oven type.

In creating this book, the team wanted to make every recipe easy to use and understandable to professionals and amateurs alike. To achieve that, we decided to provide Master Dough recipes: recipes that represent particular styles broadly rather than featuring every unique recipe possible. That allows multiple recipes throughout this book to rely on the same Master Dough that can be more easily learned by readers. And, as any good cook will do, take these Master Dough recipes and tweak them to your personal liking. That's exactly what the pros do.

Base Dough Recipe

BY TONY GEMIGNANI

This dough is for New York, Sicilian, Grandma, Detroit, and thin-crust pizzas cooked between 500°F and 600°F. 68% hydration is the starting point for this recipe. As you get more comfortable making dough, feel free to raise the hydration.

Makes a little over 1 kilogram of dough

PREFERENCES

Flours: Tony Gemignani California Artisan Flour Blend or All Trumps High-Gluten Flour (non-bromated)

Low diastatic malt: AB Mauro

Salt: fine sea salt

Video: Mike Bausch demonstrates the correct dough-balling technique.

INGREDIENTS

	Amounts makes a little over 1 kilogram	Baker's Percent
high-protein, high-gluten flour	600 g	100%
ice water, at 40°F	308 g	51%
warm water, at 85°F	100 g	17%
TOTAL WATER		68%
active dry yeast	3 g	0.5%
low diastatic malt	6 g	1%
salt	12 g	2%
extra-virgin olive oil	12 g	2%

1. Whisk the yeast and warm water together in a small bowl until the yeast has dissolved, about 45 seconds.

2. In a separate bowl, blend the malt and flour by hand.

3. Pour 70 percent of the cold water (reserving about 6 tablespoons/88 grams) into the bowl of a stand mixer fitted with the dough hook attachment. Add the flour-malt to the bowl and start the mixer on the stir setting (speed 1) for 1 minute to begin to combine. Increase speed to low (speed 2), then with the mixer running, add the warm water-yeast mixture and then mix the dough for about 2 minutes while gradually adding the remaining cold water.

4. Increase speed to medium (speed 4), add the salt and continue mixing for 2 minutes. Drizzle in the oil, increase to high (speed 8) and mix for 1 minute more. Total mix time should be approximately 6 minutes. (It is best not to exceed this time and overwork the dough).

5. Stop the mixer, pull the dough away from the hook, transfer to a clean work surface, gathering the dough into a ball. On a clean work surface, press the top of the dough ball away from you with the heel of your hand, while turning the dough 45 degrees with the other. Repeat this pushing and turning motion until the dough is smooth.

6. Lightly oil a large bowl (keeping in mind the dough could double or triple in size) with olive oil. Place the dough in the bowl, cover and let rest for 1 hour.

7. Remove the dough from the bowl to the work surface and press down slightly. Fold the top edge down towards the center, then bring the bottom up to overlap it, folding into thirds as if folding a letter. Repeat from the sides doing a second letter fold. Return to the bowl, cover

and let rest for 30 minutes. Repeat this folding and resting three more times. After the final 30 minute rest, cover the dough in plastic wrap or seal in an airtight container and transfer the dough to the refrigerator for 24 to 36 hours.

8. Remove the dough from the refrigerator and put in the bowl of the stand mixer fitted with the dough hook attachment. Mix on the stir setting (speed 1) for 30 seconds to degas the dough (removing any air bubbles). Using a dough cutter/bench scraper, divide the dough for the desired recipe(s). Form into balls **(see Floriana's video on page 174)** and set on a clean baking sheet or container, cover, and refrigerate for at least 24 hours, but preferably up to 48 hours.

If making your own pizza, you will need 285 to 370 gram portions for a classic 12-to-14-inch New York-style; 900 to 1,100 grams for a 12-by-18-inch Sicilian; 370 to 500 grams for a 12-by-12-inch Grandma; 500 to 570 grams for an 8-by-12-inch Detroit; or 735 to 900 grams for an 18-to-20-inch by-the-slice New York-style; 200–220 grams for a thin crust.

9. At this point, follow the instructions in the recipe(s).

If making your own pizza(s), remove the containers from the refrigerator, keeping the dough covered. Let warm at room temperature (65 to 68°F) for 1 to 2 hours. (Avoid setting the dough on any warm surfaces like the stovetop, which could parcook the dough.)

Sourdough Pizza Dough

BY WILL GRANT

This recipe is special to me because using our 129 year-old starter is the foundation of everything I do. Because the dough is mixed by hand it lends itself to easily making a larger batch.

Makes 1.3 kilograms of dough

PREFERENCES

flours: Shepherd's Grain
salt: fine sea salt

When calculating baker's percentages it is necessary to consider the flour and water in the starter as part of the total percentages.

Total flour (100%) is 750 grams: 670 grams (89%) for the dough plus 80 grams from the starter (11%)

Total water (68%) is 430 grams: 430 grams (57%) for the dough plus 80 grams from the starter (11%)

INGREDIENTS	Small Batch makes 1319 g	Baker's Percent
Will's Sourdough Starter (recipe follows, page 31)	160 g	11% flour 11% water
high-protein, high-gluten flour	670 g	89%
cold water	430 g	57%
granulated sugar	23 g	3%
active dry yeast	2.5 g	0.3%
salt	17 g	2.2%
canola oil or another neutral oil	17 g	2.2%

A NOTE ON YEAST

When using straight sourdough and no commercial yeast, double the percentage of sourdough to 20% and let the dough cold proof for 4-5 days under 38 degrees but over 34 degrees Fahrenheit.

Watch Will Grant's video on shaping sourdough pizza dough.

1. Fill a small bowl with water to have nearby just to moisten your fingers if the dough sticks too much. (This is a sticky dough, but it needs to be workable.)

2. Put the flour in a large bowl (large enough to mix the dough by hand) and set aside.

3. In a separate bowl, combine the water, starter and sugar. Mix with a large spoon until the starter is almost completely broken down and the water is a milky color and frothy. Stir in the yeast.

4. Add the starter mixture to the flour and roughly combine by hand. Next, take a portion of the dough, pull it out slightly and fold it back on itself towards the center. Pull up a piece of dough, from right next to the edge where you just were, and stretch and fold inward towards the center, while turning the dough slightly. Continue working your way around the dough, stretching and folding as you turn the bowl, until the water is

Video: On making and shaping sourdough pizza dough.

fully incorporated into the flour and you have a shaggy dough.

Gather the dough together and lift it above the bowl to shape into a large dough ball. Set back in the bowl. Cover the top of the bowl with plastic wrap and let rest at room temperature for 20 minutes.

5. Sprinkle the salt on the top of the dough ball and scrape down the sides of the bowl. Return to the stretch and fold motion while turning the bowl to incorporate the salt. Take the dough out of the bowl and knead on a work surface until the dough is completely smooth.

6. Return the dough to the bowl and drizzle the oil over the top. Once again, continue the stretch and fold motion while turning the bowl, until the oil is completely incorporated.

This portion of the process is the most difficult, as the oil and dough won't easily combine. It will happen slowly. Move the dough to your work surface and continue kneading until the dough has a satiny appearance.

7. Using a dough cutter/bench scraper, divide the dough into the weights desired for the recipe. Working with one piece at a time, pick up the dough and fold in the sides, tucking underneath in an inside out technique, with the same motion you would use to fold socks together. Then hold the piece up like a mini-UFO saucer in your dominant hand. Slide it between your outstretched thumb and middle finger on your opposite hand, bringing those fingers together to pinch the top as the dough slides through while turning the ball with your dominant hand to

smooth it out. Fold it in on itself a couple times and place seam side down on the work surface.

8. Transfer the dough balls to a baking sheet, reusable plastic bags, or a storage container that is twice the size of the dough. Cover the baking sheet with plastic wrap. Refrigerate for at least 24 hours but no more than 96 hours (4 days). This dough reaches its peak at around 48 hours.

9. When getting ready to make a pizza, remove the dough from the refrigerator and keep it covered. Let warm at room temperature (65°F to 68°F) for 1 to 2 hours. (Avoid setting the dough on any warm surfaces like the stovetop, which could parcook the dough.)

Will's Sourdough Starter

BY WILL GRANT

Making sourdough is straightforward, but takes some time. This process happens over five days, with the starter ready to be used on the sixth.

Makes 494 grams of sourdough starter

Day 1: In a small bowl thoroughly combine 240 grams of cold tap water with 240 grams of high-protein, high-gluten flour. Transfer to a storage container or jar with a lid. Store in a warm, dark area for 24 hours.

Day 2: Stir the water and flour mixture with a spoon. Scoop out 14 grams and place into a clean bowl. Discard the remaining mixture in the container. *Yes, that's correct: The remaining starter mixture gets discarded. The reasons are twofold and simple. First, we're building flavor and aroma complexity with each successive day, and doing that only requires a small amount of mixture from the previous batch. Second, if you do not discard the starter mixture as directed and continue adding to the existing batch, you'll have way more starter than you'll need for multiple pizzas. Even once a starter is established it will continually be refreshed.*

Whisk 240 grams of cold tap water into the 14 grams of starter mixture in the bowl until the water appears milky and frothy, with nearly all of the starter mixture absorbed. Next, add 240 grams of high-protein, high-gluten flour and mix with a silicone spatula or wooden spoon until no longer lumpy. Transfer this mixture to a clean storage container or jar, cover with its lid, and store in a warm, dark place.

Days 3 through 5: Repeat the process from day 2 on each day.

Day 6: You will now have 494 grams of active starter, ready to use in Will Grant's Sourdough Pizza Dough (page 28) or another recipe. You will know that it's ready because it will have a fresh yogurt aroma when it is bubbling on the surface.

NOTE ON MAINTAINING THE STARTER

To continue your starter's life, you can use and feed it every day like I do. Alternatively, when the starter is young, you can refrigerate it and feed it once a week. Once it is more established (after a few months) you can continue to refrigerate and feed once a month. The key to using a refrigerated starter is scheduling your baking day, and taking the starter out of the fridge to feed (reserve portion, water, then flour, while discarding the rest as outlined at left in Day 2) 24 hours before you plan to mix your dough.

LAURA MEYER

OWNER, PIZZERIA DA LAURA
BERKELEY, CALIFORNIA

WPC MEMBER SINCE 2013

Laura Meyer's introduction to the pizza industry began as an after-school hustle that evolved into a career that would take her across the globe and lead her to owning her own pizzeria.

"My friend worked at Pyzano's Pizzeria and she said I should come there and apply," Meyer said, referring to the Castro Valley, California, pizzeria co-owned by WPC founder, Tony Gemignani. "I also had a job at a sandwich shop, and when doing both became too much, I picked the most fun one—the pizzeria."

Pyzano's California riffs on pizza were simple for cooks and consumers alike. It was a busy shop at which Meyer learned to cook quickly and where she became a manager. After college graduation, Gemignani offered Meyer a kitchen manager's position at his San Francisco operation, Tony's Pizza Napoletana. "I jumped at that offer," she said. "I needed to get out of my small town and do something different. San Francisco was where it all exploded for me."

When Meyer joined Gemignani on a trip to the 2010 World Pizza Championships in Salsomaggiore, Italy, he said, "'You know, you can compete if you want to,'" she recalled. "But when I did, I didn't do well at all that first time." It was a short-lived shortfall. At the world championships in Parma, Italy, in 2013, Meyer placed first in the competition's Pan Pizza division, a first for an American and a female.

The following year, she placed first in the non-traditional division at Pizza Expo in Las Vegas. In 2019, Meyer won first place at the Caputo Cup in Naples, Italy, for best American-style pizza. This win was the first time the longstanding Caputo Cup had allowed an American-style category into the prestigious competition.

During her almost 18-year-long tenure alongside Tony Gemignani, Meyer learned a vast skill set beyond pizza making. She became a regular speaker at Pizza Expo, a columnist for Pizza Today magazine, and a teacher in her own right. Meyer is currently an ambassador for Women in Pizza, an organization devoted to championing women in the pizza industry, of which she is highly lauded and respected as a pillar of its mission and vision.

In 2023, after over a decade of mastering her craft, Meyer branched out and started her own restaurant, Pizzeria Da Laura, a full-service restaurant in Berkeley, California, serving a variety of styles. "It's a simple concept, but it's about executing very well on that simplicity and being as approachable as possible," she said. "It's an expression of all I've learned over the years. I'm really proud of it."

Basic Indirect Dough

BY LAURA MEYER

A direct dough recipe does not use a preferment, so every ingredient is mixed together in a single phase of production. This versatile dough using a pre-ferment is a dough that is suitable for New York, Sicilian, Detroit, and Grandma pizzas cooked in any oven at 650°F/345°C and below.

INGREDIENTS	Small Batch makes 682 g	Large Batch makes 1.1 kg	Baker's Percent
high-protein, high-gluten flour	350 g	595 g	87.5%
cold water, at 65°F	160 g	272 g	40%
warm water, at 80°F	50 g	85 g	12.5%
TOTAL WATER	*260 g*	*442 g*	*65%*
Poolish starter	100 g	170 g	12.5% flour 12.5% water
active dry yeast	2 g	3.4 g	0.5%
low diastatic malt	4 g	6.8 g	1%
salt	8 g	13.6 g	2%
extra-virgin olive oil	8 g	13.6 g	2%

PREFERENCES

Flours: All Trump's High-Gluten Flour (non-bromated), Tony Gemignani California Artisan Flour Blend, Caputo '00' Americana, or King Arthur Bread Flour

Salt: fine sea salt

Video: The differences between doughs that have a preferment and those that are bulk fermented

NOTE ON MIXERS

Depending on the model of mixer, the dough mixture might need to be mixed at a higher speed. This may not be recommended by the mixer's manufacturer's instructions. I would suggest if a liquid element is not incorporating (additional water or oil), increase to the next highest speed just to get things going and then lower back to the instructed speed.

TO MAKE THE DOUGH

1. Whisk the yeast and warm water together in a small bowl until the yeast has dissolved.

2. In the bowl of a stand mixer fitted with the dough hook attachment, combine the flour and malt on the stir setting (speed 1) and mix for 15 to 30 seconds. With the mixer running, still on the stir setting, add 75 percent of the cold water (reserving about ⅓ cup/ 65 grams of water for a small batch or ⅔ cup/130 grams for a large batch), followed by the yeast mixture. Scrape any yeast remaining in the small bowl. Continue to mix on stir until combined to a shaggy dough, approximately 1 to 2 minutes.

3. Stop the mixer and use your fingers to pull any dough away from the hook. Scrape the bottom and sides of the bowl as needed.

4. Add the starter into the middle of the bowl and mix the dough on medium-low (speed 3 or 4) for 1–2 minutes or until fully incorporated.

5. Stop the mixer and use your fingers to pull any dough away from the hook. Scrape the bottom and sides of the bowl as needed.

6. Pour the salt into the middle of the dough. Mix the dough on low (speed 2) for 1 minute, then

increase to medium-low (speed 3 or 4) and mix for 1 additional minute. Reduce the speed back to low (speed 2) and slowly drizzle in the remaining cold water. This should take about 2 minutes. Do not add the water too quickly. Once Incorporated, mix for 1 minute more on low (speed 2), and then increase to medium-low (speed 3 or 4) and mix for 1 minute more.

7. Stop the mixer and pull the dough away from the hook. Pour the olive oil into the center of the dough and mix on low (speed 2) for 30 seconds to 1 minute to begin to incorporate the oil.

Increase to medium-low (speed 3 or 4) for 1 minute, then to medium-high to high (speed 6–8) for 2 minutes. Turn the mixer off when the dough is smooth and slightly tacky. The total mix time should be around 10 to 12 minutes. It is best not to exceed this time as this will overwork the dough. Form the dough into a ball **(see Mike demonstrate on page 26)**.

8. Let the dough rest at room temperature for a minimum of 10 minutes and up to an hour.

9. Using a dough cutter/bench scraper, divide the dough to the weights needed for the desired recipe. For some recipes, the dough will not be divided. Form the divided dough Into balls and place on a clean baking sheet or in a sealable container, cover and refrigerate for at least 24 hours and up to 3 days.

10. When getting ready to make a pizza, remove the dough from the refrigerator and keep it covered. Let the dough warm at room temperature (65 to 68 degrees Fahrenheit) for 1 to 2 hours. (Avoid setting the dough on any warm surfaces like the stovetop, which could parcook the dough.)

MICHAEL AND JOEY MERCURIO

OWNERS, MERCURIO'S GELATO AND PIZZA
PITTSBURGH, PENNSYLVANIA

WPC MEMBERS SINCE 2019

Some children grow up working for their parents . . . and then flee the first chance they get. Anna, Joey and Michael Mercurio aren't among that group. They spent their childhoods making and scooping gelato for their parents and loved it. Even college educations didn't turn them on to other career options.

But the trio's bigger vision for the family business—adding pizza to the mix—meant someone had to learn that skill. The task fell to Michael, who studied under famed New York City Neapolitan pizza instructor, Roberto Caporuscio, also owner of Kesté Pizza & Vino. Michael's father, to help his adult children master the skill, built a wood-fired pizza oven in his backyard. In 2011, they opened Mercurio's Gelato and Pizza, and the business did well enough to eventually add a second unit.

Though their authentic Neapolitan pizzas were a hit, requests for a gluten-free version became so frequent that the Mercurios set out to perfect one.

"We felt it was necessary to include gluten sensitive customers," says Michael. Perfecting it took nearly a year, "but as gluten-free technology improved greatly, we continued improving the pizza. What we have now acts like real Neapolitan dough, proofing and rising because of the flour we use."

Confident their pizzas were potential award winners, Michael entered a pizza in the Neapolitan division at the 2018 North American Caputo Cup—and won. Joey entered the gluten-free division that same year and took second place. The following year, Anna grabbed another second place in the Gluten-Free division.

Delighted as they are with their pizzas, Michael says the siblings are proudest of the way the trio runs their business.

"The most compelling aspect of the business is how we maintain our healthy relationships after working together for over a decade," he says. The secret to that unusual success is having their own roles and responsibilities.

"Our two pizzerias are full-service restaurants spaced 15 minutes apart. We say, 'One day I'll work here, then you work here and we'll switch.' That way we all understand what's happening in both of our restaurants."

In 2019, when Michael and Joey were taking a master pizzaiolo class, they met some World Pizza Champion team members.

"I think they noticed our passion and love of the craft, and they invited us to join the team in 2019," Michael says. "Our experiences being around such talented and genuine people who never hesitate to offer help or guidance have been incredibly fulfilling. We've been fortunate to go to Italy, Las Vegas, and Atlantic City and travel with some of the best pizza makers in the world. Yeah, we like being a part of that."

Gluten-Free Pizza Dough

BY MICHAEL AND JOE MERCURIO

This recipe showcases just how good Italian gluten-free flour really is. So many gluten-free doughs just don't bake or chew like ours. It's taken work to develop it, but we're really pleased with how it bakes. Our customers are also!

Makes about 900 grams; enough for three 300 gram dough balls

PREFERENCES

Salt: finely ground kosher

INGREDIENTS

	Amounts makes 900 grams	Baker's Percent
Caputo gluten-free flour	500 g	100%
water, 90°F to 100°F	400 g	80%
active dry yeast	7 g	1.4%
salt	13 g	2.6%
extra-virgin olive oil	18 g	3.6%

MAKING THE GLUTEN-FREE DOUGH

* If you prefer, this dough is easily made by hand, but the mixing steps will take about twice as long.

1. Whisk the yeast and warm water together in a small bowl until the yeast has dissolved. Let sit at room temperature for 5 minutes.

2. In the bowl of a stand mixer fitted with the dough hook attachment, add the gluten-free flour followed by the yeast-water mixture. Mix on the stir setting (speed 1), stopping to scrape the sides and bottom of the bowl as needed, until the ingredients are combined, 1 to 2 minutes. Increase to low (speed 2) and mix for 5 minutes. With the mixer still running, add the salt and mix for 2 minutes more. Drizzle in the olive oil and mix for an additional minute.

3. Remove the bowl from the mixer, and pull the dough away from the hook, leaving the dough in the bowl. Cover the top of the bowl with a damp towel and let sit at room temperature for 1 hour.

4. Rub a little olive oil on your hands and transfer the dough to a clean work surface. Using a dough cutter/bench scraper, cut the dough into three equal pieces and weigh to check each is 300 grams. Form into tightly rolled balls **(see Mike demonstrate on page 26)** and wrap each individually in plastic. Put into a larger storage container and refrigerate for at least 1 hour or up to 3 days.

SHAPING AND BAKING GLUTEN-FREE DOUGH

Unlike other pizza doughs, this gluten-free dough should be cold when shaped for a pizza.

1. Position an oven rack in the center of the oven with a baking steel or stone on top of the rack. Preheat to 500°F for at least 30 minutes.

2. Dust the work surface and a peel (or flat baking sheet) generously with gluten-free flour.

3. Remove the dough from the refrigerator and unwrap.

4. **Watch Michael and Joseph's video on pressing or rolling gluten-free dough into a round.**

Video: Pressing or rolling gluten-free dough into a round

Gluten-free dough is very forgiving but fragile (almost like cookie dough), so if you roll it too thin or put a hole in the dough, just re-ball and reshape.

To press the dough into a round by hand: Using your fingertips, press the dough into a disc, about a half-inch thick, and then continue pressing down gently, rotating as you press, until the dough is about 10 inches in diameter. Add flour as needed to keep the dough from sticking, but do not lift the dough too high from the work surface or the bottom will crack.

To roll the dough into a round with a rolling pin: Using your fingertips, press the dough into a disc, about a half-inch thick, and then with a rolling pin, roll out dough from the center to its edges, rotating as you roll to keep at an even thickness, until it's about 10 inches in diameter.

5. Form a raised edge by positioning your hands next to each other, with one on the interior edge and one on the exterior edge of the dough. Using the fingertips of the inside hand, press the dough against the fingertips of the other to gently pinch and raise a small vertical edge, working your way around the dough.

6. At this point, if baking at home, parbake the dough. (If baking in a pizzeria, slide the peel under dough, sauce, cheese and top as usual.) Slide the dough onto the dusted peel and brush the top of the dough lightly with olive oil. Slide onto the steel or stone on the oven rack and bake until the dough has set with some slight browning on the underside, 4 to 5 minutes. This crust will not have the typical golden brown color of traditional pizza doughs.

Sauce and top using ingredients of your choice. Return to the oven and bake for an additional 4 to 5 minutes, or until your desired doneness.

OUR RECIPES

In an effort to streamline and standardize this book, our pizza makers shared specific recipes, such as doughs and sauces, which can be used on a wide range of recipes featured in these pages. Following is a collection of those shared recipes.

TONY GEMIGNANI

GEMIGNANI RESTAURANT GROUP

WORLD PIZZA CHAMPIONS FOUNDER 2004

Like any kid, Tony Gemignani didn't know how good he had it when dinner was served. Fresh produce from his grandparents' California farm was a staple in his mother's dishes, and family dinners were Italian-lively. He hadn't a clue those experiences would lay the foundation for his life as a restaurant owner—with more than 30 locations under his belt—and entrepreneur of Slice House, which has a hundred franchises in development. Gemignani is a 13-time World Pizza Champion, his restaurants regularly land on national and international best-pizzeria lists, and he has appeared on "The Tonight Show," "Good Morning America," "The Early Show," and the Food Network. The man is a legend.

His public popularity is equally matched by insider accolades. Soon after Gemignani cofounded the World Pizza Champions in 2004, he became the first American certified master instructor from the Scuola Italiana Pizzaioli in Italy, one of the oldest and most prestigious schools in the industry. He is also the first non-Neapolitan pizzaiolo to win the World Pizza Cup in Naples, Italy, and the first American to win cooking in the Pizza in Pala Roman division at the World Pizza Championships in Parma, Italy. He later became the only Triple Crown winner for baking at the International Pizza Championships in Lecce, Italy.

It all started after high school, when his brother, Frank, hired Tony to work with him at Pyzano's Pizzeria in Castro Valley, California. From there, Gemignani's interests grew ever broader. For example, when he opened his first restaurant, Tony's Pizza Napoletana, in San Francisco, he wanted to honor all styles of pizza—not just Neapolitan, but also New York, Detroit, Romana, St. Louis, California, Tavern, Grandma and others—even though he needs seven specific ovens to bake them all.

"So many people point to one pizza style and insist, 'This is the best!' That's just not true," he says. "So, I wanted to create a place where you could taste my versions of all the best styles from Italy and America."

Having mastered making and serving pizza, he moved to teach the craft to other professionals at his International School of Pizza in San Francisco. Many of his students integrate the new styles they've learned into their own operations across the globe. He has also authored three books on pizza, most notably, "The Pizza Bible," and is now teaching pizza making on the prestigious online-education platform Master Class.

"One goal I had for the World Pizza Champions was for us to become educators, writers, speakers, owners and operators in the industry, and we've really done that," Gemignani says. He always looked at the team as being the best of the best in the industry, and hand selected most of the current members. He's not always looking for multi-award winners. It is more about the individual and who they are, their work ethic, personality, drive, enthusiasm and passion for pizza. As Tony says, "My success is your success," and "always respect the craft."

The Cortopassi

Dino Cortopassi was the owner of Stanislaus, a tomato processor in California, and a longtime friend. Also an Italian-American, we were proud that we were from the same town in Italy, Lucca, and the fact that he was a farmer like my grandfather. His company's tomato products are some of the finest available to the American foodservice industry, and I have used them in all my restaurants since I started in 1991. Sadly, he passed away in 2022 at age 84. This pizza is my tribute to him.

PREFERENCES

Whole milk mozzarella: Grande
Ground tomatoes: Stanislaus 7/11 or Cento
Super heavy pizza sauce: Saporito or Super Dolce (or Contadina tomato paste)
Whole peeled tomatoes: Valoroso, Alta Cucina or Bianco di Napoli (or another quality brand using whole San Marzano tomatoes)
Extra-virgin olive oil: Corto
Salt: fine sea salt

TONY'S PIZZA SAUCE

Makes 150 grams (generous ½ cup)

84 grams ground tomatoes
28 grams super heavy pizza sauce
2 whole peeled tomatoes sliced in half
Generous pinch of salt
Pinch oregano
Pinch onion powder

1. Put the ground tomatoes, super heavy tomato sauce, salt, oregano and onion powder in a bowl, and use an immersion blender to blend until smooth. The sauce can be made a day in advance and refrigerated. Bring to room temperature before using.

THE CORTOPASSI PIZZA

Makes one 10-inch pizza

One 336 gram ball Base Dough by Tony Gemignani (page 26)
Three 14-gram slices (preferably done to order at the deli counter) whole milk mozzarella
Extra-virgin olive oil
150 grams Tony's Pizza Sauce (from left)
2 whole peeled tomatoes sliced in half
4 full basil leaves
56 grams fresh basil, chiffonade
One (114 gram) burrata
Salt and freshly ground black pepper, to taste
Grated Pecorino Romano cheese, optional

1. Remove the dough from the refrigerator 1 to 1½ hours before baking and keep covered or in the container at room temperature (65°F to 68°F). The dough should come to room temperature before stretching and shaping, but should not be too warm. (Avoid setting the dough on any warm surfaces like the stovetop, which could parcook the dough.)

2. Position oven racks in the upper and lower third of the oven with baking steels or stones on each. Preheat to 550°F (or as hot as possible for your home oven) for at least 30 minutes. Alternatively, you can use one steel or stone, set on an oven rack positioned in the center of the oven.

Video: Cutting a Canotto-style pizza

3. Dust a smooth work surface with just enough flour to keep the dough from sticking, then dust the dough and a peel. Place the dough on the work surface and push and stretch it out to a 10-inch round **(watch Thiago demonstrate on page 82)**, and slide onto the peel.

4. Brush the dough with olive oil. Arrange the mozzarella slices all around, leaving a 1½-inch border from the dough's inner edge. Using a ladle or spoon, add the sauce on top of the cheese.

Before you start cooking, put your oven on broil or convection bake. Slide the pizza onto the top steel and bake until you get micro-blistering with a mixed golden brown and/or charred crust, 3 to 4 minutes. Lift the pizza with the peel, rotate it 180 degrees and transfer to the bottom steel. Bake until the bottom crust is a rich golden brown and the cheese is bubbling with some browning in spots, 5 to 7 minutes. *Baking time will vary depending on the max temperature of the oven.*

Alternatively, if baking on one steel or stone, bake for 8 to 11 minutes, rotating the pizza 180 degrees once during the baking.

5. Transfer the pizza to a cutting board. Place the four tomato halves and 4 basil leaves on the pizza. Add the chiffonade of basil in the middle and place the burrata over it. Drizzle with extra-virgin olive oil, and season with salt and pepper. Sprinkle with Pecorino Romano, if using.

6. Watch Tony's video on cutting a Canotto-style pizza on page 46.

For best results, the pizza should be cut with shears. Cutting with a rolling cutter or a rocker knife will crush and decompress the cornicione (the puffy crust edge). Using the tips of the shears, poke a hole and then snip the top of the crust. Make a second cut from the side and then continue to cut to the center of the pizza. Repeat the snipping and cutting to make slices.

WILL GRANT

OWNER, THAT'S A SOME PIZZA, BAINBRIDGE ISLAND, WASHINGTON
OWNER, SOURDOUGH WILLY'S PIZZA, KINGSTON, WASHINGTON

WPC MEMBER SINCE 2018

Will Grant was only six when his parents opened a pizzeria on Bainbridge Island, Wash., and just two years later, he was working alongside them in its kitchen. After the family opened its fifth pizzeria, they spent two months traveling Europe to research fine dining restaurants in preparation for opening one of their own.

"For those two months, I ate a Margherita pizza every day," Grant says of the Italy-centric odyssey. Not settling for mere travel souvenirs, the family returned home with a Sicilian master chef who helped them open the restaurant. "I spent the next four years apprenticing under him and three other chefs learning the art of Italian food."

Grant loved the restaurant business, and after working in every position in his family's operations, he left to work for Wolfgang Puck and chains such as Red Robin and Bertucci's. Eventually he returned to the Pacific Northwest, and as owner of his family's pizzeria, That's A Some Pizza, he opened up another store, Sourdough Willy's Pizza, in 2020. The name alludes to the story of his family's pizza.

"Since 1984, we've used a sourdough starter that was created in 1894, so it's one of the oldest in the world," Grant says. When a representative from Quest for Sourdough—an actual sourdough library in Belgium—visited Bainbridge to make a documentary about the Grant family sourdough, he returned home with a sample and stored it there as sourdough #104. "I'm pretty proud that it still lives on there. But I'm most proud of the effect that starter has on the flavor of our pizzas."

Grant has used that sourdough to good effect, winning and placing high in multiple pizza contests. The natural-born student of restaurants credits some of his skills to his studies to become a certified pizzaiolo at Tony Gemignani's International School of Pizza, and the Scoula Pizzaiolo Italiana, where he became one of only three certified master pizzaiolo instructors in the U.S. He eventually opened his own kitchen of higher dough education called the Pacific Northwest School of Pizza.

Not surprisingly, his bona fides caught the attention of the World Pizza Champions, and he was invited to join in 2018.

"Joining the team has been a life-changing event for me because it validated that I was making the best pizza possible," says Grant, a WPC board member overseeing strategic alliance partnerships. "It gave me the confidence to compete in Portugal and London and teach classes in Italy and Belgium. Being on the team has catapulted our company into the competitive pizza and restaurant world, and before that, we were just hiding out on Bainbridge Island in Washington."

Gorgonzola Vegetarian Pizza

This is my most famous sourdough crust pizza, and a Caputo Cup Non-Traditional winner.

GORGONZOLA SAUCE

Makes 245 grams (1 cup)

85 grams mayonnaise
64 grams buttermilk
28 grams sour cream
7 grams rice wine vinegar
4 grams minced garlic
.5 gram finely ground black
   pepper
.5 gram Lawry's Seasoned Salt or
   a pinch of salt
56 grams crumbled gorgonzola
   cheese or other high-quality
   blue cheese

1. In a medium bowl, combine all of the ingredients, except for the gorgonzola, with an immersion blender at the lowest speed. Next add the gorgonzola and blend just until combined, while leaving some chunks of cheese. The sauce can be refrigerated in a storage container until ready to use or up to 3 days. Bring to room temperature before using.

GORGONZOLA VEGETARIAN PIZZA

Makes one 14-inch New York-style pizza

One 438 gram ball Sourdough
   Pizza Dough (page 28)
43 grams Gorgonzola Sauce
   (see left)
113 grams block mozzarella
   cheese, shredded
71 grams button mushrooms sliced
   thinly
29 grams red onion, thinly sliced
2 grams minced garlic
14 grams raw pine nuts
28 grams feta cheese, finely
   crumbled

1. Remove the dough from the refrigerator 1 to 2 hours before baking, but keep covered or in the container at room temperature (65°F to 68°F). The dough should come to room temperature before stretching and shaping, but should not be too warm. (Avoid setting the dough on any warm surfaces like the stovetop, which could parcook the dough.)

2. Position oven racks in the upper and lower third of the oven with baking steels or stones on each. Preheat to 525°F (or as hot as possible for your home oven) for at least 30 minutes. Alternatively, you can use one steel or stone set on an oven rack positioned in the center of the oven.

3. Dust a smooth work surface with just enough flour to keep the dough from sticking, then dust the dough and a peel. Place dough onto the work surface and stretch out to a 13- to 14-inch round **(watch Joe's demonstration on page 264)**, and slide onto the peel.

4. Using a spoon, drizzle and spread the gorgonzola sauce evenly across the dough, leaving a 1-inch border. This will be a thin layer. Spread the mozzarella evenly over the sauced area.

Intersperse the mushrooms, red onions, garlic, and raw pine nuts on top of the cheese.

5. Slide the pizza onto the top steel and bake for 5 to 7 minutes or until the crust is beginning to brown and the cheese has melted, but isn't browning. Lift the pizza with the peel, rotate it 180 degrees and transfer to the bottom steel. Bake until the bottom crust is a rich golden brown and the cheese is bubbling with some browning in spots, 3 to 5 minutes. * *Baking time will vary depending on the max temperature of the oven.*

Alternatively, if baking on one steel or stone, bake for 8 to 12 minutes, rotating the pizza 180 degrees once during the baking.

6. Remove the pizza from the oven. Sprinkle the feta cheese evenly over top and return to the oven to melt, 30 seconds to 1 minute. Transfer the pizza to a cutting board and cut into 8 wedges.

JOHN ARENA

CO-OWNER/FOUNDER METRO PIZZA
LAS VEGAS, NEVADA

WPC MEMBER SINCE 2014

John Arena can't recall a time when pizza wasn't at the center of his life. In a family full of bakers and pizza makers, a child is all but destined for an education by osmosis at his family's pizzeria.

"When I turned 13, my uncle allowed me to make my first pizza," Arena recalled. "I burned my arm putting that pie in the oven, but it was worth it."

The transaction was mind opening to the boy: A product of his hands went into an oven, was transformed from pale and flat to puffy, bubbly and golden, placed into a box and traded to a woman for $1.75 (for a 16-inch cheese pie in 1967!), which made both parties happy.

"Our little pizzeria was an integral part of the daily lives of people who came through the door generation after generation," Arena said. "It made me dream of creating a similar place of my own."

Arena's cousin, Sam Facchini, shared that dream, and the pair fantasized about it aloud for years. During one dinner table conversation, an uncle rose from his seat and looked sternly at his nephews.

"He reached into his pocket and pulled out a rumpled ad for a pizzeria for sale in Las Vegas—which, to a couple of kids from Brooklyn, may as well have been Mars," Arena said. "He challenged us: 'Are you going to talk about it the rest of your lives, or are you going to actually do something about it?'"

They called the shop. The owner was an old-school New York-style pizza maker, who, after moving to Nevada, hated it so badly that he offered the cousins the pizzeria for a down payment and a five-year plan to pay him the rest. The cousins sold everything they had to raise funds, their parents helped with the down payment, and they were off. Once settled in Las Vegas, they opened Metro Pizza, on June 1, 1980. It's since become a seven-unit, full-service restaurant group serving pizza and other Italian standards.

In 1984, Arena and Facchini helped create The Pizza Olympics for dough acrobats. That event became a springboard for the formation of the World Pizza Champions 11 years later. Arena was invited to join the WPC team in 2014.

"I watched with admiration as the WPC changed the perception of pizza making and presented our craft as a respected career choice," Arena said. "Being named to the team was the highlight of my 50-plus years in the industry. The WPC has been a passport to friendships and growth opportunities that I never could have imagined as an 8-year-old kid."

Little Charlie's Fried Calzone

The basics required for pizza—dough, sauce and cheese—is one of the most versatile ingredient combinations ever made. That the combination works so well as a calzone, which is fried, not baked, isn't surprising. Just as pizzas adapt well to a variety of toppings, so do calzones. In this case, I chose fried shrimp as part of the filling. Pro tip: This is an easy dish that does require precise technique. Follow the frying instructions exactly for the best result.

D'AVOLA SAUCE

Makes 230 grams (1 generous cup)

60 grams extra-virgin olive oil
1 medium garlic clove, minced
1/2 anchovy filet
1 gram crushed red pepper flakes
250 grams tomato puree
7 grams clam juice
.5 gram dried oregano

1. Heat the olive oil in a medium saucepan over medium heat. Add the garlic and sauté until just starting to sizzle, 30 seconds to 1 minute. Add the anchovy, mashing it with a wooden spoon. Remove from the heat. Stir in the red pepper flakes to toast, quickly followed by the tomato puree, stirring to combine. Lastly, stir in the clam juice and oregano.

2. Return to medium heat and simmer, adjusting the heat as needed until the sauce is reduced by about one-quarter (about 1 cup). Transfer to a storage container and let cool. Refrigerate until needed or up to 3 days. Bring to room temperature before using.

LITTLE CHARLIE'S FRIED CALZONE

Makes 1 calzone

PREFERENCES

Mozzarella cheese: Galbani

168 grams raw shrimp (approximately twelve 12 shrimp, 31–35 count/size), peeled and deveined
Wondra flour, about 50 grams
One 196 gram ball of Tony Gemignani's Master Dough (page 26)
84 grams ricotta cheese
84 grams D'Avola Sauce (see left)
112 grams shredded whole milk block mozzarella cheese
1 gram chopped flat leaf Italian parsley
5 grams grated Parmigiano-Reggiano, optional

1. Remove the dough from the refrigerator 1 to 2 hours before baking, but keep covered or in the container at room temperature (65°F to 68°F). The dough should come to room temperature before stretching and shaping, but should not be too warm. (Avoid setting the dough on any warm surfaces like the stovetop, which could parcook the dough.)

2. Preheat a deep fryer to 350°F. Alternatively, fill a high-sided pot one-third of the way with oil for frying. Keep in mind there needs to be enough depth of oil and width of the pan to fry the

Video: Folding a calzone

calzone on one side and then turn over in the oil. Attach a candy/deep-fat thermometer to the pot and heat the oil to 350°F.

Line a small baking sheet or plate with paper towels. Dust the shrimp on all sides with the Wondra flour. Fry until a light golden brown, about 1 minute.

3. Flour the work surface and the dough. Using a rolling pin, roll the dough to a 9-inch circle. Spoon and spread the ricotta on half of the dough, leaving a ½-inch rim of dough. Arrange the fried shrimp on the ricotta, then spoon on the sauce. Top with the mozzarella.

4. Watch John's video on folding a cheese calzone on page 56.

Position the round so that the uncovered portion of the dough is in front of you. Gently pull the uncovered half of the dough up and over the filling towards the opposite edge, stopping ¼-inch from matching up the edges. By folding this way, the rounded edge of the calzone will conform to the shape of your hand to help form a tight seal. Press the top edge into the bottom. Fold the lower piece of dough at the outer edge over the top piece, crimping with your fingertips. The tighter the better. Lastly, press along the inside edge of the crimp to be sure it is sealed tightly.

5. Place the calzone in the fryer by dragging it through the oil and releasing it away from

you. As it fries on the first side, carefully spoon or ladle hot oil over the raw dough side in a slow basting motion. (If you don't baste this side with oil, it will puff up and flip itself over.) Fry until the underside is a rich golden brown, 2 to 3 minutes. Using a ladle or spoon, carefully turn the calzone over to fry on the second side until golden brown, about 2 minutes more.

6. Transfer to the paper towel lined baking sheet and pat off any excess oil. Serve with with a small ramekin of D'Avola sauce and sprinkle with the parsley and the Parmigiano-Reggiano, if using.

ADAM SACHS

ARTISAN BREAD AND PIZZA MAKER
SAN FRANCISCO, CALIFORNIA

WPC MEMBER SINCE 2020

Adam Sachs's path to pizza was literally magical. A veteran bread baker at the time, Sachs was also performing magic in a weekly stage show. One night after a show, a fellow magician mentioned he knew Tony Gemignani. Sachs, eager to up his pizza game, asked his friend to relay a sauce question to the WPC founder. A week later, Gemignani sent over three No. 10 cans of tomatoes, an herb blend and a pizza-sauce recipe.

"I was blown away by Tony's generosity, and wanted to thank him," recalls Sachs. "I brought him a loaf of bread I'd made with my old starter and a blend of flours. Tony asked me about the flour in the bread, and we discovered right away that we spoke the same language of doughs."

Their conversation flowed quickly into flour varieties, fermentation practices, adjusting hydrations and other critical elements of doughs. Not long after, Gemignani invited Sachs to a class at his International School of Pizza in San Francisco. The experience forever changed Sachs's outlook on pizza.

Today, Sachs specializes in natural preferments and high hydration doughs, mills many of the grains he uses, and also uses cracked and sprouted grains. When he talks about dough with his pizzaioli peers, he almost always asks whether using freshly milled grains might work in their operations.

"When you mill your grains, you feel a more direct connection to the ingredients. Nuances of texture and flavor and aroma become more apparent to you. You have a deeper understanding of the elements of the dough," he explains. "While freshly milled grains are less consistent and less predictable than flour from high quality, large-scale mills, you learn to make adjustments."

After that first pizza class with Gemignani, Sachs was hooked, and he started helping Gemignani with other classes and pizza demonstrations, and traveled with him to tradeshows. Time with Gemignani also meant time around World Pizza Champion team members. Sachs calls that time "learning from the best." Being asked to join the team in 2020 "was an honor, I couldn't believe. When I was traveling and working with them, they treated me like I was on the team. The camaraderie was incredible."

Gemignani went even further by asking Sachs to develop a New York-style bagel dough for a bakery concept Gemignani was developing. Ever the student, Sachs read numerous books and articles on the subject, consulted other experts and started developing a recipe. Sachs would bring a new batch to Gemignani and his staff each week, and after some refinement, he hit the final formula that would become Dago Bagel's flagship product. Sachs used a variation of that formula to bake the bagel that won the East Coast Traditional Bagel competition at the Artisan Bakery Expo in 2022, among many other titles he's won.

The Carny Time Pizza with Corny Sicilian Dough

This pizza pays homage to the carnitas tacos from Primavera, a vendor at the San Francisco Ferry Building farmer's market, where I worked. Primavera is run by El Molino, which mills the corn for its tortillas, and the pizza seeks to bring both the freshly milled element and the flavor profiles of that taco to a pizza.

Video: Performing the windowpane test

Video: A four fold with a high-hydrated dough

ADAM SACHS'S NOTES ON FRESHLY MILLED GRAINS

I use a Mockmill to mill grains finely for flour and coarsely for cracked grains. For Corny Sicilian Dough, depending on the texture and flavor profile you want, you may substitute a freshly milled flour, cracked grains, or sprouted grains for the cornmeal. I recommend making the dough once with the amounts given, but after that you can increase the amount of those inclusions to as much as 25 percent of the flour weight; up to 115 grams cornmeal with 422 grams high-protein, high-gluten flour.

When I use any of these elements (freshly milled flour, cracked grains or sprouted grains), I refer to them as inclusions. I think about how they will affect the flavor, texture, and appearance of the crust. As a general rule, if inclusions make up less than 25 percent of the flour weight, they will have only a small effect on how the dough handles. Even when inclusions are as little as 5 percent of the flour weight, they add flavor and change the textural bite of the crust.

I usually soak the coarsely milled grains in water for 1 day before using them. I also sprout whole grains, which I then process through a meal grinder to create mashed sprouted grains.

When I use soaked or sprouted grains, I generally count the dry weight of the grains as a portion of the flour and adjust the salt percentages to include that weight. I also take into account the inclusion's level of hydration and adjust the amount of water in the dough accordingly.

NOTE ON STARTER

I use a natural starter with 100% hydration. You may use Will's Sourdough Starter on page 31 or a poolish. If using a poolish, prepare it the night before making the dough: pour 55 grams of water into a small airtight storage container and stir in 0.05 grams of yeast until dissolved. Add 55 grams of flour, then mix until thoroughly combined. Cover and let sit at room temperature for 18 hours.

For example, when I make the sprouted grains, I weigh the grains before and after they have sprouted and the difference in the weights tells me how much water the grains have absorbed. So if I started with 50 grams of dry grains, and they weigh 70 grams after they've been sprouted, they've absorbed 20 grams of water, and I can subtract 20 grams of water from the final recipe. I would add salt based on the 50 grams of dry grain, so if the salt percentage is 2 percent, I would add 1 gram of salt.

CORNY SICILIAN DOUGH

Makes 1.1 kilograms; enough for one 12-by-18-inch Sicilian pizza

PREFERENCES

Salt: fine sea salt

Flour: Tony Gemignani California Artisan Flour Blend

---

1 gram instant yeast

60 grams water, at 75°F (lukewarm)

12 grams low diastatic malt

29 grams cornmeal (see Adam Sachs's Notes on Freshly Milled Grains, on page 62)

498 grams high-protein, high-gluten flour

380 grams cold water, 55°F to 60°F

110 grams starter (see Note on Starter, on page 62)

13 grams salt

TO MAKE THE CORNY SICILIAN DOUGH

1. Whisk the yeast and lukewarm water together in a small bowl until the yeast has dissolved and blooms.

2. In the bowl of a stand mixer fitted with the dough hook attached, combine the malt, cornmeal and flour on the stir setting (speed 1) until thoroughly combined, about 30 seconds. With the mixer running, still on the stir setting (speed 1), slowly pour about one-third of the cold water into the dry ingredients. Next, slowly pour in the water-yeast mixture, followed by another one-third of the cold water. Mix until the dry ingredients are incorporated, but the dough is still shaggy, 1 to 2 minutes.

3. Add the starter, increase the speed to low (speed 2), and then mix until incorporated, about 2 minutes. Slowly pour in the remaining cold water. Increase to medium-low (speed 3 or 4) and mix until there is medium gluten development; the dough will become smoother and have a little strength and elasticity. To test the development, stop the mixer. Gently and slowly pull a golf ball-size piece of dough away from the whole. As you pull, the dough should stretch a little and have some elasticity before it tears.

Alternatively, just after the remaining water has been added and just mixed in, turn off the mixer and remove the dough hook attachment, scraping any dough back into the bowl. Cover the top of the bowl with a damp dish towel and let the dough rest for 30 minutes to 1 hour.

4. Pour the salt into the middle of the dough and mix on medium high to high (speed 6 to 8) until the dough is close to full development, about 2 more minutes.

See Adam performing the windowpane test in the video on page 62.

To test the development of the dough, do a windowpane test. Remove a golf ball–size piece of dough and hold it between your hands. Slowly and gently move your hands apart to stretch the dough. If a thin membrane forms near the center of the piece of dough without tearing and you can see light through that membrane, the dough is almost fully developed. If the dough tears, continue to mix on medium high to high (speed 6 to 8), stopping after 1 minute and checking again.

In the center of the area of the dough that is translucent, poke a hole. If the interior edges of the hole are smooth, the dough is ready. (If those edges are ragged, the dough needs to be developed a little more.)

5. Transfer the dough to a rectangular container or a large bowl that's at least twice as large as the dough. Cover the container with a lid or plastic wrap to prevent the dough's surface from drying. Let sit at room temperature for 45 minutes.

6. See Adam demonstrate the four fold with a high-hydrated dough on page 62.

Lightly dust the top surface of the dough and the work surface with flour. Moisten your hands with a little water. With your moistened hands, separate the sides of the dough from the sides of the container and flip the dough out onto the work surface, floured side down.

Pull the edges of the dough as needed to create a rectangular shape. To do a four fold on the dough, lift the top edge (the side farthest from you) down towards the bottom edge (the side closest to you), stopping just short of the bottom edge. Lift the bottom edge up, folding it towards the top over the rest of the dough. Take care to not incorporate any air pockets into the dough with this step. Gently flatten the folded dough a little bit.

In the same manner, gently grasp the left side of the dough

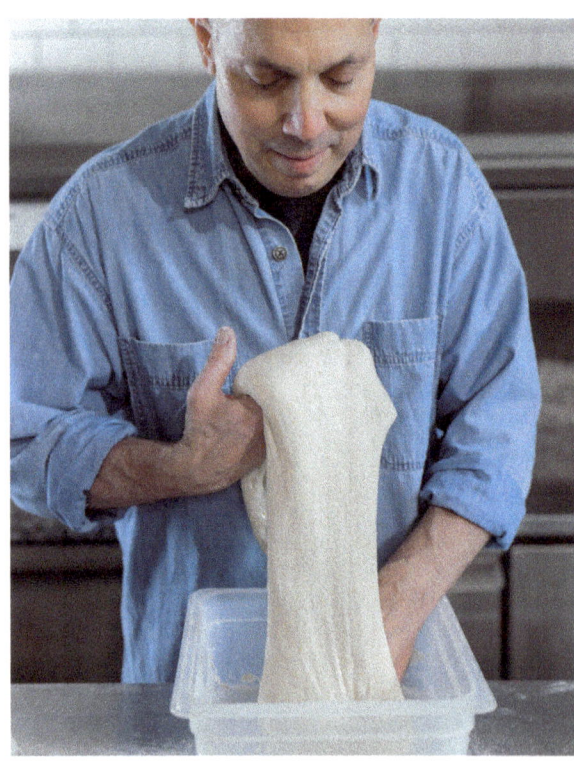

and fold it over to the right, stopping just short of the right edge. Next, gently grasp the right side of the dough and fold it over to the left, stopping just short of the left edge. Gently turn the dough to be seam-side down, tuck in the edges, and lift back into the container.

7. Repeat the four fold every 45 minutes until the dough is fully developed, which is usually after two to three sets of four folds.

To determine whether the dough is fully developed, perform the windowpane test described on page 64, but continue to pull until the window tears, or take your finger and poke a hole in the middle of the window. If the dough isn't fully developed, the edges of the hole will be slightly ragged. If the hole's edges are smooth, the dough is fully developed.

8. Once the dough is fully developed, ball the dough **(see Mike demonstrate on page 26)** and set it on a baking sheet. Mist the dough surface lightly with water and cover the dough with plastic wrap. Refrigerate for 24 to 72 hours.

TO PUSH OUT AND PARBAKE THE DOUGH

1. About 6 hours before you would like to parbake the pizza, remove the dough from the refrigerator and let the dough warm to room temperature, for about 4 hours (this time might be shorter if the room is warm), while covered in its container. (After 4 hours, the dough will go into the pan to proof.)

2. When the dough is at room temperature, lightly oil a 12-by-18-inch Sicilian-style pan. Lift the dough from the baking sheet or storage container and place in the prepared pan. Gently stretch the dough evenly outward from the center. Using your fingertips, start to push the dough to the edges of the pan from the center to the edges, turning the pan 180-degrees with each pass. Press the dough with your fingers one last time to ensure it is even. At this point, the dough will not reach the sides. Oil the dough surface lightly to prevent the surface from drying as the dough proofs. Cover the top of the pan with its lid or plastic wrap.

Set the pan in a warm area and let the dough rise for 30 minutes.

3. Lightly press out and stretch the dough again so that the edges reach the sides and corners of the pan. Re-cover the pan and continue to let the dough rise until almost doubled in size, another 1½ to 2 hours.

4. Meanwhile, position a rack in the center of the oven, preferably with a baking steel or stone and preheat to 450°F. Set the pan in the oven. Bake, rotating the pan 180 degrees midway through baking, until golden brown, 8 to 10 minutes.

5. Using a large spatula, carefully remove the parbaked dough from the pan to a cooling rack Cool for 15 minutes if continuing to topping and baking. If making ahead, cool the parbaked dough completely on the rack. The dough is okay at room temperature for up to 8 hours. For longer storage, wrap completely in plastic wrap for up to 1 day or double wrap (with foil, another layer of plastic wrap, or in a bag) and freeze for up to 2 weeks.

CARNY TIME PIZZA

Makes one 12-by-18-inch Sicilian pizza

PREFERENCES

Mozzarella cheese: Grande
Cheddar cheese: Cabot
Olive Oil: Corto

Olive oil
One parbaked Corny Sicilian
    Dough (see page 63)
240 grams shredded whole milk
    mozzarella cheese
60 grams shredded sharp cheddar
    cheese
240 grams pulled pork
50 grams peppadew peppers, cut
    in halves
30 grams pickled jalapeño rings
20 grams cilantro leaves
20 grams curly or flat-leaf parsley
    leaves
100 grams jalapeño pepper jelly
½ lime, cut into wedges
½ lemon, cut into wedges

1. Preheat the oven to 500°F, with the same oven setup from parbaking the dough.

2. Wipe out the pan and brush generously with olive oil. Return the parbaked dough to the pan.

Leaving a ½-inch border, sprinkle the mozzarella and the cheddar cheese over the dough. Arrange the pulled pork in small stacks in the center of what will be each slice when the pizza is cut. (I usually cut the pizza into 6 pieces, but the pizza is large enough to cut into 8 or 12 pieces.)

3. Set the pan in the oven. Bake, rotating the pan 180 degrees, midway through baking, until

the cheese is bubbling and the crust is golden brown, 8 to 14 minutes. About 2 minutes before you remove the pizza from the oven, use a metal spatula to elevate the pizza from the pan to check that the bottom is well browned and crisp. If the bottom is still light brown, carefully remove the pizza from the pan and place it directly on the baking steel or stone. Remove the pizza from the oven and transfer to a cooling rack for 1 to 3 minutes to cool slightly.

4. Spoon and gently spread the jelly in small portions onto the pork. Sprinkle the peppadew peppers and pickled jalapeño slices across the pizza followed by the chopped cilantro and parsley. Squeeze lime and lemon juice over the top.

TARA HATTAN

CO-OWNER, ZASA'S PIZZA & WINGS
GENERAL MANAGER, ANDOLINI'S
TULSA, OKLAHOMA

WPC MEMBER SINCE 2019

Tara Hattan was not only bright enough to graduate high school at age 16, she had the brains and self-confidence to pursue pharmaceutical chemistry.

But then a job in the pizza business came along and hooked her in ways she didn't expect. In an age when new hires typically join restaurant crews as a result of heavy incentives, Hattan merely saw a banner saying a new pizzeria was opening and applied.

"I don't know why it sounded fun to me, but it did to a 16-year-old kid who needed some independence," Hattan says. "I'd always worked with my mom in the kitchen; we'd see how fast we could make a meal and clean it up. So it was like I was training my whole life for this."

Not only was Hattan a natural in the pizzeria's kitchen, she was a natural leader who earned promotions to assistant kitchen manager and kitchen manager. Before long, she was training managers to open other stores at Andolini's Pizza, a five-unit company owned by WPC president Mike Bausch.

Around that time, Hattan discovered pizza acrobatics during Andolini's annual crew contest. In her first attempt, her boss was pleased enough to promise a trip to Pizza Expo in Las Vegas to compete when she turned 21.

"Looking back on that video of my routine, it was not great at all," Hattan says. "But they thought I had potential, so I started practicing."

When 2018 rolled around and she met her first competition, she finished dead last. But instead of quitting, she committed to practicing constantly and studying other dough acrobats' routines. When she returned to Las Vegas, she won the event's preliminary round, a first for a woman. That victory paved the way for her to compete in London, where her presence was received with mixed reviews.

"Most of the competitors there were guys from Italy who gave me the dirtiest looks I've ever seen," Hattan says. Not surprisingly, she won them over in short order with her skills. "In a people's choice vote, they voted for me! They were congratulating me and saying, 'Good job!'"

As Hattan's wins continued piling up, she was invited to join the World Pizza Champions.

"I can't say I ever expected that," she says, laughing. "That was just too cool."

Bausch had even bigger news for his protégé. The multi-concept restaurant owner wanted to partner with Hattan in the creation of Zasa's Pizza & Wings. Unit one opened in 2021, and the second came online a year later.

"It's a lot to have two of my own, but I'm more prepared for it than I thought I'd be," she says. Asked whether her experience working among some of the world's most talented pizzeria operators has helped, she affirms it has. "I'm around the best there is, and I can get their wisdom on anything just by asking. . . . Yeah, I'd say I'm really lucky."

Acrobatic Dough

Acrobatic dough isn't for eating, it's for spinning and throwing and stretching. Since this tough dough is created for pizza acrobatics, it's built to maintain that beautiful circular shape when the acrobat is spinning and tossing it. It's also not just for pizza competitions, it's nice to have around to put on a show for customers. Either way, acrobatic dough is built to entertain!

This is a very stiff dough and can overstress a stand mixer, particularly one made for home use. If it is straining your mixer, remove the dough from the bowl and knead by hand. It is a workout!

small batch makes 1.2 kilograms; three double doughs
large batch makes 3.5 kilograms; nine double doughs

PREFERENCES

Flour: King Arthur Bread Flour or Shawnee Mills
Salt: fine sea salt

INGREDIENTS	Small Batch makes 1.2 kg	Large Batch makes 3.5 kg
cold water, at 65°F	434 g	1240 g
salt	32 g	92 g
high-protein, high-gluten flour	770 g	2200 g

1. Pour the water into a large bowl, and whisk in the salt until almost completely dissolved.

2. In the bowl of a stand mixer fitted with the dough hook attachment, mix the flour on low (speed 2), while slowly adding in the water-salt mixture. Be sure to add any undissolved salt from the water into the mixer bowl. Increase the speed to medium (speed 3 or 4) and continue to mix until the dough is uniform, dryish, and extremely tough, 7 to 10 minutes.

Alternatively, if mixing by hand, put the flour in a large bowl and gradually work in the water-salt mixture. Once it is a shaggy dough, transfer to a generously floured work surface. Knead until smooth.

3. Remove the dough from the mixer bowl to the work surface.

4. Watch Tara's video on dividing, balling, and over-the-shoulder tossing technique for acrobatic dough.

Using a dough cutter/bench scraper, cut the dough into 198 gram portions. The less you cut the dough, the better. Trying to compress little pieces of cut dough back into a larger ball is certainly doable, but can be challenging. If you do have a lot of small pieces, set them aside to form a single portion at the end of scaling.

Working with one 198 gram portion at a time, gather the pieces together as needed into a ball. Hold the dough with your fingers on the underside with the smoother side of dough up. Work the dough's edges towards the center, folding in the underside (which will maintain and stretch the smooth side) and making a more distinct ball with as few air pockets as possible. Turn the ball seam side up. Continue to tuck the edges in, turning as you do to make

Video: Dividing, balling and over-the-shoulder tossing technique for acrobatic dough

a tighter ball. Set on a baking sheet, seam side down. Repeat with the remaining portions of dough. Wrap the entire baking sheet securely in plastic wrap or with food-grade garbage bags. Refrigerate for 24 hours.

5. When ready to use, pick up two of the dough balls and press their flat undersides together with just enough pressure for them to stick. Using your fingertips, press them towards your palms to crimp the edges of the balls together where they meet, but don't flatten the centers together.

Flour the dough and roll to a 10-inch round with a rolling pin or, if you're a professional and have a dough sheeter, use it.

6. The dough is ready for acrobatics.

For the over-the-shoulder tossing, hold a pizza round by the crust in one hand. Stick your opposite arm out and look towards the fingertips of that hand (where you will be tossing the pizza). Toss the dough in a rolling motion, over your back, towards your outstretched fingers, catching the round in your outstretched hand.

Now, keep practicing!

SILER CHAPMAN

OWNER, KING OF FIRE
FORT MILL, SOUTH CAROLINA

WPC CO-FOUNDING MEMBER SINCE 2004

"I was lying awake and praying hard for an idea," Siler Chapman recalls. "At about 3 a.m., the idea came to mind: I was going to open up a pizza shop. And I was only 18."

After graduation, Chapman enrolled in college to pursue an engineering degree, but the confines of the classroom bored him. Knowing he'd soon be a dropout, he grasped for a post-college plan.

That he knew next to nothing about business didn't deter him. He committed to making it work by learning all he could quickly. One thing he did know: he was really into pizza. At age 12, when most kids play team sports on weekends, Chapman was playing around in a pizzeria owned by his friend's mother.

"That's where I found my love for pizza," says Chapman. "My best friend and I would help out there. Then when I was high-school aged, I started working for her."

So his decision to open the shop was also just the next step on a path he'd walked for years. "We're all scared to totally jump into something so blindly," Chapman says. "But when you are patient and fully focused on one thing, you will never let it fail."

He grew Si's Pizzeria to three 100-seat, full-service delivery and carryout locations in North and South Carolina. When a franchisee of a midwestern pizza chain approached Chapman about converting his pizzerias to his brand and helping open 12 more, Chapman signed on. Years later, when the franchisee sold his interests in the company, "We all did well," Chapman says.

The two-year non-compete clause in the deal led him to cofound a pizza consulting business.

On one client visit, he spied a wood-fired pizza oven on a trailer which the client was using at special events. He was convinced the model was duplicable, and in 2018, he founded King of Fire.

"It's now crazy busy all the time," Chapman says. "People really like that they can be at a wedding and get great pizza right on the spot."

Years before Chapman converted Si's Pizzerias, a consultant told Chapman he should become a pizza dough acrobat. Again, despite knowing nothing about competitive dough tossing, Chapman entered a competition in New York City soon after.

"And I sucked! No other way to say it," he says. Tony Gemignani, who was also at the contest, gave Chapman a DVD of his routines and told him to practice. "He also told me I sucked, and I thought, 'Man, these New York guys are tough!' I didn't even know he lived in California."

Practice he did and he became good enough to win a competition in Los Angeles. That qualified him to compete at the World Pizza Championships in Salsomaggiore, Italy, where his improvements caught the attention of Gemignani and four other American pizza makers. In 2004, the group of five dough-acrobats co-founded the World Pizza Champions.

"Sometimes you have to be in the right place at the right time, and that was so true for me," Chapman says. "I was blessed to be around such a great group of guys who pushed me hard every time I was with them. I'm still blown away at how big the team's become."

Honey Pie

This is a simple, but really good pizza with great dough and a lot of flavor. We sell a ton of these, and once you bake it and taste it, you'll understand why it's so popular.

DOUGH FOR A WOOD-FIRED OVEN

Makes 970 grams; enough for three 12-inch pizzas with some leftover dough

POOLISH

28 grams flour
28 grams water
.05 grams instant yeast

DOUGH

542 grams high-gluten flour
3 grams instant yeast
343 grams water, at 65°F
14 grams sea salt
11 grams extra-virgin olive oil

TO MAKE THE POOLISH

1. Blend all of the ingredients thoroughly together in a small bowl. Cover and let rest at room temperature for 18 hours.

TO MAKE THE DOUGH

1. Put the flour in the bowl of a stand mixer fitted with the dough hook attachment. With the mixer running on the stir setting (speed 1) add the yeast, followed very slowly by the water.

2. With the mixer still running, add in the poolish and continue to mix until the dough is no longer shaggy, about 2 minutes. Stop the mixer and, using a

Video: Setting up a wood-fired oven (including an Ooni)

WATCH SILER CHAPMAN SET UP A WOOD-FIRED OVEN (INCLUDING AN OONI)

Choose a wood-fired starter (compressed wood fibers that allow a fire to catch quickly), a grill lighter, and dried kindling/seasoned firewood. Set 2 larger pieces of the wood parallel to each other on the stone on the front face of the oven. Put the starter between them. Lay 2 more pieces of the wood on top, orienting them perpendicular to the first two pieces. Put 2 smaller pieces of wood on top (going the same way as the original 2 pieces). Light the fire and let burn for about 10 minutes.

Slowly with a peel, push the full fire set-up to the center of the oven and let that burn for 20 minutes. Push the pile to the left side of the oven and burn for 20 minutes, then the back of the oven for 20 minutes more. Finally, move the pile to the right side of the oven for 20 minutes. After that the oven will be ready for baking.

bowl scraper or spatula, scrape the sides and bottom of the bowl to be sure the flour is all incorporated. Continue to mix on the stir setting (speed 1) for 3 minutes.

3. With the mixer running, stream in the salt and mix for 2 minutes to incorporate. Next, with the mixer still running, slowly add the oil. Increase the speed to low (speed 2) and mix until the dough comes together and is tacky, but not sticky, about 2 minutes.

4. Transfer the dough to a work surface and knead by hand for 1 minute or until the dough is smooth and satiny in appearance and no longer sticky.

5. Using a dough cutter/bench scraper, divide the dough into three 268 gram portions. Ball the dough **(see Mike demonstrate on page 26)**. Transfer the dough to a baking sheet or storage container that is twice the size of the dough. Refrigerate for 36 to 48 hours.

HONEY PIE

Makes one 12-inch pizza

71 grams shredded whole milk mozzarella cheese
71 grams Joe's Pizza Sauce (page 266) [This is Joe Carlucci's Sauce.]
45 grams pepperoni
14 grams crushed red pepper flakes
Local honey, for drizzling

1. Remove the dough from the refrigerator 1 to 1½ hours before baking, but keep covered or in the container at room temperature (65°F to 68°F). The dough should come to room temperature before stretching and shaping, but should not be too warm. (Avoid setting the dough on any warm surfaces like the stovetop, which could parcook the dough.)

2. Preheat an outdoor Ooni oven to 650°F. If your oven doesn't have a built-in temperature gauge, use an infrared thermometer to determine the oven stone's temperature. If using wood, brush away any ash or wood embers off the baking surface before adding the pizza.

3. Dust a smooth work surface with just enough flour to keep the dough from sticking, then dust the dough and a peel. Push and stretch the dough out to a 12-inch round **(watch Joe's demonstration on page 264)**, and slide onto the peel.

4. Using a large spoon or pizza spoodle, spread the sauce onto the dough, leaving a ½-inch border from the dough's edge.

Sprinkle the mozzarella evenly over the sauce and then arrange pepperoni across the top.

5. Slide the pizza into the Ooni, close the door (if your Ooni has a door), and bake for 1 to 2 minutes until the cheese has melted and the crust has started to brown. Lift the pizza with the peel, rotate it 180 degrees and continue to bake until the crust is golden brown and the cheese is bubbling, 1 to 2 minutes more.

6. Transfer the pizza to a cutting board. Cut into 8 wedges, sprinkle with red pepper flakes and drizzle with honey.

THIAGO VASCONCELOS

OWNER, PEDROSO'S PIZZA
AUSTIN, TEXAS

WPC MEMBER SINCE 2013

Thiago Vasconcelos' pizza story didn't begin in his homeland of Brazil. It started when he immigrated to San Francisco in 2005 and was hired at his twin uncles' pizzeria.

"Pizza making was definitely not love at first sight," Vasconcelos says. "It was way more difficult than it looked and, in the beginning, I didn't have a concept of what good pizza or bad pizza was."

The sight of his uncles as entrepreneurs did make him yearn to follow their path to ownership, and he'd bounce around the Bay Area working at other pizzerias before that happened. A long stop at Tony's Pizza Napoletana in the city's North Beach area made certain he'd go down that road.

"I always joke that the first time I had real pizza in my life was at Tony's, where I learned that I didn't actually know how to make pizza," he says. "But my skills were at least enough to secure my job."

After two years at the pizzeria, Gemignani hired him to work at his International School of Pizza next door. For the next seven years he helped teach pizza making while working at the pizzeria as head Neapolitan pizzaiolo. In 2013, Gemignani encouraged Vasconcelos to compete at Pizza Expo's International Pizza Challenge.

"Since it was my first time, he wanted me to just compete and have some fun," Vasconcelos says. The contest's judges, however, assessed his entry more seriously. "I ended up winning first place in the Traditional division that first time."

That victory and his dedication to pizza making also earned him an invitation to join the WPC team.

"The level of knowledge that's shared between the members helped me get to where I am today," he says. "I'm happy that these guys have also become great friends."

Though Vasconcelos loved working for Gemignani, he and wife Alissa Gibson moved to Austin, Texas, in 2019, to open a small pizza shop. But when the onset of the Covid-19 pandemic spooked his initial investors, the couple spent their own funds on a 7' × 12' trailer from which to serve four different styles of pizza, calzones and stromboli.

"For the next seven months, we produced everything out of that trailer in temperatures that ranged from 30 degrees to 107 degrees," Vasconcelos says. Eventually they leased a commissary kitchen and bought an 8' × 20' trailer. "We have opened up a second trailer and are planning for brick and mortar within the next few years. I never imagined I would be part of any of this when I started making my first pizzas at my uncles' pizza shop."

Pomodorini con Burrata

This recipe is inspired by classic Neapolitan pizza blending different grains to make the pizza more healthy and digestible without overly affecting the integrity of the dough and its texture. You can make it at home using an Ooni outdoor oven or in a restaurant using a wood-fired or high-temperature commercial grade electric oven. This recipe works best when baked between 750°F and 900°F.

Video: Pushing out Neapolitan-style dough into a round

MULTIGRAIN NEAPOLITAN-INSPIRED DOUGH

Makes 670 grams; enough for three 10-inch or two 12-inch pizzas

PREFERENCES

Flour: King Arthur White Whole Wheat Flour can be substituted for the Caputo Tipo 1

Polselli or 5 Stagioni Neapolitan Flour can be substituted for the Caputo 00

Salt: finely ground sea salt

POOLISH

40 grams warm water, at 80°F
0.4 grams active dry yeast
40 grams Caputo Tipo 1 flour

DOUGH

320 grams Caputo 00 flour
40 grams spelt flour
170 grams ice cold water
50 grams warm water, at 80°F
2 grams active dry yeast
8 grams salt

TO MAKE THE POOLISH

1. Twenty-four hours before making the dough, in a small bowl combine the warm water and yeast, followed by the flour. Cover the top of the bowl with plastic wrap and let rest at room temperature for 24 hours.

TO MAKE THE DOUGH

1. Whisk the yeast and warm water together in a small bowl until the yeast has dissolved.

2. In the bowl of a stand mixer fitted with the dough hook attachment, combine the flours on the stir setting (speed 1) until combined, about 1 minute. With the mixer running, slowly add the ice water and the yeast-water mixture. Scrape in any yeast remaining in the small bowl. Mix until combined, 1 to 2 minutes.

3. Stop the mixer and use your fingers to pull any dough away from the hook. Scrape the bottom and sides of the bowl as needed. Add the poolish and mix on the stir setting (speed 1) for 4 minutes.

4. Stop the mixer again and use your fingers to pull any dough away from the hook. Pour the salt into the middle of the dough. Mix the dough on the stir setting (speed 1) for 4 minutes more. Remove the dough from the mixing bowl onto a clean work surface. Form into a large ball, cover with a damp towel, and let rest for 10 minutes.

5. Using a dough cutter/bench scraper, divide the dough into three 200-gram portions for 10-inch pizzas or two 255-gram portions for 12-inch pizzas. Form into balls **(see Floriana's video on page 174)**. Transfer to a baking sheet, or storage container leaving 2 to 3-inches between. Cover with plastic wrap or the lid and refrigerate for 24 to 36 hours.

SAUTÉED CHERRY TOMATOES

Makes 175 grams (about 1 cup)

14 grams olive oil
225 grams cherry or grape tomatoes, cut into halves or quarters depending on size
Sea salt

1. Heat the olive oil in a sauté pan over medium-high heat until shimmering. Add the tomatoes and, using a spatula or spoon, move them around gently until the skins have softened, 3 to 4 minutes. Season with salt to taste and set aside to cool at room temperature.

NOTE ON BAKING A NEAPOLITAN PIZZA

If using a commercial wood-fired oven, start heating your oven early, 2 to 3 hours before baking, to ensure it is ready when you are. The temperature should be about 900°F for a classic Neapolitan look. Bake, rotating 180 degrees midway through baking until the cheese is completely melted and browning in spots, and the crust is golden brown with some charring on the crust, 60 to 90 seconds.

POMODORINI CON BURRATA

Makes one 10-inch pizza
Makes one multigrain Neapolitan-inspired dough.

85 grams whole-milk block mozzarella, shredded
100 grams sautéed cherry tomato medley (see left)
1 garlic clove, minced
Finely ground sea salt
55 grams burrata cheese
Dried oregano sprig(s)
3 leaves fresh basil
Extra-virgin olive oil
5 grams pecorino cheese, grated

NOTE ON BAKING A NEAPOLITAN PIZZA

For a traditional Neapolitan pizza, the oven should be set at 900°F to obtain the classic, blistered and slightly-blackened crust. In this recipe, it is baked at a lower temperature, 750°F to 800°F, for a longer amount of time, resulting in a firmer crust that is more golden brown and less blistered. When using an outdoor oven like an Ooni, if you have an infrared thermometer, use it to check the oven deck temperature to maintain as close to desired temperature as possible.

1. Remove the dough from the refrigerator 1 to 2 hours before baking, but keep covered or in the container at room temperature (65°F to 68°F). The dough should come to room temperature before stretching and shaping, but should not be too warm. (Avoid setting the dough on any warm surfaces like the stovetop, which could parcook the dough.)

2. Meanwhile, preheat an outdoor Ooni oven 750°F to 800°F (see Note on Baking a Neapolitan Pizza) for about 30 minutes. **(Watch Siler set up an oven on page 76.)** If using wood, brush away any ash or wood embers off the baking surface before adding the pizza.

3. Dust a smooth work surface with just enough flour to keep the dough from sticking, then dust the dough and a peel.

Watch Thiago's video for pushing out a Neapolitan-style dough into a round on page 82.

Using a plastic scraper, gently lift the dough a little at a time, putting your hands underneath. Flip the dough top-side down onto your work surface, dust with a little flour and flip it over again. Press on the dough around the perimeter, rotating it as you do to create edges. Flip over and repeat the pressing and turning, continuing to form the edge. Continue, popping any bubbles until there is a distinct, raised edge. Put your left hand underneath the dough, slide it over your right forearm, and then slap it back on the work surface, holding it against the table and stretching it up. Repeat it over again a few times until you reach the desired size, then, with the smooth top side up, slide dough onto the peel.

4. Spread the mozzarella evenly across the dough, leaving a ½-inch border from the dough's edge. Spoon the cherry tomatoes on top and add the garlic around the tomatoes. Sprinkle with a little salt and drizzle with the olive oil.

5. Slide the pizza into the Ooni, close the door, and bake for 1 to 2 minutes until the cheese has melted and the crust has started to brown. Lift the pizza with the peel, rotate it 180 degrees and continue to bake until the crust is golden brown and the cheese is bubbling, 1 to 2 minutes more.

6. Transfer the pizza to a cutting board. Arrange the pieces of burrata, sprinkle with pecorino and rub the dried oregano between your palms to crumble leaves over the pizza. Tear the basil over the top and cut pizza into six slices.

CHRISTOPHER DECKER

MANAGING PARTNER, METRO PIZZA
LAS VEGAS, NEVADA
MANAGING PARTNER, TRULY PIZZA
DANA POINT, CALIFORNIA

WPC MEMBER SINCE 2018

The neighborhood of Christopher Decker's youth in Binghamton, N.Y., was not just predominantly Italian, the normally white lane dividers on its streets were painted green, white and red.

"That gives you some idea of the place, right?" Decker says.

Eager for income to pay for community college, he got a job "making 'drunk' pizza" from 9 p.m. to 5 a.m. for barhopping college kids. Unglamorous as it was, he enjoyed the business.

"Even in snow, they'd been out drinking and we were the only thing open," he says. "When you see the same people so often, you learn a lot about your customers. I liked that."

His lone beef with Binghamton was its commonly dreary weather. Craving sunshine and warmer temps, he applied to the University of Nevada Las Vegas and was accepted.

"I go there and I didn't want to go home," Decker says. "Las Vegas has 300 days of sunshine, so why would I want to go back to walking to class in the snow and rain when I could live in paradise?"

He also had a job in Vegas that he liked: pizza maker at the legendary Metro Pizza, co-owned by his fellow WPC teammate, John Arena. He applied in June of 1996, loved it and never left. Not only was he learning a lot from Arena, he was hooked on pizza making.

"I'd wanted to be a cop my whole life, but when I went to Vegas, I saw what real crime was like!" Decker says. Making pizza for others, he believes, is also an important service to his community. "When I started making pizza, I loved the handmade part of it; rolling the dough, stretching it, feeling it, smelling it—it's magic."

Despite years of living in Las Vegas, Decker dragged his heels on visiting the city's annual Pizza Expo tradeshow. On that first visit, he was awestruck to see so many peers in one place and surrounded by every resource needed for his trade.

"I remember walking the show floor and seeing those (WPC) guys in their jackets," Decker recalls. "I wanted to be involved in all of it and help out as much as I could."

That service mindset was one factor that earned him an invitation to the team.

"To be selected by the all-time greats in your profession is a true honor," he says. "Think about how many pizza makers there are in the world, and you were selected to be part of this group. I'm thinking, 'Me?' You go to Metro and I'm still the guy on the line just stretching the dough every day."

86th Street Sicilian

Decker likes all pizza but considers himself partial to panned varieties. In this pizza, he combines favorite flavors of his youth with a light and airy Sicilian crust.

Makes one 12-by-18-inch Sicilian-style pizza

PREFERENCES

Extra-virgin olive oil: Corto
Pepperoni: cup and char

Video: Pushing out Sicilian dough for parbaking

Extra-virgin olive oil
One 1105 gram ball of Tony Gemignani's Master Dough (page 26), cold fermented three to five days
425 grams pizza sauce (such as Anthony Berghela's on page 122)
340 grams thinly sliced (preferably at the deli counter) whole milk mozzarella cheese
142 grams pepperoni
50 grams grated Pecorino Romano cheese
12 to 15 fresh basil leaves

TO PUSH OUT THE DOUGH

1. Remove the dough from the refrigerator 1 to 2 hours before baking, but keep covered or in the container at room temperature (65°F to 68°F). The dough should come to room temperature before stretching and shaping, but should not be too warm. (Avoid setting the dough on any warm surfaces like the stovetop, which could parcook the dough.)

2. Watch Christopher's video on pushing out Sicilian dough for parbaking.

Lightly brush a 12-by-18-inch Sicilian-style pan with olive oil. Lift the dough from the baking sheet or storage container and place top-side down into the prepared pan.

Using your fingertips, gently start to push the dough to the edges of the pan, starting in one corner and working your way around all four edges and corners. Next, work your fingers up the middle of the dough. Repeat, working your way around the edges and corners, and then back over the center. Take your time with all of these steps. If at any point the dough resists and begins to pull back, don't force it. Wait a couple minutes and then continue.

3. Cover and let rest overnight at room temperature.

TO PARBAKE THE DOUGH

1. Position a rack in the center of the oven, place a baking steel or stone on the rack, and preheat to 450°F.

2. Set the pan in the oven on the steel or stone. Bake, rotating the pan 180 degrees midway through baking, until golden brown, 10 to 12 minutes.

3. Transfer to a cooling rack and cool in the pan for (1 hour. This is a large, soft dough and needs that time in the pan.) Turn the parbaked dough out onto the cooling rack, bottom-side up. Let sit on the rack until the bottom is dry.

4. If making ahead, cool the parbaked dough completely on the rack. The dough is okay at room temperature for up to 4 hours. For longer storage, wrap completely in plastic wrap and refrigerate for up to 1 day or double wrap (with foil, another layer of plastic wrap, or in a bag) and freeze for up to 2 weeks.

TO COMPLETE THE PIZZA

1. Position an oven rack in the center with a pizza steel or stone and preheat to 550°F (or as hot as possible for your home oven) for at least 30 minutes.

Wipe out the pan and drizzle about 25 grams of extra-virgin olive oil into the pan. Brush to spread evenly. Return the parbaked dough to the pan.

2. Position the pan with a long end in front of you. Spread a light layer (about 84 grams) of sauce on the dough, leaving a ½-inch border from the dough's edge. An easy way to do this is using your hand to spread the sauce. A ladle also works, if you prefer. Maintaining the border, arrange the mozzarella slices in four rows of three to ensure each finished slice will have a single slice of mozzarella. Using a small ladle, stripe the remaining sauce on the diagonal across the pizza. Sprinkle with half of the Pecorino Romano. Lastly, arrange the pepperoni over the top.

3. Baking time will vary depending on the max temperature of your oven (set between 500°F to 550°F). Set the pan in the oven. Bake, rotating the pan 180 degrees midway through baking, until the cheese is bubbling with some browning in spots and the crust is golden brown, 8 to 12 minutes.

4. Check the bottom of the crust to confirm it's crisp and golden brown. If the bottom isn't crisp and golden brown, lift the pizza from the pan with a peel, and return the pizza to the steel, stone, or directly to the oven rack for 1 minute more.

5. Transfer the pizza to a cooling rack carefully, using a large spatula. Let rest for 1 to 3 minutes to cool slightly while keeping the bottom crisp.

6. Slide onto a cutting board and cut into 12 pieces. Sprinkle with the remaining Pecorino Romano and tear the basil leaves over the top (or keep whole if they are on the smaller side).

NICOLE BEAN

OWNER, PIZARO'S PIZZA NAPOLETANA
HOUSTON, TEXAS

WPC MEMBER SINCE 2019

"I was wrangled into my family's pizza business, but it wasn't what I'd ever dreamed of doing," says Nicole Bean. "We started making pizzas at my parents' house in 2009, and that hobby turned into a passion. My dad (Bill Hutchinson) wanted to open his own pizzeria."

Hutchinson wasn't just dreaming either. He wanted Neapolitan-style pizza to be his restaurant's centerpiece, and he pursued and received a Vera Pizza Napoletana certification prior to opening the doors.

Bean was proud of him and loved her family, but she wanted a career in fashion merchandising instead, and she landed a job in sales. Eventually she was charged with overhauling the store's floor displays every month, which she loved.

"Creating window displays was my favorite thing ever," she says. Promotions to store manager and regional transitions followed. "I really enjoyed what I did and could have done it for a long time."

That made the request from her father to work at the family's restaurant, Pizaro's, all the more stressful. The year following its 2011 opening, Pizaro's had done so well that Hutchinson wanted a second location and wanted Nicole to join the family in opening it.

"I asked myself, 'What do I need to learn from this current business to do well in pizza?'" Bean recalls. "The answer was to know the ins and outs of operations and managing a team to meet and exceed expectations numerically. I'd gotten very good at metrics, hitting sales goals and staying organized, so that's what I knew I could bring."

Corporate successes aside, she was a restaurant newbie needing to work long hours to learn the ropes in short order. In retail, she'd managed a diverse staff across several locations, but working in two restaurants with her family "was really interesting. I dealt with a lot of personalities in retail, but adjusting to the family dynamic was different," says Bean, who moved to her hometown of Houston and joined the company in 2012, along with husband, Brad Bean.

Sticking to her plan to improve Pizaro's operations, she made successful upgrades that helped grow Pizaro's already strong following. Bean worked alongside her brother, Matt Hutchinson, and they added Detroit-style pizza to the menu, followed by New York-style and even a gluten-free Detroit-style after that. Expectedly, sales rose and "best of" praise from Houston publications piled up.

Certain she still had much to learn, Bean visited Pizza Expo, where she met members of the World Pizza Champions. A former competitive athlete, Bean knew what it was like to work on a great team and mused that someday she'd "get the call to join." It came in 2019, and her "Yes," came easily, she says.

"I felt so lucky to have been chosen to be a part of such a fantastic group of people who are wildly talented, smart and hardworking individuals," Bean says. "We're not like any other group out there that I know of. When I have a problem to solve, I put out a text and get 17 answers. That's amazing to me because those come from such busy people who just want to help."

Sweetpea Pizza

This is a unique take on the traditional Napoletana dough in that it can be used in multiple ways and oven types. The blend of flours allows for high- and mid-temperature baking. The dough keeps the integrity of a Neapolitan pizza with blistering and char. The dough texture will change slightly in each oven and as temperatures vary.

I am using this dough to make our Sweetpea pizza, which is named after my mother. She created this pizza one evening during our original pizza home trials and it's always been a staple on the menu. The delicate balance of sweet and savory lingers through each bite and is quite simple to recreate with a little patience.

Video: Making a poolish

NEO-NAPOLETANA DOUGH

Makes 615 grams dough; enough for 2 neo-Napoletana pizzas

PREFERENCES

High-protein, high-gluten 00 flour: Captuo Americana 00 or King Arthur 00
High-protein, high-gluten flour: All Trumps bleached and bromated, King Arthur or Ceresota
Salt: fine sea salt

POOLISH

17 grams water
17 grams high-protein, high-gluten flour
0.01 gram (pinch) active dry yeast

DOUGH

283 grams high-protein, high-gluten 00 flour
57 grams high-protein, high-gluten flour
6.8 grams salt
231 grams water, at room temperature
3.4 grams active dry yeast
Extra-virgin olive oil, for your hands

TO MAKE THE POOLISH

1. Watch Nicole's video on making a poolish.

Twenty-four hours before making the dough, weigh the yeast into the bowl, followed by the flour. Pour in the water and stir until incorporated. Cover and let sit in the refrigerator for 24 hours.

Alternatively, to develop more flavor and complexity, the poolish can be made a few days in advance and fed every 24 hours. To do this, discard half of the existing poolish (17 g), and to the remaining poolish, stir in 8.5 grams of water and 8.5 grams of flour.

TO MAKE THE DOUGH

1. Combine the flours in a medium bowl and set near the mixer. Have the salt in a ramekin or small bowl ready to go.

2. In the bowl of a stand mixer fitted with the dough hook attachment, combine the water and yeast on the stir setting (speed 1) until the water begins to look murky, about 2 minutes.

3. Stop the mixer, add half of the flour blend to the mixer. Continue to mix on the stir setting (speed 1) until just incorporated and like a pancake batter, 1 to 2 minutes. Stop the mixer and add the remaining flour blend. Mix on low (speed 2) until fully incorporated and slightly tacky, 2 to 3 minutes more.

4. Stop the mixer and add the poolish to the bowl. Continue mixing on low (speed 2) until incorporated and smooth, 3 to 4 minutes. Stop the mixer and pull the dough away from the hook and add the salt. Continue mixing on low (speed 2) until

the salt is fully incorporated, 1 to 2 minutes.

5. Stop the mixer and test the dough for a windowpane. Pinch off a small ball of dough and slowly stretch it into a square until there is a thin windowpane in the center. You should be able to see light through it without the dough tearing. If the pane is strong, stop mixing. If the dough breaks, continue mixing for another minute and then test again. Continue mixing and testing at 1 minute intervals until there is a windowpane.

6. Stop the mixer and rub a few drops of olive oil on your hands. Remove the dough from the mixer to a clean work surface. Gently stretch the dough into a small oval, then take one end of the dough and fold it over to the other end. Seal the ends together. Turn the dough 45 degrees and repeat, sealing the other ends together. The result should be a roughly circular dough ball. Form into a ball **(see Floriana's video on page 174).**

Oil a large bowl or a storage container (keeping in mind the dough could double or triple in size). Set the dough ball inside, cover with plastic wrap or a lid, then let rest at a warmer room temperature (70°F) for 3 hours.

7. Using a dough cutter/bench scraper, divide the dough in half and roll into balls, closing the bottoms tightly. Transfer to a dough tray, baking sheet, or storage container. Cover with plastic wrap or the lid and refrigerate for 48 hours.

SWEETPEA MIX

Makes 630 grams (about 3½ cups)

350 grams red bell peppers
350 grams yellow bell peppers
325 grams yellow onion
113 grams light brown sugar
28 grams salted butter
Pinch of Salt

1. Preheat the oven to 500°F.

2. Keeping them separate, cut the peppers into ¼-inch strips and the onion into ¼-inch slices.

Spread the onions in the bottom of a small roasting pan or large Dutch oven. Top with the peppers and sprinkle with a pinch of salt. Cover the top with aluminum foil and roast until the onions and peppers soften, about 30 minutes. Since a lot of liquid will be released into the pan, take care not to slosh it when removing the pan from the oven.

3. Uncover the pan, and stir in the brown sugar, mixing thoroughly. Return the pan, uncovered, to the oven and bake until the onions start to brown around the edges, about 15 minutes more.

4. Remove the pan from the oven. Cool the peppers and onions in the pan and pour off excess water. Once cooled the onions can be refrigerated for up to 3 days, but should be brought to room temperature before using.

SWEETPEA PIZZA

Makes one 12-inch Neo-Napoletana pizza

One ball neo-Napoletana Dough
    (see page 94)
113 grams fresh mozzarella
    cheese, diced or hand-pulled
    into small pieces
113 grams Sweetpea Mix (see
    page 96)

1. Remove the dough from the refrigerator 1 to 2 hours before baking, but keep covered or in the container at room temperature (65°F to 68°F). The dough should come to room temperature before stretching and shaping, but should not be too warm.

2. Position oven racks in the upper and lower third of the oven with baking steels or stones on each. Preheat to 550°F (or as hot as possible for your home oven) for at least 30 minutes. Alternatively, you can use one steel or stone set on an oven rack positioned in the center of the oven.

3. Dust a smooth work surface with just enough flour to keep the dough from sticking, then dust the dough and a peel. Place dough onto the work surface then push and stretch it out to a 12-inch round **(watch Thiago demonstrate on page 82),** and slide onto the peel.

4. Spread the mozzarella evenly across the dough, leaving a 1-inch border. Arrange the sweetpea mix on top of the cheese.

Slide the pizza onto the top steel and bake for 5 to 7 minutes

or until the crust is beginning to brown and the cheese has melted, but isn't browning. Lift the pizza with the peel, rotate it 180 degrees and transfer to the bottom steel. Bake until the bottom crust is a rich golden brown and the cheese is bubbling with

some browning in spots, about 5 minutes more. Baking time will vary depending on the max temperature of the oven.

Alternatively, if baking on one steel or stone, bake for 10 to 12 minutes, rotating the pizza 180 degrees once during the baking.

5. Transfer the pizza to a cutting board and cut into 8 slices.

If using a wood-fired oven, start heating your oven early to ensure it is ready when you are. The temperature should be 650°F to 750°F. Bake, rotating 180 degrees midway through baking until the cheese is completely melted and browning in spots, and the crust is golden brown with some charring on the crust, 5 to 6 minutes.

MASSIMILIANO SAIEVA

OWNER, ASR PIZZALAB ACADEMY AND
PIOTTA ROMANA PIZZERIA, MADRID, SPAIN

WPC MEMBER SINCE 2018

Palermo, Italy, native Massimiliano Saieva learned to cook under the guidance of his mother and grandmother. But it was a move to a small town near Rome, where he took his first pizzeria job, that ignited his passion for the work. Always seeking to improve and innovate, Saieva soon found himself studying under "the old masters" at the National University of Pizza in Rome.

After a first (and successful) foray as a restaurant owner, in Caracas, Venezuela, Saieva headed for Miami to pursue what would become his signature—a Roman-style pizzeria. "Saieva is a massive figure in the pizza world," explains World Pizza Champions president, Mike Bausch. "He's basically responsible for bringing Roman pizza to the states."

This was 2011 and, as Saieva recalls, "Roman pizza was totally new to Miami," he says. Customers were puzzled by it at first, so to convince them it was really good, "I promised myself that my product would be unique, definitely something they'd never seen before."

Over the four years that Saieva tweaked and adjusted his long-fermented, highly hydrated Roman dough, business picked up. His pizzeria became one of Miami's best regarded spots. Consulting work followed, and Saieva began traveling the globe. He also taught his innovative dough and pizza making techniques to students who went on to win U.S. pizza competitions.

"One guy, who took my two-day class in New York, had never baked Romana pizza, and two months later, he went to Parma, Italy," for the World Pizza Championships, he says. "He finished in fifth place, which made him the top American competitor. There were guys there who'd done Romana pizza for 40 years, but he did better than them."

The pull to become a full-time pizza instructor and consultant freed Saieva to move once again, this time to his current home of Madrid. As one of the foremost experts on Roman pizza, he teaches that style and others to Michelin-starred chefs, restaurant and hotel franchises, and at culinary schools across the globe.

According to Saieva, owner of ASR PizzaLab, a consultancy, being asked to lead a Roman pizza demonstration at Pizza Expo in 2019 was the pinnacle of his teaching career. When he entered the presentation hall, he was astonished to see 200 chairs.

"I said to Tony Gemignani, 'No way we need 200 chairs!'" he recalls. Gemignani also knew it was the wrong number—and told Saieva more would attend. "That day, 600 people came to the demo! I thought, 'This is absurd!'"

A year earlier, when Saieva was invited to join the WPC team, "I cried like a baby. When Tony gave me the team jacket, I was happy that finally, somebody was taking me seriously," says Saieva. "That was the award I was looking for. It was an extraordinary feeling and I felt honored."

Pizza Romana

When I learned to make Roman pizza from the pizza masters, I always thought that the dough's lightness and could be raised to much higher levels. Ten years ago, I started working on my direct method, which I make using ice water. After four years of hard work, I had a dough that I think is perfect, and it can also be used for many baked products such as bread and round, pala and teglia pizzas.

Video: Stretching Romana Dough for baking

ROMANA DOUGH

1,000 grams Caputo Chef's Flour
5 grams Caputo dry yeast
800 grams of water, divided (see Note on Water, below)
25 grams finely ground sea salt
25 grams extra-virgin olive oil

NOTE ON WATER

One of the keys to my Romana dough is keeping the ingredients cool, particularly the water when it is added to the dough. For that reason, I recommend measuring the water into two separate containers and checking the temperature with an instant read thermometer at Step 2.

Container 1: 650 grams water, at 68°F (250 grams crushed ice mixed with 400 grams water)

Container 2: 150 grams water, at 68°F (60 grams crushed ice mixed with 90 grams water)

TO MAKE THE DOUGH

1. Refrigerate the flour for at least 30 minutes prior to starting the dough.

2. In the bowl of a stand mixer fitted with the paddle attachment, combine the flour and the yeast on the stir setting (speed 1) for 15 to 30 seconds.

(Weigh out the water as suggested in the Note On Water, above.)

3. With the mixer running on the stir setting (speed 1), slowly add 80 percent of the water from container 1, then wait about 45 seconds before adding the final 20 percent from that container. Increase the mixer speed to low (speed 2) and mix for 4 minutes. Next, with the mixer running, stream in the salt.

With the mixer still running, very slowly (you can use a turkey baster or a syringe) add half of the water from container 2. Continue to mix until the dough comes together, about 2 minutes, then very slowly add the remaining water from container 2. Continue to mix until the dough comes together again, about 2 minutes more.

4. Stop the mixer and switch to the dough hook attachment. Turn the mixer back to low (speed 2) and slowly drizzle in the olive oil. Continue to mix for 1 minute.

5. Transfer the dough to a container large enough to allow the dough to double, and with a tight fitting lid. Refrigerate for 48 hours.

TO DIVIDE THE DOUGH

1. Remove the dough from the refrigerator. Turn out onto a lightly floured work surface. Using a dough cutter/bench scraper, divide the dough into the desired sizes.

For 8-by-24-inch Romanas,

such as *Nerano alla Romana* (Zucchini-Pancetta) or *All'Orto* (Tomato-Red Pepper-Olive), divide into 500 gram portions. For a sandwiched 8-by-24-inch Romana, such as *Romanità* (Mortadella-Pistachios), divide into one 450 gram and one 400 gram portion. Form each portion into a ball **(see Floriana's video on page 174).** Put into a dough box or into a storage container with a lid (I recommend 48-ounce GladWare Big Bowls.) Let proof at room temperature for 5 to 6 hours.

TO STRETCH THE DOUGH

1. Watch Massimiliano's video on stretching Romana Dough for baking.

Using a brush or your hands, brush the bottom and sides of an 8 × 24-inch pan or pans with a few ounces of olive oil. Be sure to brush the oil into every corner.

Flour the work surface generously with 00 flour and have more flour nearby.

For a single crust Romana with toppings such as the *Nerano alla Romana* (Zucchini-Pancetta) or *All' Orto* (Tomato-Red Pepper-Olive)

Invert the dough box or container with a 500 gram portion of Romana Dough over the floured area of the work surface. Let the dough naturally drop onto the flour, and then flour the top of the dough generously.

Important! Remember that Romana dough should be handled as little as possible. The less the dough is touched, the better. If you have not watched the video demonstration, it's advised to do so before going further.

Lift the dough slightly and pull the edges a little as needed so the dough is in a more

rectangular shape. Spread your fingers to open your hands over the dough, positioning them at the bottom of the dough. Using the pads of your fingertips, press the outside edges of the dough working up towards the top and then coming back down. Repeat the pressing, but this time go up the center of the dough and back down.

As demonstrated in the video, slide your right hand under the dough and gently lift the dough up and over onto your left forearm. Lift the dough off of the work surface, tapping the dough with your right hand to remove excess flour, and allow the dough to naturally stretch. Next, go under the dough with your right hand and tap with your left hand to remove excess flour and to allow the dough to naturally stretch. Go under the dough with your left hand so that it is

now resting on both hands and lay into the prepared pan.

Lift the dough at one of the short ends and stretch it to the edge of the pan. Press the right hand against the dough in the center along the edge and use the left hand to press the dough into the corner. Then, as shown in the video, gently press and lift the dough (stop and go) to meet up with the edge on one long side of the pan until you get to the corner. Repeat the stop and go along the other long side until you reach the other corner. Press the dough along the edge of the remaining short side. The dough should reach all of the edges, but if there are a couple spots that don't reach, press in as needed.

Lastly, the signature move of shaping a Romana pizza is to spread your hands out again, this time with your pointer fingers facing each other and press and ever so slightly turn your fingers to push up any air in the dough. Starting at the short side of the pan facing you, go up the pizza just one time, gently pushing up any air with all of your fingers.

Repeat this process for any remaining dough and pans.

FOR A SANDWICHED 8-BY-24-INCH ROMANA, SUCH AS ROMANITÀ (MORTADELLA-PISTACHIOS)

Extra-virgin olive oil
Sea salt

Invert the dough boxes or containers with the 450 gram and 400 gram portions of Romana Dough over the floured area of the work surface. Let the dough naturally drop onto the flour, and then flour the top of the dough generously.

Starting with the 450 gram portion, repeat the stretching steps on page 102 through putting the dough in the pan. Drizzle olive oil over the top of the dough.

Stretch the 400 gram portion and lay it directly onto the oiled dough in the pan. Stretch it right on top of the other piece until it reaches all of the edges and corners and then do the stop and go pressing on the top. Drizzle the top of this piece of dough with olive oil and sprinkle it with sea salt. Press holes in the top to dock and to let any steam escape while baking.

NERANO ALLA ROMANA (ZUCCHINI-PANCETTA)

Makes one 18-by-24-inch Romana pizza

Olive oil
113 grams zucchini, thinly sliced,
    preferably on a mandoline
Finely ground sea salt, optional
One 450 gram portion of dough
    stretched in the pan (see
    To Stretch the Dough, on
    page 102)
200 grams thinly sliced pancetta
100 grams shredded provolone
Small water bottle, for misting
    (optional)
110 grams burrata or mozzarella
    di bufala, pulled or cut into thin
    strips
One small piece Parmigiano-
    Reggiano cheese to be grated
    over the finished pizza

SETTING UP THE OVEN

1. Position an oven rack in the center of the oven with a baking steel or stone on top. Preheat to 550°F (or as hot as possible for your home oven) for at least 30 minutes.

TO FRY THE ZUCCHINI

1. Pour 1-to-2-inches of olive oil into a high-sided saucepan for frying. Attach a candy/deep-fat thermometer to the pot and heat the oil to 350°F. Set a cooling rack in a sheet pan. (Draining the zucchini on a rack will keep it crisp.) Alternatively, line a plate with paper towels.

2. Working in batches as needed to not overcrowd the oil, add the zucchini and fry until golden brown, 3 to 4 minutes, depending on thickness. Using a spider or large slotted spoon, transfer to the rack. Season to taste with salt.

ASSEMBLE AND BAKE THE *NERANO ALLA ROMANA*

1. Set the pan with the dough in front of you. Arrange the pancetta evenly over the top and then sprinkle with the shredded provolone. If you have a water bottle with a sprayer, mist with the water.

2. Set the pan in the oven. Bake, rotating the pan 180 degrees midway through baking, until golden brown, 15 to 18 minutes.

3. Transfer the pan to a cooling rack. Arrange the burrata in five diagonal strips along the top of the pizza and return to the oven for a couple minutes just for it to begin to melt. Return to the cooling rack.

Using a long spatula, remove the pizza to a cutting board. Divide the fried zucchini in strips between the burrata. Grate the Parmigiano-Reggiano directly over the top. Cut into eight 6-by-4-inch pieces.

USING A COMMERCIAL-GRADE ELECTRIC OVEN

These pizzas are best baked in a commercial grade electric oven at 610°F.

For the single crust pizzas with toppings, bake for 6 minutes, rotate the pan 180 degrees and continue to bake until the crust is golden brown on the top and the underside. If there is cheese it should be completely melted with some light browning, about 5 minutes more.

For the sandwiched doughs, bake for 3 minutes, rotate the pan 180 degrees and continue to bake until the crust is golden brown on the top and the underside, about 5 minutes more.

ALL' ORTO (TOMATO-RED PEPPER-OLIVE)

Makes one 18-by-24-inch Romana pizza

200 grams grape or cherry
    tomatoes
3 grams finely ground sea salt
10 grams extra-virgin olive oil
1 large basil leaf, cut into
    chiffonade
One 450 gram portion of dough
    stretched in the pan (see
    To Stretch the Dough, on
    page 102)
200 grams roasted red peppers,
    julienned
100 grams whole, pitted black
    olives
200 grams mozzarella di bufala
15 to 18 small-medium basil leaves

SETTING UP THE OVEN

1. Position an oven rack in the center of the oven with a baking steel or stone on top. Preheat to 550°F (or as hot as possible for your home oven) for at least 30 minutes.

(See the note on page 105 for baking in a commercial grade electric oven.)

TO PREPARE THE TOMATOES

1. Cut the tomatoes in half or quarter depending on their size and put them into a bowl. Sprinkle with the salt, drizzle with the olive oil, and then break into medium and small pieces.

TO ASSEMBLE AND BAKE THE *ALL' ORTO*

1. Set the pan with the dough in front of you. Arrange the tomatoes evenly over the top, followed by the peppers, and then the olives.

2. Set the pan in the oven. Bake, rotating the pan 180 degrees midway through baking, until golden brown, 15 to 18 minutes.

3. Transfer the pan to a cooling rack. Using a long spatula, remove the pizza to a cutting board. Tear the mozzarella di bufala into pieces over the top, then add the basil. Cut into eight 6-by-4-inch pieces.

A bit different, this recipe uses two pieces of dough stretched and baked one atop the other, seasoned with extra-virgin olive oil and salt. Once baked, the top dough is separated from the bottom and used like bread slices for a sandwich.

Makes one sandwiched 18-by-24-inch Romana pizza

One sandwiched 8-by-24-inch Romana dough in the pan (see To Stretch the Dough, on page 102)

450 grams thinly sliced mortadella

200 grams mozzarella di bufala, pulled apart into thin strips

50 grams finely chopped pistachios

1 lemon, zested

Extra-virgin olive oil in a squeeze bottle

Sea salt, coarsely ground, for sprinkling onto dough

Pans needed for recipe: two 24 × 16-inch (60 × 40 centimeters) pans or four 24 × 8-inch (60 × 20 centimeters) pans

SETTING UP THE OVEN

1. Position an oven rack in the center of the oven with a baking steel or stone on top. Preheat to 550°F (or as hot as possible for your home oven) for at least 30 minutes.

(See the note on page 105 for baking in a commercial grade electric oven.)

2. Set the pan in the oven. Bake, rotating the pan 180 degrees midway through baking, until golden brown, 12 to 15 minutes.

3. Transfer the pan to a cooling rack. Let cool for a few minutes and then using a long spatula, remove the pizza to a cutting board. Using your fingertips, carefully remove the top piece from the bottom. Spread the mortadella in small piles on the bottom piece, followed by the *mozzarella di bufala*. Sprinkle with the pistachios and, using a microplane, zest half of the lemon over the top. Replace the top crust. Using a serrated knife, cut across into six 4-by-8-inch slices or eight 3-by-8-inch slices.

AUDREY KELLY

CO-OWNER, AUDREY JANE'S PIZZA GARAGE
BOULDER, COLORADO

WPC MEMBER SINCE 2010

That Audrey Kelly grew up believing she'd have a career in foodservice isn't surprising given her parents ran bagel businesses, in Boulder. Her parents wanted her to explore broader horizons by pursuing a college degree before settling down to a restaurant career. She sought a balance by studying journalism in the hope that she'd write about food and restaurants.

A college internship that sent her to Italy fueled that fire by turning her on to that nation's pizza styles.

"I became obsessed with making the perfect pie," Kelly said. "When I came home from Italy, I moved to San Francisco to continue college, and I got into the food scene there."

Hoping to write about the Golden City's eateries, Kelly sought jobs there in journalism. Unfortunately, publications were laying off more people than they were hiring, which led Kelly to a creative educational detour: Tony Gemignani's International School of Pizza. Better educated than ever on pizza, she was convinced she was on the right track. Even better, Gemignani hired her to work at Tony's Pizzeria Napoletana next to the school.

"I eventually ran the Neapolitan line at the pizzeria," she said. Impressed with her work, Gemignani asked her to join the WPC team in 2010. "I started to see that I had an intuitive sense with pizza. When I pick up dough, it works with me."

Kelly later returned to Boulder to open Audrey Jane's Pizza Garage with her brother, Peter Sherman, in 2015. The New York slice house offers three styles of sourdough pizza in addition to salads and grinders. The concept quickly gained attention among locals, and even the Food Network's "Diners, Drive-ins and Dives" and Travel Channel's "Food Paradise" took notice.

As a World Pizza Champion, Kelly has competed in Parma, Las Vegas, Naples and Atlantic City, N.J. She is an Ambassador for Women in Pizza and has been featured in the New York Times, on National Public Radio and in The Denver Post. She scratches her never-lost itch to write, as a regular columnist in Pizza Today magazine.

"I love pizza because of the simplicity of it and the creative freedom it allows," Kelly said. "There's lots of science behind dough. But unlike the precision of fancy restaurants, where every piece has to be the same size, pizza can be inexact. I like that."

Pizza Amatriciana Patty-Style with Sesame-Crusted Dough

As amatriciana implies, the sauce on this pizza is based on a traditional Italian pasta sauce from the town Amatrice. But the recipe as a whole is a tribute to a pizza my mom Patty made at home. Making it from a sourdough starter—just like every pizza at Audrey Jane's—lends complexity and flavor to the final product. As a pan pizza, it's a fantastic option for home cooks who don't have a fancy oven.

AUDREY JANE'S DOUGH

Makes 800 grams;enough for one 14-by-14-inch Grandma-style pizza

NOTE ON SOURDOUGH STARTER

I use a natural starter with 100% hydration. You may use Will's Sourdough Starter on page 31. Because there is no additional yeast in this recipe, it is important that this is a well-established starter and that it is fed the night before and/or the morning of making the dough.

PREFERENCES

Flour: King Arthur
Salt: fine sea salt

420 grams all-purpose flour, 11 to 12% protein
3 grams low diastatic malt
336 grams ice cold water
50 grams sourdough starter (see Note on Sourdough Starter)
12 grams fine sea salt
12 grams extra-virgin olive oil

1. Put the flour, malt, and 270 grams of the water in the bowl of a stand mixer fitted with the dough hook attachment. Mix on low speed (speed 2) for 3 minutes.

2. Stop the mixer. Add the sourdough starter and mix on low (speed 2) until everything is combined, about 6 minutes.

Let the dough rest in the mixing bowl uncovered for 20 minutes.

3. Add the salt and the remaining 66 grams of water to the mixing bowl and mix on low (speed 2) until the salt and water are absorbed into the dough, about 6 minutes. With the mixer running, pour in the olive oil and mix for 1 minute more. Increase the mixer speed to medium-high (speed 6) and mix for 2 minutes.

4. Remove the dough from the mixer and put in a plastic container (not oiled) with a lid that will allow it to double in size. Let the dough rise at room temperature for 4 hours and then refrigerate for 12 to 18 hours.

Video: Preparing the pan with sesame seeds and pushing out a Grandma-style dough

AMATRICIANA SAUCE

Makes 486 grams (2 cups)

20 grams diced guanciale

78 grams diced onion

3 grams thinly sliced (paper thin) garlic

5 grams sea salt

2.5 grams finely ground black pepper

.3 grams crushed red pepper flakes

400 grams crushed Roma tomatoes

15 grams tomato paste

50 grams heavy cream

1. Set a medium saucepan over medium heat. When it is hot, add the guanciale and reduce the heat to medium-low, cooking slowly, rendering all of the fat and crisping the meat, about 10 minutes.

2. Using a slotted spoon, remove the crisp guanciale to paper towels to drain, leaving the fat in the pan. Add the diced onion and cook at medium-low heat until translucent, about 5 minutes. Stir in the garlic and cook for another 2 minutes. Season with the salt, black pepper, and red pepper flakes, and cook for an additional minute. Stir in the tomato paste, crushed tomatoes and guanciale, and cook for 2 minutes. Whisk in the heavy cream and cook for 2 minutes more. Remove from the heat and set aside to cool at room temperature.

3. The sauce can be refrigerated in a storage container up to 3 days. Bring to room temperature before using.

PIZZA AMATRICIANA PATTY-STYLE

Makes one 14-by-14-inch Grandma-style pizza

Extra-virgin olive oil

25 grams sesame seeds

One ball Audrey Jane's Dough (see page 110)

225 grams whole milk block mozzarella, shredded

70 grams finished Amatriciana sauce (see left)

40 grams shaved Pecorino Romano cheese

9 basil leaves

1. Remove the dough from the refrigerator 1 to 2 hours before baking, but keep covered or in the container at room temperature (65°F to 68°F). The dough should come to room temperature before stretching and shaping, but should not be too warm. (Avoid setting the dough on any warm surfaces like the stovetop, which could parcook the dough.)

2. Meanwhile, position a rack in the center of the oven, preferably with a baking steel or stone and preheat to 575°F (or as hot as possible for your home oven) for at least 30 minutes.

3. Watch Audrey's video on preparing the pan with sesame seeds and pushing out a Grandma-style dough.

Drizzle 30 grams of olive oil in a 14-by-14-inch Grandma-style pan. Using your hands, rub the oil over the bottom of the pan, getting into the corners. Sprinkle the sesame seeds evenly across the bottom of the pan.

Lift the dough and lay bottom-side down in the pan on top of the seeds. Drizzle the top of the dough with olive oil and spread it across the top of the dough with your hand. Starting in the center of the dough, press on the dough, working your way out pushing towards the edges of the pan. As the dough is pressed, the sesame seeds

may slide to the corners. Lift
the corners of the dough and lay
them back on the sesame seeds
to ensure the bottom is evenly
coated. With this push, get the
dough as close to the corners
of the pan as possible. Cover
and let the dough rest for 20
minutes.

Push out the dough in the same
manner to reach the edges and
the corners. Cover and let rise
until about doubled, 2 hours.

4. Sprinkle the mozzarella
evenly across the dough taking
care to line the pan edges with
cheese. Spoon the sauce over the
cheese in five diagonal stripes.

5. Set the pan in the oven. Bake,
rotating the pan 180 degrees
midway through baking, until
the cheese is bubbling with
some browning in spots and the
crust is golden brown, 12 to 17
minutes.

6. Transfer to a cooling rack.
Using a large spatula, scrape
the browned cheese edges
carefully from the sides of the
pan. Remove the pizza from the
pan to the cooling rack or onto
a pizza peel. Check the bottom
of the crust. If needed, to crisp
the bottom, return to the steel,
stone or directly to the oven
rack for 1 to 2 minutes more.

7. Transfer the pizza to a cooling
rack for 3 to 5 minutes to cool
slightly while keeping the bottom crisp. Slide onto a cutting
board and cut into 9 pieces. Top
with the shaved pecorino and
set a basil leaf on each slice.
Finish with a drizzle of olive oil.

LEE HUNZINGER

PIZZALEE33 CONSULTING
TEXAS

WPC MEMBER SINCE 2020

When Lee Hunzinger made pizza at age 13 in his family's shop, his first interaction with dough was love at first touch. That something so remarkably pliable and bland was transformed into crisp, chewy and delicious when baked hooked him for good.

"I was blown away when others would taste my pizza and enjoy it," Hunzinger said. "The feeling was super-rewarding and it made me want to get better at the craft."

Like most who've had great mentors, Hunzinger remembers his "Uncle" Joe Sciara fondly. Sciara, a Sicilian immigrant, regularly picked up his protégé in the afternoon, and on the hour-long drive to his pizzeria, taught him about pizza, the business and life. "He'd stand over my shoulder and watch me, telling me, 'Work neat and slow down. The speed will come naturally with repetition.'" During summer breaks, Hunzinger would work from 4 p.m. to 4 a.m. under Sciara's watch. "He'd just say to me, 'Write down your hours,' and that's how I got paid. He's retired now, but he's such a gem and we stay in touch."

Hunzinger's pizza path would take him to many restaurants up and down Long Island, and after 37 years cooking for diners, he started a bread and pizza-centered consulting business. That work took him to Dallas for a long-term gig with a restaurant company he helped grow from one unit to 10. Not surprisingly, the concept's menus featured three types of pizza.

"Teaching has always been a passion of mine, and being able to pass on the information and techniques I've gathered through the years has been rewarding," he said. "What I do is more than a business, it's a lifestyle."

Eager to test his pizza chops in competition, Hunzinger traveled to Pizza Expo in Las Vegas in 2017. It was the first time he'd heard of the World Pizza Champions. They were recognizable in their team jackets and seeing them doing demonstrations and leading seminars "convinced me they were leaders in the industry. I instantly wanted to be a part of their mission."

Undeterred by his middle-of-the-pack finish that year, Hunzinger entered the Pan Pizza division of the 2019 Caputo Cup and won with his Momma Theresa pizza, named after his mother. At the 2020 Pizza Expo, he was invited to join the WPC team.

"Getting selected was surreal, just a tremendous honor," he said. "It feels great to be approved by your peers, and these guys, they do so much for the industry. I know it sounds crazy, but I still get chills every time I put on my WPC jacket!"

Momma Theresa

This recipe reflects memories of my mother's pizza I enjoyed growing up. This pizza has it all: sweet, savory, a little spice and it's visually stunning. Thin, crispy and packed with flavor, this pizza style is an ode to Italian grandmothers who would make pizza like this for their families. In this recipe, the pizza is baked with whole milk mozzarella and Pecorino Romano cheeses, crushed tomatoes, Sicilian oregano and extra-virgin olive oil.

Video: Stretching a New York-style Grandma pizza

HOT SOPPRESSATA MARMALADE

Makes 475 grams (2 cups)

3 medium-large jalapeños, about 85 grams
Extra-virgin olive oil
227 grams very finely diced hot soppressata
100 grams finely diced red onion
10 grams minced garlic
60 grams sherry vinegar
250 grams granulated sugar
25 grams sambal oelek chili paste

1. Position an oven rack on the top shelf and preheat the broiler to high.

2. Rub the jalapenos with a little olive oil and put on a baking sheet. Set on the top oven rack and broil, turning as needed to blister on all sides, 2 to 3 minutes per side. Because broiling intensities can vary significantly, keep a watchful eye so as not to burn.

Transfer to a metal bowl and cover the top tightly with plastic wrap. Let rest for 15 minutes to steam and loosen the charred skin. Remove the skin, cut open, and remove the seeds. (To maintain the jalapeños' flavor, do not rinse under water to remove the seeds.) Finely chop and set aside.

3. Put the soppressata in a sauté pan over medium heat and cook slowly to render fat, about 10 minutes. Strain fat from soppressata and set aside.

4. In the same sauté pan over medium-high heat, add 15 grams of olive oil. Sauté the red onion until beginning to lighten, 3 to 5 minutes. Stir in the garlic and continue to sauté until the onions and garlic are caramelized and fragrant, 1 to 2 minutes. Return the soppressata to the pan along with the roasted jalapenos. Mix well and sauté on medium-high to high heat to brown a bit more, about 2 minutes.

Lower the heat to medium. Stir in the sherry vinegar, scraping to loosen any bits on the bottom of the pan. Sprinkle in the sugar and cook, stirring often, until the sugar has melted and the liquid is thickened and coating the other ingredients, 8 to 10 minutes. Remove from the heat and stir in the sambal oelek. Spoon the mixture from the pan onto a plate to cool.

Transfer to a storage container. The marmalade can be stored in the refrigerator for up to 3 days. Bring to room temperature for the pizza.

MOMMA THERESA PIZZA

Makes one 12 × 12-inch Grandma-style pizza

PREFERENCES

Oregano: dried Sicilian oregano bunches

1 420 gram ball of Tony Gemignani's Master Dough (page 26)

175 grams whole milk block mozzarella cheese, shredded

200 grams crushed tomatoes

5 grams thinly shaved garlic

40 grams thinly sliced hot soppressata

10 grams extra-virgin olive oil

15 grams grated Pecorino Romano cheese

Dried oregano sprigs

75 grams ricotta, whipped

75 grams Hot Soppressata Marmalade (see page 116)

12 basil leaves

1. Remove the dough from the refrigerator 1 to 2 hours before baking, but keep covered or in the container at room temperature (65°F to 68°F). The dough should come to room temperature before stretching and shaping, but should not be too warm. (Avoid setting the dough on any warm surfaces like the stovetop, which could parcook the dough.)

2. Position an oven rack in the lower third of the oven, preferably with a baking steel or stone, and preheat to 500°F.

3. See Lee's video on stretching a New York-style Grandma pizza.

Lightly coat a 12-by-12-inch Grandma or Sicilian-style pan with olive oil, using your hands to spread it evenly. Lift the dough from the baking sheet or storage container and place top-side down into the prepared pan.

Gently pull the dough evenly outward from the sides towards the edges of the pan. Press the edges just a little bit (with no pressing in the center of the dough). Repeat this stretching until the sides nearly reach the edges of the pan. Once you are close to the edges, use your fingertips in a straight motion to press the dough into one of the edges and a corner. Turn the pan 90 degrees and repeat on the next side. Continue this until you press all four sides and corners. Press the dough with your fingers to ensure it is even.

Using a dough docker or a fork, lightly dock the full surface of the dough. Pinch the dough's edges against the sides of the pan to create a ½-inch frame. Press the top of the dough to release any air pockets and ensure an even thickness. Using your fingertips, dimple the top of the dough. Cover and let proof at room temperature until the dough has raised slightly and some bubbles form on the top, 30 to 45 minutes.

4. Spread the shredded mozzarella evenly across the dough up to the raised edge (½-inch frame). Spoon the crushed tomatoes on top of the mozzarella in small dollops about one inch apart. (Work around the outer perimeter of the pizza, framing the pizza, and then work your way toward the center.) Add the thinly shaved garlic across the top. Keeping in mind the pizza will be cut into 9 slices, then lay the sliced soppressata on top. Drizzle lightly with extra-virgin olive oil and sprinkle with the Pecorino Romano.

5. Set the pan in the oven. Bake, rotating the pan 180 degrees midway through baking, until the cheese is bubbling with some browning in spots and the crust is golden brown, about 15 minutes.

6. Transfer to a cooling rack. Carefully, using a large spatula, remove the pizza from the pan to the cooling rack for 3 to 5 minutes to cool slightly while keeping the bottom crisp. Next, slide onto a cutting board and cut into 9 slices. Working around the perimeter (like the tomatoes), pipe small dollops of ricotta cheese around the pizza, and then spoonfuls of the soppressata marmalade. Tear the basil leaves over the top and and rub the dried oregano between your palms to crumble over the pizza.

ANTHONY BERGHELA

OWNER, ROMO'S PIZZERIA & RESTAURANT
GLENMONT, NEW YORK

WPC MEMBER SINCE 2019

A conversation in high school was prophetic for Anthony Berghela's future, but that prediction was slow to manifest.

"A friend and I were just talking about what we'd do for a living when we got older, and when he said he'd become a bar owner, I said I would open a pizzeria," Berghela recalled. "Funny thing was I'd never worked in one. . . . Growing up I'd hung around a pizzeria where my uncles worked, but I just watched them do the work."

Closest he came to the actual exertion was in college. Living next door to a pizzeria where his cousins worked, he called to order a pie and his cousin told him, "'Come in and make the pizza yourself,'" he recalled. To do that, "I had to walk inside the kitchen. And there I could see how it all happened—the fryer guy doing his thing, the pizza guys doing their thing—and it really got my attention; this could be something for me someday."

But someday wasn't the next day or next month. It took five years of hopping between jobs "that gave me no feeling of passion or pride before I bought a business in 2009," he said.

That enterprise was a pizza shop in a C-minus location: 680 square feet with zero road visibility and a poor reputation as a pizzeria. Not only did Berghela have to learn the craft, he had to convince customers the pizzeria was even open for business. Tougher still, he had to convince them his pizza was better than the previous owner's. Fortunately, his girlfriend, mother, uncles, and brother stepped in to help the business move from days of $100 gross sales to respectability and profitability.

Berghela eventually upgraded to a 1,000 square-foot location that merely springboarded him to a 4,200 square-foot spot. The ambitious jump to a larger space necessitated a full-service restaurant to maximize its potential.

In 2013, his girlfriend, mother and sisters chipped in to send him to Pizza Expo, a bucket list trip that required him leaving his restaurant for the first time in years. There, he met other pizzaioli who were equally passionate about food and growing their businesses, and he attended seminars to learn how. Three years later, he traveled to Tony Gemignani's International School of Pizza, where he learned multiple pizza styles that became standards on Romo's menu. In 2019, he was invited to join the World Pizza Champions team.

"It's been a mind-opening experience to compete in Las Vegas and Italy against the best pizza makers in the world," he said. "But the experience of being around the men and women of the WPC, I can't say enough about them and what it's done for me and Romo's. It's changed my life."

Gracie Pie

I like naming menu items after people and places that inspire me. My daughters Gracelyn and Antonia are reasons I continue to grow and do what I do, so when putting this pizza on the menu years ago, instead of calling it an upside down pie like others would, I named it after my eldest, Gracelyn. The name Gracie Pie is synonymous now with our restaurant.

Video: Pushing out Sicilian dough for parbaking

PIZZA SAUCE FOR GRACIE PIE

Makes 500 grams of sauce; about 2 cups

196 grams canned crushed tomatoes
196 grams canned whole, peeled tomatoes, crushed by hand
98 grams tomato concentrate or paste
3.5 grams extra-virgin olive oil
3.5 grams fine sea salt
2.5 grams granulated sugar
0.5 grams finely ground black pepper
1 bunch of large fresh basil leaves (about __ leaves), coarsely torn

1. In a high-powered blender, combine both tomatoes with the tomato paste. This also can be done in a bowl using an immersion blender.

2. Add the olive oil, salt, sugar, pepper and basil leaves and blend until smooth.

3. Set the sauce aside or transfer to an airtight container and refrigerate for up to 3 days. Bring to room temperature before using.

GRACIE PIE

Makes one 12-by 16 to 17-inch Sicilian-style pizza

125 grams extra-virgin olive oil
One 906 gram ball Master Pizza Dough (page 26)
12 grams finely chopped garlic
12 slices thinly sliced (preferably at the deli counter) whole milk mozzarella cheese, about 310 grams
332 to 392 grams Pizza Sauce for Gracie Pie (see left)
84 grams grated Pecorino Romano cheese (56 grams for parbake and 28 grams for post bake)

TO PUSH OUT AND PARBAKE THE DOUGH

1. Remove the dough from the refrigerator 1 to 2 hours before baking, but keep covered or in the container at room temperature (65°F to 68°F). The dough should come to room temperature before stretching and shaping, but should not be too warm. (Avoid setting the dough on any warm surfaces like the stovetop, which could parcook the dough.)

2. Watch Anthony's video on pushing out Sicilian dough for parbaking.

Pour 56 grams of extra-virgin olive oil onto a half sheet pan or a 12-by-16-inch Sicilian-style pan. (This will also work in a 12-by-18-inch Sicilian pan, but the dough may not quite reach the corners. If using this

pan, keep a watchful eye when baking since it will be thinner.) Using a brush or your fingers, spread the oil evenly throughout the pan, being sure to cover all sides and corners.

3. Lift the dough carefully, bringing it into an oval shape and place in the prepared pan, turning it over to coat both sides in the oil. Using your fingertips, begin to press out the dough (smooth side up) towards the top edge of the pan, and then back towards the bottom. If any air bubbles appear, gently pop them. Continue to push out evenly towards all sides. With the dough covering about three-quarters of the pan, it will begin to resist and draw back. Cover and let it rest for 45 minutes to 1 hour.

4. At this point the dough should be much easier to press out. Continue pressing the dough towards the edges with your fingertips until the dough reaches the edges of the pan. Cover and proof at room temperature until the dough has risen to the top of the sheet pan (or about three-quarters of the way up the sides of a Sicilian-style pan with 1½-inch sides), 1 to 2 hours.

5. Meanwhile, position a rack in the center of the oven, preferably with a baking steel or stone and preheat to 450°F. Set the pan in the oven and bake, rotating the pan 180 degrees midway through baking, until golden brown, 10 to 12 minutes.

6. Transfer to a cooling rack and use a large spatula to carefully remove the parbaked dough from the pan. Cool for 15 minutes if continuing to topping and baking. If making ahead, cool the parbaked dough completely on the rack. The dough is okay at room temperature for up to 4 hours. For longer storage, wrap completely in plastic wrap and refrigerate for up to 1 day or double wrap (with foil, another layer of plastic wrap, or in a bag) and freeze for up to 2 weeks.

TO COMPLETE THE GRACIE PIZZA

1. Increase the oven temperature to 500°F.

2. Wipe out the pan and drizzle about 25 grams of extra-virgin olive oil into the pan. Using a brush or your fingers, spread the oil evenly over the bottom of the pan. Return the parbaked dough to the pan.

Combine the garlic with 42 grams of extra-virgin olive oil.

3. Position the pan with a long end in front of you. Create a ¼-inch border from the dough's edge by arranging the mozzarella slices in four rows of three to ensure each finished slice will have a single slice of mozzarella. Spoon the pizza sauce over the mozzarella followed by 56 grams of the Pecorino Romano over the sauce and then drizzle with the garlic oil.

4. Set the pan in the oven. Bake, rotating the pan 180 degrees midway through baking, until the cheese is bubbling with some browning in spots and the crust is golden brown, 10 to 12 minutes.

5. Transfer to a cooling rack and carefully, using a large spatula, remove the pizza from the pan to the cooling rack or onto a pizza peel. Check the bottom of the crust for crispness and, if needed, move the pizza to the steel, stone or directly on the oven rack for 1 to 2 minutes more.

6. Transfer the pizza to a cooling rack for 3 to 5 minutes to cool slightly while keeping the bottom crisp. Slide onto a cutting board and cut into 12 pieces. Sprinkle the remaining 28 grams of Pecorino Romano across the top and drizzle lightly with the garlic olive oil.

DOMENICO "MIMMO" TOLOMEO

CORPORATE CHEF, ORLANDO FOOD SALES, GLEN ROCK, NEW JERSEY
CO-OWNER, TAGLIO PIZZA, MINEOLA, NEW YORK

WPC MEMBER SINCE 2021

First-generation Italian-American, Domenico Tolomeo, learned the food-ways of his ancestors in delis and bakeries along Long Island. A product of Elmont, N.Y., he learned to butcher meat, make fresh mozzarella, dig into the essentials of classic dishes and managed one of the largest gourmet Italian markets on Long Island.

But when he turned 32, he turned his focus to one thing: mastering pizza. Under the tutelage of famed pizzaiolo Roberto Caporuscio, U.S. president of the Association of Neapolitan Pizza Makers (APN) and his daughter, award-winning pizzaiola Giorgia Caporuscio, Tolomeo received his APN certification. While working at Kesté Pizza e Vino, he dove into pizza competitions in Italy and the U.S. That helped him be named Caputo Rising Star Pizzaiolo at the 2019 Pizza Expo in Las Vegas. Three years later, Domenico would become the corporate chef of Orlando Foods, the exclusive importer of Caputo flour and Ciao tomatoes in the United States.

While training for the Trofeo Caputo in Naples, Italy, Tolomeo worked for months on ingredient selection, dough stretching technique, proper fermentation and finding the right baking temperature for his entry. In that process he created a hybrid style he named Pizza Americana.

"Pizza Americana combines the best characteristics of pizza Napoletana and New York-style pizza into one new style of pizza," he says. "It's an ode to Napoli and New York, two cities very near and dear to my heart."

Tolomeo's pizza maintains the pronounced airy *cornicione* (crust edge) of a tender 12-inch pizza Napoletana and the crispness and overall aesthetics of an 18-inch New York-style pizza.

"People would see the pizza and think, 'It looks Neapolitan,' but they knew it wasn't because it's the size of a traditional New York-style pie," Tolomeo says. "The most important ingredient required to do this is Caputo Americana 00 flour, which is milled in Napoli."

Selecting the finest ingredients not only ensures a great outcome, he says they give him the upper hand on competitors.

"Ciao Pomodori tomatoes from Italy are something else I insist on," he begins. "They help bridge the gap between Napoli and New York and provide the authentic Italian flavor I want."

Like a lot of World Pizza Champions members, Tolomeo was honored to be asked to join the team. The best way to improve your craft, he says, is to work with others of equal passion and high skill level.

"For me, the World Pizza Champions were always the best of the best pizza makers all on one team, and it's amazing to be a part of that," says Tolomeo, now co-owner of Taglio Pizza Mineola, N.Y. and Corporate Chef of Orlando Food Sales. "But the support you receive and the friendships made are a breath of fresh air in a highly competitive industry."

Americana Pizza

I chose to share this dough recipe for the Pizza Americana below because it's my perfect hybrid between New York and Neapolitan Pizza. This highly versatile and flavorful dough is easy to prepare. Although it takes just a little time to make its essential starter and requires a longer fermentation, the end result will surely put a smile on your face.

AMERICANA DOUGH

Makes 943 grams; enough for three 12-inch pizzas

PREFERENCES

Salt: Sicilian sea salt

BIGA

216 grams Caputo Americana 00 flour
0.5 grams Caputo dry yeast
97 grams cold water at 65°F

DOUGH

280 grams cold water at 55°F
14 grams honey
0.5 grams Caputo dry yeast
270 grams Caputo Americana 00 flour
54 grams Caputo Tipo 1 flour
14 grams salt
11 grams extra-virgin olive oil

NOTE ON HONEY FOR THIS RECIPE

If this pizza is made in a commercial grade electric oven, eliminate the honey from the dough.

TO MAKE THE BIGA

1. In a large bowl combine the flour, yeast and water and mix with a wooden spoon until yielding a shaggy dough, about 2–3 minutes. Break up into small pieces and put in a proofing box or bowl. Cover the top with plastic wrap and poke holes across the top to allow the biga to breathe. Leave at room temperature for 12 to 18 hours.

TO MAKE THE DOUGH

1. In the bowl of a stand mixer fitted with the dough hook attachment, combine the water, honey, biga, and the yeast on the stir setting (speed 1) for 1 minute, then increase to low (speed 2) until the mixture is frothy, 4 to 5 minutes.

2. Add both of the flours and mix on the stir setting (speed 1) for 5 minutes. Stop the mixer, cover, and let rest for 30 minutes.

3. Mix the dough on the stir setting (speed 1) for 2 minutes. With the mixer running, stream in the salt and continue to mix for 5 minutes. With the mixer still running, drizzle in the olive oil. Increase to low (speed 2) and mix until the oil is completely absorbed and the dough is smooth and well combined.

4. Lightly dust the work surface and turn the dough out. Cover with a damp towel and let sit at room temperature for 30 minutes.

5. Divide the dough into thirds, trimming to 300 gram portions. Form into balls **(see Floriana's video on page 174)**. Put each into a lightly oiled dough box or storage container with a lid. Refrigerate for 24 hours.

AMERICANA PIZZA

Makes one 12-inch pizza

One Americana Dough ball
(see page 128)
100 grams crushed Ciao
Authentica tomatoes
Pinch dried oregano
Pinch grated Pecorino Romano
cheese
3 basil leaves
120 grams burrata, pulled apart
by hand into strips
Olive oil for finishing

1. Remove the dough from the refrigerator 1 to 2 hours before baking, but keep covered or in the container at room temperature (65°F to 68°F). The dough should come to room temperature before stretching and shaping, but should not be too warm.

2. Position one of the oven racks on the lowest rungs and another in the upper third of the oven with baking steels or stones on each. Preheat to 550°F (or as hot as possible for your home oven) for at least 30 minutes. Alternatively, you can use one steel or stone set on an oven rack positioned on the lowest rung.

3. Dust a smooth work surface with just enough flour to keep the dough from sticking, then dust the dough and a peel. Push and stretch the dough out to a 12-inch round **(watch Thiago demonstrate on page 82)**, and slide onto the peel.

4. Spoon the crushed tomatoes onto the dough, leaving a ½-inch border from the dough's edge. Sprinkle with the oregano and then the grated Pecorino Romano.

5. Slide the pizza onto the bottom steel and bake for 3 to 5 minutes or until the crust is beginning to brown and the cheese has melted, but isn't browning.

Lift the pizza with the peel, rotate it 180 degrees once, and continue to bake until the bottom crust is a rich golden brown and the cheese is bubbling with some browning in spots, 4 to 5 minutes. Baking time will vary depending on the max temperature of the oven.

Alternatively, if baking on one steel or stone, bake for 7 to 10 minutes on the bottom steel rotating the pizza 180 degrees once during the baking.

If the crust top does not have the desired doneness, move to the top steel or stone, turn the oven to broil, keep the pizza on the peel and then hold it under the broiler to brown. Keep a watchful eye so as not to burn it!

6. Transfer the pizza to a cooling rack for 30 seconds to 1 minute. Slide onto a cutting board. Arrange the basil leaves and burrata over the top. Finish with a drizzle of olive oil. Cut into 8 wedges.

In a professional setting, this pizza is best baked in a commercial grade electric oven at 620°F. Bake, rotating 180 degrees midway through baking until the cheese is completely melted and browning in spots, and the crust is golden brown with some charring on the crust, 6 to 7 minutes.

TONY CERIMELE

OWNER, NEW COLUMBUS PIZZA CO., NESQUEHONING, PENNSYLVANIA

WPC MEMBER SINCE 2018

Tony Cerimele got his work ethic the old-fashioned way: growing up in a busy family catering business. Started in the 1950s by his grandparents and uncles, the catering company's menu included pizza, which Cerimele learned to make. But by the time he was ready for college, "I didn't want my family's pizza anymore," says the Nesquehoning, Pennsylvania, native. "You can imagine I'd eaten plenty of it, so I was sick of it."

His uncles viewed it differently when they were his age. When their mother made it for their meals, they'd take the pizza to fire halls and bars and sell it. It quickly became popular, so in addition to the hours required to run a booming catering business, the family sold carryout pizza to the public every Friday.

"And that's what they became known for, the pizza," Cerimele says, adding that the business eventually closed when its older partners retired. "Eventually I wanted to bring the business back."

That wish would lie dormant as Cerimele got through college and began working in fields such as medical device sales. But reminders of those great pies would follow in the least expected places. A woman he met at his first job out of college was from Old Forge, Pennsylvania, and she led him there on their second date to taste the eponymously named pizza style.

"I'm expecting a round pizza, but this pizza comes out and it's rectangular," Cerimele recalls. (His date, Marianne, became his wife.) The Sicilian-like pie featured onions, black pepper and a cheese blend he didn't recognize, but liked. "That was the spark that started me thinking about making pizza again and doing the Old Forge style."

Several years later, Cerimele reopened his family's catering business under the name of New Columbus Pizza Co. His family's 60-year-old pizza recipe would feature prominently in the business's offerings, and over time he added other styles. To increase his pizza knowledge, he attended classes at the International School of Pizza in San Francisco and became a certified pizzaiolo. As his skills grew, he added a mobile wood fired pizza catering option.

"This is a family-run operation, and my mother, Marguerite, who is 84, can outwork anyone," Cerimele says proudly. "My sister Theresa and nephew Sam have all been working since we reopened." "My father, who we called Zeppy, was also a huge part of the business when he was alive."

As in the past, Friday is the only day New Columbus serves pizza to the public. Not surprisingly, Cerimele runs out of pizza before he runs out of customers.

"We have had some pretty upset customers when they couldn't get a pizza, but we've been doing that since 1958 and will continue that tradition," he says.

Cerimele credits his pizza peers with inspiring him to make phenomenal pies and helping him sort through business challenges. That he was invited to join the World Pizza Champions in 2018 implies he's equally inspiring and wise.

"The best part of being on the team is being with an amazing group of people with the same goals," he says. "The chance to see the world through the eyes of other pizza makers is incredible. I'm just lucky to be around such people."

Old Forge

This Old Forge double crust pizza is very simple to make, though the dough requires some patience. When you make it, you might find it similar to what your parents or grandparents made when you were a kid. Think homemade pizza or bread on a Sunday morning or the first thing you eat on a Friday night after a high school football game. Just try it, you'll love it.

PREFERENCES

Flour: Sir Galahad or King Arthur
Salt: fine sea salt

Video: Assembling an Old Forge pizza

OLD FORGE DOUGH

Makes 926 grams; enough for 1 12-by-17-by 2.8-inch Old Forge pizza

330 grams cold water at 65˚F
16 grams granulated sugar
14 grams salt
550 grams all-purpose flour, 11% to 12% protein
5.5 grams fresh cake yeast or 3.5 grams instant yeast
11 grams Crisco, plus additional for the pan
Extra-virgin olive oil

TO MAKE AND PROOF THE OLD FORGE DOUGH

1. In the bowl of a stand mixer, whisk the water, sugar and salt together until the sugar and salt have dissolved.

2. Add the flour and crumble fresh yeast over the top. If using instant yeast, sprinkle it over the top.

3. Fit the mixer with the dough hook attachment and combine on the stir setting (speed 1), 2 to 3 minutes. Increase the speed to medium (speed 3 or 4) and mix until the dough is more developed and has a smooth and satiny appearance, 3 to 4 minutes.

4. Turn off the mixer and add the Crisco. Mix on medium (speed 3 or 4) until fully incorporated, about 2 minutes.

5. Transfer the dough to a lightly floured work surface. Wipe out the mixing bowl (or grab a clean bowl) and lightly coat with olive oil. Return the dough to the bowl, cover and let rest for 20 minutes.

6. Liberally coat a 12-by-17-by 2.8-inch Detroit-style pan with Crisco.

7. Turn the dough out onto a lightly floured work surface and sprinkle with flour. Using a rolling pin, roll into a rectangle about 10-by-15-inches. Lay the dough top-side up in the pan. With your fingertips, gently press the dough to reach all sides of the pan. If the dough resists, cover, and let it rest a few minutes before pressing it out a bit more. Cover the pan with its lid or plastic wrap and refrigerate overnight.

8. Remove the pan with the dough from the refrigerator and let sit, still covered at room temperature for 6 to 8 hours until the dough has doubled in size. (Avoid setting the dough on any warm surfaces like the stovetop, which could parcook the dough.)

OLD FORGE PIZZA

Makes one 12-by-17-by-2.8-inch Old Forge pizza

1 medium onion, cut in half and sliced paper thin on a mandoline

15 grams extra-virgin olive oil

3 grams granulated garlic

3 grams fine sea salt

.5 grams freshly ground black pepper

1 medium onion

15 grams extra-virgin olive oil

680 to 850 grams of mixed shredded cheese (see Note on Shredded Cheese Mixture, page 137)

.5 grams dried rosemary, crushed gently with hands or 1 gram chopped fresh rosemary

1. During the last hour of the dough proofing, position a rack in the center of the oven, preferably with a baking steel or stone, and preheat to 450°F.

2. Peel the onion and cut in half through its equator and then slice as thinly as possible on a mandoline. Toss the slices with the olive oil, breaking into individual rings.

Combine the granulated garlic, salt and pepper in a small bowl and set aside.

3. Watch Tony's video on assembling an Old Forge pizza on page 134.

Once the dough is ready, gently press on the surface with your fingers to deflate any large air bubbles that may have formed underneath. Position the pan with a short edge facing you. Gently press the dough into the bottom and side edges of the pan so it "crawls" towards the top of the pan. Lift the top edge of the dough and drape it over that end of the pan.

Arrange the shredded cheese on top of the dough, covering about three-quarters of the surface while being sure to get it into the bottom corners. The surface area will be dense with cheese.

Take the cheeseless portion of the dough from the opposite short edge of the pan and carefully stretch and fold it over to completely cover the cheesed portion. Be sure that all the edges match up and join together. Use your fingertips to pinch the dough together around all of the edges, gently folding them together. (This sealing method is similar to how you would close the edges of a calzone.) Once it's sealed on all three sides, gently press on the top to redistribute the cheese and to cover about three-quarters of the bottom of the pan with the filled dough.

Tear four small holes on the top of the pizza to allow steam to escape.

4. Sprinkle with the granulated garlic mixture, followed by the rosemary, and then the onions, piling them generously on top. Finish with a little more rosemary.

5. Set the pan in the oven. Bake for about 8 or 9 minutes. Carefully check the bottom of the crust. If at any point you notice it is browning too quickly, use the "double pan" method described below. After checking the bottom, rotate 180 degrees and return to the oven. Continue the baking process until you have golden-brown crusts and crisp onions, usually 20 to 25 minutes depending on the oven.

The hallmark of an Old Forge White Pizza is a golden-brown top with crispy onions, as well as a golden-brown bottom crust. The color of both the top and bottom should be similar to the picture here. Since oven temperatures and heating elements can vary greatly, it's best to check throughout the baking process (especially the bottom crust) to ensure even baking. Have another pan on hand (a baking sheet will work); if the bottom begins to brown too quickly, simply take the pizza out of the oven, place it on the second pan, and return it to the oven. This "double pan" method will allow the bottom cooking to slow while the top continues.

6. When baking is complete, transfer to a cooling rack. Carefully, using a large spatula (sometimes two are needed), move the pizza from the pan to the rack. Let stand for 3 to 5 minutes for the cheese to firm up before cutting. Lastly, slide the pizza onto a cutting board and divide into 12 "cuts."

NOTE ON THE SHREDDED CHEESE MIXTURE

The amount of cheese used depends on how much cheese you like in your Old Forge Pizza. Once you make this recipe a few times, you'll decide on the amount you like. I suggest starting on the lighter side, using about 685 grams. (This is still a generous amount of cheese.)

My favorite grated cheese blend is 35 percent whole milk mozzarella, 25 percent brick cheese, 25 percent white cheddar, and 15 percent white American cheese. And, if you can't find brick cheese you can substitute mozzarella and cheddar.

For 685 grams that would be 235 grams grated whole milk mozzarella, 174 grams grated brick cheese (or muenster, but brick is worth seeking out), 174 grams grated white cheddar, and 102 grams grated white American cheese.

TONY TROIANO

OWNER, J.B. ALBERTO'S PIZZA
CHICAGO, ILLINOIS

WPC MEMBER SINCE 2015

That Tony Troiano became a highly successful pizzeria operator isn't all that surprising when you learn that he started at age five. Yeah, five. You can do that when your family owns the pizza shop.

"I was clearing tables, cutting bread and grinding cheese at that age," Troiano says. "By the time I was 10, I was making pizzas as good as the seasoned veterans who'd worked there for years."

Like many of his WPC teammates, his true love for the business came from watching people happily eat food he'd made. That simple connection confirmed he'd be a pizza lifer—though that didn't happen automatically.

When he was a teenager, his father sold the pizzeria to fund a partnership in a high-end full-service Italian restaurant and bar. But some partnerships end on a sour note, and Troiano's father sold out and prepared to move the family back to Italy.

Still, none of it distracted Troiano from pizza work. Midway through high school, his boss at a pizzeria asked if he wanted to partner on a recently closed pizzeria.

"I didn't even have a driver's license yet, and I was flattered and interested in the opportunity," he said. "But I had to ask my parents."

Turns out the ask wasn't necessary. Just a few days later, a foodservice distributor called his father about a pizzeria for sale in a densely populated neighborhood. Father and son liked the spot, struck a deal with its owners and took over the business, Alberto's Pizza.

"After a few years of hard work, tweaking recipes and promoting Alberto's, we began to win over the community and grow the business," Troiano recalls. "In 1981 our largest competitor, J.B.'s Pizza, came up for sale. We purchased it and merged the two pizzerias into J.B. Alberto's Pizza. We've since grown to be one of the busiest delivery-carryout operations in the country."

Ever the student of the business, Troiano was a regular at the annual Pizza Expo in Las Vegas. When he first saw the WPC team there, the crew was tossing dough to music.

"They were pizza makers, athletes and dancers all rolled into one," he recalls. "It was so fun to watch and they wore some pretty cool looking chef coats donning the WPC logo."

Though Troiano and some WPC team members became friends, he hadn't been invited to join the team until they surprised him during the fiftieth anniversary celebration of J.B. Alberto's. As Troiano's crew gave away free slices and T-shirts to about 3,000 loyal customers, WPC teammates Tony Gemignani and Scott Anthony celebrated the milestone by presenting Troiano with the WPC team patch.

"I cannot explain how much it meant to me," he says. "To be surrounded by the best pizzaioli in the world, people who help and develop each other to be better at our craft, is simply amazing. Being part of the WPC team is the pinnacle of my pizza career and I'm fortunate to be a small part of the team."

Italian Beef and Giardiniera Pizza

In this recipe I combine two truly Chicago items: our Chicago-style thin pizza (a.k.a. cracker thin) and Italian beef and giardiniera, a classic sandwich filling used as a pizza topping. This is a real Chicago treat!

Video: Rolling out a cracker thin crust

CRACKER THIN CRUST DOUGH

Makes 981 grams; enough for two 12-to-14-inch pizzas and one 8-inch pizza

PREFERENCES

Flour: Ceresota
Salt: iodized

325 grams cold water, at 65°F
24 grams half-and-half
3 grams granulated sugar
2 grams fresh cake yeast (see Note on Fresh Cake Yeast, below)
12 grams vegetable margarine, softened
12 grams corn oil, plus additional for brushing the dough
3 grams salt
600 grams all-purpose flour, 11 to 12% protein

NOTE ON FRESH CAKE YEAST

Cake yeast is the preference here, but if unavailable, substitute 0.8 grams of instant or active dry yeast. Instant yeast can be added at the same point as the cake yeast. If using active dry yeast whisk the yeast into 50 grams of the water in a small bowl prior to beginning the dough. It then can be added to the larger mix of water and half-and-half.

1. In the bowl of a stand mixer, whisk together the water, half-and-half, sugar, cake yeast and margarine to combine. Add the corn oil and salt and whisk again. Fit the mixer with the dough hook attachment. Add the flour. Mix on the stir setting (speed 1) for 1 minute. Increase the speed to low (speed 2) and continue to mix until smooth, 6 to 7 minutes more.

2. Transfer the dough to a clean work surface. Cover with a damp cloth and let rest at room temperature for 1 hour.

3. Using a dough cutter/bench scraper, divide the dough into two 370-gram pieces. The remaining dough, about 220 grams, can be used for a smaller 8-inch pizza. Form into balls **(see Mike demonstrate on page 26)** and set on a clean baking sheet or container. Rub with a little corn oil, cover and refrigerate for at least 24 hours and up to 2 days.

PIZZA SAUCE FOR CRACKER THIN CRUST

Makes 577 grams (about 2¼ cups)

PREFERENCES

Salt: iodized

368 grams tomato puree

200 grams crushed tomato

14 grams grated Parmigiano Reggiano cheese

3 grams salt

3 grams finely ground black pepper

1.7 grams granulated sugar

1.7 grams dried oregano

1. Whisk all of the ingredients together until completely combined.

2. The sauce can be used at this point or refrigerated for up to 3 days. Bring to room temperature before using.

ITALIAN BEEF AND GIARDINIERA PIZZA

Makes one 14-inch pizza

One 370-gram ball Cracker Thin Crust Dough (see page 140)

Cornmeal, for dusting

150 grams of Pizza Sauce for Cracker Thin Crust (see left)

150 grams thinly sliced Italian roast beef

75 grams hot giardiniera, drained (more or less depending on your heat tolerance)

180 grams whole milk block mozzarella, shredded

Generous pinch dried oregano

1. Remove the dough from the refrigerator 1 to 2 hours before baking, but keep covered or in the container at room temperature (65°F to 68°F). The dough should come to room temperature before stretching and rolling, but should not be too warm. (Avoid setting the dough on any warm surfaces like the stovetop, which could parcook the dough.)

If the sauce has been refrigerated, set on the counter at this point as well.

2. Position an oven rack in the center of the oven with a baking steel or stone on top. Preheat to 500°F for at least 30 minutes.

3. Dust a smooth work surface with just enough flour to keep the dough from sticking. Sprinkle cornmeal on a pizza screen or peel.

4. Watch Tony's video on rolling out a cracker thin crust on page 140.

Push the ball with your fingertips to make a basic circle. Next,

using a rolling pin, roll the dough out to a 14-to-15-inch round. Using a dough docker or a fork, dock the dough to keep it from puffing up as it bakes. *Optional step:* To make a perfect 14-inch circle, trim the edges with a pizza wheel. (A 14-inch pizza screen or dish inverted on the top will help when cutting an even round.) Transfer the dough round to the pizza screen or peel.

5. Spoon the pizza sauce evenly on top, leaving a ¼ inch border from the dough's edge. Arrange the beef evenly over the sauce. If you like extra sauce, drizzle a bit more on top of the beef. Keeping your heat tolerance in mind, intersperse the giardiniera. Top with the mozzarella and then sprinkle with the oregano.

6. Slide the pizza from the peel onto the steel and bake until the crust is golden brown and the cheese is bubbling, 9 to 12 minutes (depending on thickness), rotating 180 degrees once during the baking. If your pizza is on a screen, bake the same way.

7. Transfer the pizza to a cutting board and cut in a grid pattern into 3-inch squares. Correct! Squares, not wedges. That's how we do it in Chicago!

ANTHONY (TONY) SCARDINO

OWNER, PROFESSOR PIZZA
CHICAGO, ILLINOIS

WPC MEMBER SINCE 2019

Typical of dinner at an Italian-American home in Chicago, food was always front and center during family gatherings in Tony Scardino's youth. Early on, Scardino found the kitchen to be his combination of comfort zone and classroom, where he watched his mother make sauce, his grandmother shape meatballs, and his aunts and grandfather bake cookies.

"As I got older, it became apparent that my passion and profession would be in the kitchen in one capacity or another," Scardino says.

Starting with Inspiration Kitchens in Chicago, his training moved from the simple (his uncle's hot dog stand) to trendy restaurants such as Publican Quality Meats and Au Cheval. He says that fine dining refined and sharpened his kitchen skills, "but my roots were calling, and nothing made me want to make my mark on this industry quite like pizza."

Fully focused on the humble, savory pie, he sought training from the best and traveled to Tony Gemignani's International Pizza School for a deep dive.

"I was totally mind blown by that," he says. "It was the most formative experience that had ever happened in my pizza education—probably in all of my culinary training to that point."

In addition to his two-week stay at the school, he *staged* at some of Gemignani's restaurants. Upon returning to Chicago, he introduced Detroit-style pizza to the city when helping open Paulie Gee's Logan Square pizzeria. He later managed Dough Bros, a New York-style slice joint in the heart of downtown, but when the Covid pandemic hit, he pivoted to pop-up dinners under the Professor Pizza brand.

When Gemignani encouraged Scardino to help him with Pizza Expo instructional demonstrations and seminars, Scardino jumped at the chance to be around top-level pizza makers from across the globe. Eventually, that led him to begin competing against them, and in 2019, he was invited to join the WPC team.

"We were at an awards ceremony, and they were announcing new inductees to the team in front of about 200 people," Scardino begins. "They announced a couple of people's names, and then someone said, 'You're next, buddy.' I said, 'I don't know what you're talking about,' Then they called my name. It was hard to process that I would be joining this elite team. The whole thing was humbling then, and it still is."

Gyros Grandma Pizza

While I love hot dogs and Italian beef sandwiches, there was always something special about my Uncle Fred's gyros served at his hot dog stand, Mandino's. A toasted pita, perfectly crispy shaved gyros strips, cucumber, tomato, and tzatziki sauce ties it together. I have recomposed all the elements of this food memory as a grandma-style pizza designed to be cooked in an outdoor gas or wood-burning Ooni oven.

TZATZIKI

Makes about 775 grams (3¼ cups)

PREFERENCES

Calabrian chili paste: Tutto Calabria

Half English (seedless) cucumber, about 150 grams
450 grams Greek yogurt
175 grams sour cream
20 grams extra-virgin olive oil
10 grams freshly squeezed lemon juice
10 grams Kalamata olive brine
6 grams pepperoncini brine
4 grams dried oregano
2.5 grams minced garlic
2.5 grams garlic powder
1.5 grams onion powder
1.5 grams chopped dill
1.5 grams chopped mint leaves
5 grams Calabrian chili paste

1. Peel the cucumber and cut it in half lengthwise. Use a spoon to scoop out the seeds and discard. Cut the cucumber into ¼-inch dice. Set in a strainer over a bowl for 15 minutes. Dry on paper towels and put in a medium bowl. Add all of the remaining ingredients and stir together. Cover and refrigerate until ready to use, up to 3 days.

GYROS GRANDMA PIZZA

Makes one 12-by-12-inch pizza

PREFERENCES

Gyro strips: Kronos brand

One 425 gram ball of Tony Gemignani's Master Dough (page 26)
Six (28-grams each) thin slices (preferably at the deli counter) of whole milk mozzarella
Six slices fully cooked gyros strips
1 large garlic clove, shaved
Extra-virgin olive oil
5 grams dried oregano
380 grams Tzatziki (see left)
65 grams seedless cucumber slices, thinly sliced lengthwise, preferably on a mandoline
8 cherry tomatoes, cut in half
2 grams thinly sliced red onion
30 grams crumbled feta cheese
3 grams mint florets or small mint leaves
3 grams dill fronds

TO PUSH OUT AND PARBAKE THE DOUGH

1. Remove the dough from the refrigerator 1 to 2 hours before baking, but keep covered or in the container at room temperature (65°F to 68°F). The dough should come to room temperature before stretching and shaping, but should not be too warm. (Avoid setting the dough on any warm surfaces like the stovetop, which could parcook the dough.)

Video: Cutting and garnishing a Gyros Grandma Pizza

2. Lightly coat a 12-by-12-inch Grandma or Sicilian-style pan with olive oil. Lift the dough from the baking sheet or storage container and place in the prepared pan. Gently stretch the dough evenly outward from the center. Using your fingertips, start to push the dough to the edges from top to bottom, turning the pan 90 degrees with each pass. Press the dough with your fingers to dimple the top and ensure it is even. The dough will not reach the sides. Cover the top of the pan with its lid or plastic wrap and keep in a warm place for about 20 minutes.

Dimple and extend again until dough snaps back. Continue this every 20 or 30 min until dough is extended to each pan corner. (Note: If your kitchen temperature is cool, the dough will resist stretching and this step will take longer. If it's warmer, the dough will relax and this step could finish in two passes). Once the dough has been extended to all of the corners, cover, and let rise until it has doubled in size, about 2 hours.

3. Meanwhile, preheat an outdoor Ooni oven to 500°F for about 30 minutes. **(Watch Siler set up an oven on page 76.)** If your oven doesn't have a built-in temperature gauge, an infrared thermometer is recommended to measure the oven's deck temperature for accuracy. If using wood, brush away any ash or wood embers off the baking surface before adding the pizza.

4. Gently, dimple the top of the dough. This last dimpling ensures an even rise in the oven and prevents a peak in the middle during the parbake. Set the pan in the oven and then turn off the oven. Bake using the residual heat until you start to see small brown spots on top, about 5 minutes.

5. Transfer to a cooling rack and, using a large spatula, carefully remove the parbaked dough from the pan. Cool for 15 minutes if continuing to topping and baking. If making ahead, cool the parbaked dough completely on the rack. The dough is OK at room temperature for up to 4 hours. For longer storage, wrap completely in plastic wrap and refrigerate for up to 1 day or double wrap (with foil, another layer of plastic wrap, or in a bag) and freeze for up to 2 weeks.

TO COMPLETE THE GYROS GRANDMA PIZZA

1. Preheat (or return the heat) of the Ooni oven to 500°F. Once heated, keep the flame low. If you have an infrared thermometer, use it to check the oven deck temperature.

2. Lightly oil the pan and return the dough to the pan. Lay the mozzarella slices on top, leaving a ¾-inch border from the dough's edge. Arrange the gyros on top of the mozzarella and place garlic slices on top of the gyros. Drizzle with extra-virgin olive oil, favoring the gyros strips, and sprinkle with oregano. Have a cooling rack or other heat proof surface near the oven.

3. Set the pan in the oven. Bake until the cheese is bubbling and the crust is golden brown, about 6 minutes, using a peel during the baking time to rotate the pan 180 degrees to ensure even browning. Transfer the pan to the cooling rack. Carefully, using a large spatula, lift the pizza from the pan to check the bottom of the crust to be sure it is browning equally to the top. If the bottom is browning more quickly, put the rack in the oven with the pizza on top until the top is as browned as the bottom. Or, if you're skilled with a pizza peel, lift the pizza on the peel 2 to 3 inches toward the oven dome to promote top browning. If the baking is even, but could be a richer brown, return to the oven for a couple more minutes. Total baking time on the pizza is 6 to 8 minutes.

4. Slide onto a cutting board. Cut into 4 square slices. Spoon dollops of tzatziki over the top. Lay the cucumber slices, folded end to end, next to the tzatziki. Nestle the tomatoes and red onion across the whole pizza. Top with the crumbled feta, drizzle with olive oil, and sprinkle with oregano. Place the mint and dill to garnish.

Watch Anthony's video on cutting and garnishing a Gyros Grandma Pizza on page 146.

LEO SPIZZIRRI

OWNER, SPIZZIRRI MEDIA GROUP
CHICAGO, ILLINOIS

WPC MEMBER SINCE 2008

As a first-generation Italian-American, Leo Spizzirri grew up in the kitchen with his Mom and Nana Gilda, watching and assisting while they created traditional Italian dishes. He quickly developed the family passion for all things pizza, bringing also to his endeavors a fastidious perfectionism and a desire to share his expertise with the community.

Today, Spizzirri holds the distinction of being one of only a hundred worldwide Master Instructors from Venice, Italy's Scuola Italiana Pizzaioli. He's also a consultant who brings a deep knowledge of dough rheology (think: pizza physics) to manufacturers. And he's had a hand in major Chicago operations, including Giordano's Famous Stuffed Pizza. His expertise in commercial artisan bread and frozen pizza have led him to innovate for and support major national brands across the United States and Canada.

In addition to the recipe he shares in this book, Spizzirri gives advice and tutorials to both professionals and at-home foodies on his "Ask Chef Leo" social media channels and "The Pizza Garage" YouTube channels. In 2022, he created the Spizzirri Media Group which specializes in pizzeria consulting and education, and the production of high quality pizza content. And this year, he is opening his first restaurant, Pizzeria Moderna, in Austin, Texas.

All in all, Spizzirri is a chef who gets attention. Case in point, that World Pizza Championships competition, some years ago, when he was told his Chicago stuffed pizza had to be entered in the Non-Traditional division. "I was rattling the cage saying, 'It's not traditional? Says who?'" Spizzirri recalled.

His dispute had merit. Chicago stuffed pizza is a direct descendent of torta pasqualina (translated as Easter torte), a savory Italian double crusted pie filled with vegetables, eggs and ricotta cheese. For at least a century, Italian immigrants in Chicago were swapping out those ingredients with mozzarella and meats.

Tony Gemignani had Spizzirri's back, telling him not only to enter the pie, but to go big. "He says, 'Make it over the top. Make it in a 20-inch pan,'" Spizzirri says. The entry weighed a hefty 13 pounds. Since 6 pounds of its bulk was mozzarella, when sliced, the cheese pull was luxuriously thick and long. Photographers covering the contest couldn't get enough of Spizzirri and his pie.

"Tony knew that it would attract a ton of attention and that that was more important than a win," Spizzirri says. "I became forever known based on that little moment. It didn't matter that the Italian judges hated it."

None of that would have happened without being a WPC member, Spizzirri says.

"We learn so much from each other that makes us better. That kind of support doesn't happen a lot between competitors, but it happens in this group."

Chicago Stuffed Pizza

My stuffed pizza is the classic pie from Chicago. It's true to the old school formula from a time when it was still cool to use lard in a dough and not worry about offending a vegan. The dough has a beautiful flakiness to it because of the lard, yet it eats surprisingly light and is crispy enough to lift a slice to your mouth. Knife and fork not required if you prefer to pick it up!

Video: Building a traditional Chicago stuffed pizza

STUFFED PIZZA DOUGH

Makes 1.17 kilograms; enough for one 14-inch Chicago stuffed pizza

PREFERENCES

Flour: Ceresota
Salt: fine sea salt

400 grams cold water, at 55°F
14 grams salt
7 grams non-diastatic malt
700 grams all-purpose flour, 11 to 12% protein
7 grams instant yeast
45 grams lard

1. In the bowl of a stand mixer, whisk together the water, salt and malt until dissolved. Fit the mixer with the dough hook attachment. Add the flour and yeast. Combine on the stir setting (speed 1) for 3 minutes.

2. With the mixer running, break the lard into pieces and add to the bowl. Continue to mix on the stir setting (speed 1) for 5 minutes. Increase to low (speed 2) and mix for 2 minutes more. Let the dough rest at room temperature for 15 minutes.

3. Transfer the dough to a clean work surface. Using a dough cutter/bench scraper, divide into a 650 gram portion (for the bottom) and a 450 gram portion (for the top). Form into balls **(see Mike demonstrate on page 26)** and set on a clean baking sheet or container, cover and refrigerate for 24 hours.

PIZZA SAUCE

Makes 646 grams (2½ cups)

PREFERENCES

Tomato paste: double concentrated
Oregano: dried Sicilian oregano bunches
Salt: kosher

517 grams ground or crushed tomatoes
74 grams tomato paste
37 grams extra-virgin olive oil
7 grams finely chopped garlic
5 grams salt
4 grams dried oregano
2 medium-large basil leaves

1. Pour the ground tomatoes, tomato paste, olive oil, garlic, salt and oregano into a bowl. Roll the basil leaves together then smash between your hands to release the essential oils. Tear into pieces and add to the bowl. Whisk together until combined. The oil will shimmer on the top. The sauce is ready at this point, but can be refrigerated for up to 3 days. Bring to room temperature and whisk before using.

CHICAGO STUFFED CHEESE PIZZA

Makes one 14-inch Chicago stuffed pizza

Vegetable margarine
650-gram dough ball (see page 152)
450-gram dough ball
340 grams pizza sauce (see page 152)
800 grams whole milk or part-skim block mozzarella, shredded
10 grams grated Parmigiano Reggiano
Dried oregano sprigs

1. Remove the dough from the refrigerator 1 to 2 hours before baking, but keep covered or in the container at room temperature (65°F to 68°F). The dough should come to 55°F when tested with an instant-read thermometer. (Avoid setting the dough on any warm surfaces like the stovetop, which could parcook the dough.)

2. Position the oven racks in the upper and lower third of the oven with baking steels or stones on each. Preheat to 480°F to 490°F for at least 30 minutes. (Or to 500°F depending on the settings of your oven, keeping in mind baking times could be a few minutes less.) Coat the bottom and sides of a 14-inch round Chicago-style pizza pan with 2-inch sides (deep-dish nesting pan) with margarine.

3. **Watch Leo's video on building a traditional Chicago stuffed pizza on page 152.**

4. Using a rolling pin or dough sheeter, roll the 650 gram portion of dough to a 17-to-18 inch round. Lay the dough in the pan, gently easing it onto the bottom. Use your fingertips to press out any air bubbles from under the dough. Using your fingertips press the dough firmly into the pan's bottom edges and then against the sides. Once the sides are fully pressed the dough should extend over the edges by at least 2 inches.

5. Spread the mozzarella on top of the dough to fill the bottom of the pan. Gently shake the pan to spread evenly.

6. Roll the 450 gram portion of dough to 16-inches (enough to extend beyond the rim on all sides of the pan). Lay on top to cover the mozzarella. Gently press the dough against the top of the cheese and into the sides of the pan. Using your fingertips, work your way around the pan, pressing the dough into the inside edge of the pan, leaving some indentations. Using your fingertips in a gentle snapping motion, pinch 9 evenly spaced holes into the top layer of dough. Lastly, pinch a 1-inch hole at the dough's center. These holes will allow steam to escape.

7. With a sharp knife, cut any excess dough from the edges to create a uniform and smooth edge. The pizza should look like a pie at this point.

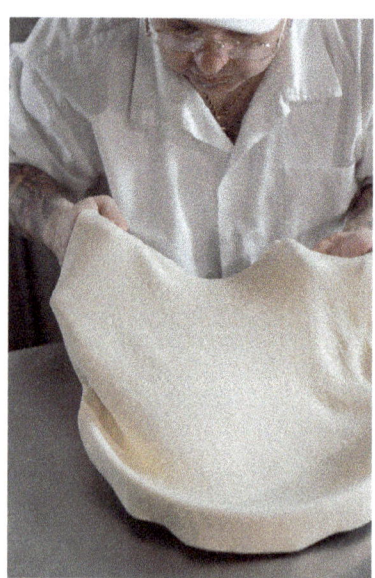

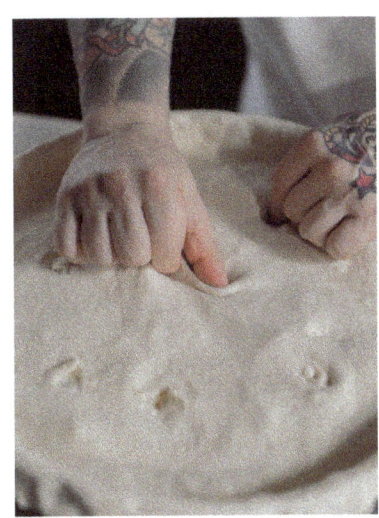

8. Spoon the pizza sauce evenly on the top layer of dough. Grate some Parmigiano Reggiano on top.

9. Slide the pizza onto the bottom steel and bake for 15 minutes. Lift the pizza with a large offset spatula or a peel, rotate it 180 degrees and transfer to the top steel. Bake until the crust is a rich golden brown, 10 to 12 minutes. Alternatively, if baking on one steel or stone, bake for 25 to 27 minutes, rotating the pizza 180 degrees once during baking. Transfer to a cooling rack for 5 minutes to cool slightly.

10. Using a large offset spatula, carefully remove the pizza from the oven onto a cutting board. Sprinkle a little more Parmigiano Reggiano on top of the sauce and rub the dried oregano between your palms to crumble over the pizza. Cut the pizza into 6 equal slices without removing them from the whole.

11. Bring the cutting board with the pizza to the table. With a pie server, remove the slices to serve. Presentation is key to the Chicago pizza, so enjoy the beauty of the cheese pull as the molten cheese oozes onto the plate!

PETE TOLMAN

OWNER, IRON BORN PIZZA
PITTSBURGH, PENNSYLVANIA

WPC MEMBER SINCE 2019

Like several WPC members, Pete Tolman dove deep into fine dining before surfacing in the pizza business. After earning a culinary school degree, he worked in five-star fine dining kitchens and became an executive chef at a high-end grocery chain.

The shift to pizza came during a 2016 vacation to Telluride, where friends insisted he visit Brown Dog Pizza, owned by WPC member Jeff Smokevitch. The shop was known for its top-notch Detroit-style pizza, and Tolman ordered it.

"I was absolutely blown away by it," Tolman recalls. "I told everyone at the table I would try to make Detroit-style pizza and open a shop in Pittsburgh."

To ensure his palate wasn't fooling him, he returned to Brown Dog the next day for another dose of that airy Detroit-style crust. This time his mind turned to its business potential.

"I saw a gap in the Pittsburgh market for that kind of pizza," Tolman says. "And with an upswing for Detroit-style pizza at that time, it was perfect timing for me."

Tolman read every book and internet article he could on Detroit-style pizza and reached out to experts such as Shawn Randazzo, owner of Cloverleaf in Detroit and a one-man pied piper who helped nationalize the style.

The Iron Born name pays homage to Tolman's birthplace in the steel city of Pittsburgh and the blue steel pans commonly used in Detroit-style pizza. Exactly one year after Tolman spoke of his hopes at the table in Telluride, the wraps came off of Iron Born Pizza. Customers swarmed to the shop, to see his fresh take on this style of pizza.

"We sold out every day for the first month," says Tolman, who has since added a second location. Iron Born made Pittsburgh's Magazine's Best New Restaurant list, and the White Pie (featured here) was named one of Pittsburgh's 20 Most Iconic Dishes by Good Food Pittsburgh. "We had to figure out how to scale up."

To tweak Iron Born's operation for greater volume, he called other operators and visited Pizza Expo to meet like minded peers. Amazed that so many operators would share their wisdom and help him succeed, he vowed to do the same for others.

"A big reason why I wanted to join this team was because so many members took time out of their days to listen to the struggles and hopes of a nobody in the pizza business," he says. "When I met these guys who'd helped me before, I thought, if they can help others in this business, why wouldn't I do the same?"

Little did Tolman know that WPC team members were assessing his potential as a member of the group. It didn't hurt that his pizza won the Northeast division, and third overall, at the International Pizza Challenge. Still, Tony Gemignani wanted to meet him personally.

"I went to his booth and chatted, and I guess he was just trying to make sure I was a normal, decent person," Tolman says of the WPC co-founder. "All I know is I was glad to be asked."

White Pie

As we prepared to open our first restaurant, I began trying to create the ideal pizza that my wife Carrie would order with a group of friends. I wanted to design something unique but had familiar flavors for anyone to enjoy. I tried a few different flavor combinations including roasted baby kale, cherry tomatoes, and caramelized onions with a gouda cheese crust. On opening day, we proudly presented this version of the White Pie and it will never leave our menu in the future.

Our final creation has roasted cherry tomatoes, caramelized onions, piped ricotta cheese and a pile of arugula topped with parmesan cheese and lemon.

I think this pizza defines Iron Born's signature look. It shows our signature ricotta dots, impactful design and flavorful local ingredients.

Video: Piping and finishing a Detroit White Pie

DETROIT-STYLE DOUGH

Makes 759 grams; enough for two 8-by-10-inch Detroit-style pizzas

PREFERENCES

Flour: Central Milling Artisan Bakers Craft flour with 11.5% protein

425 grams all-purpose flour, 11 to 12% protein
308 grams water, at 60°F
3 grams instant yeast
4 grams low diastatic malt
11 grams salt
8 grams olive oil

TO MAKE THE DOUGH

1. In the bowl of a stand mixer fitted with the dough hook attachment combine the flour, cold water, yeast and malt on the stir setting (speed 1) and mix for about 30 seconds. Increase the speed to low (speed 2) and continue mixing until just combined to a shaggy mass, but not quite a ball, 3 to 5 minutes.

2. Increase the speed to medium-low (speed 3 or 4) and stream in the salt as the dough begins to form a firmer ball and the salt is fully incorporated, about 4 minutes. With the mixer still running, slowly stream in the oil. Now increase the speed to medium-high (speed 6) and mix until smooth and satiny, about 5 minutes more. Ideally, the finished dough temperature will be about 72°F, which you can check with an instant-read thermometer. Transfer the dough to a storage container and refrigerate for at least 24 hours, but preferably for 2 days.

TO PUSH OUT AND PARBAKE THE DOUGH

Canola oil, or another neutral oil
40 grams (20 g per parbaked crust) shredded part-skim block mozzarella and provolone cheese blend

1. Oil the bottom and sides of an 8-by-10-inch Detroit-style pan. Remove the dough from the refrigerator. Using a dough cutter/bench scraper, divide the dough in half for two 375-gram portions. Place one 375-gram piece of dough into the prepared pan. Using flat, extended fingers (imagine playing a piano), press the dough toward each of the corners of the pan. Since dough is still warming and relaxing, you may need to use your knuckles for additional pressure to push the dough outwards. Be careful not to press so hard that the dough pinches and sticks to the bottom of the pan. Once it resists and begins to pull back, cover and let rest in a warm spot for 30 minutes.

2. Continue to press out with your fingertips, working towards the corners and edges,

resting as needed. This process of pressing dough to the pan's corners and edges and resting will take 1 to 2 hours. Once the dough has reached all of the edges, cover, and let proof in a warm spot until the dough has doubled in height, 1½ to 2 hours. The dough will jiggle slightly when jostled.

3. Meanwhile, position a rack in the center of the oven, preferably with a baking steel or stone and preheat to 525°F (or as hot as possible for your home oven) for at least 30 minutes. This is also a great time to prepare the caramelized onion jam and the garlic cream.

4. Set the panned pizza in the oven and bake, rotating the pan 180 degrees once, midway through baking, until golden brown, 8 to 10 minutes.

5. Transfer to a cooling rack to rest in the pan. Sprinkle a 20 gram border of the cheese blend along all sides of each pan to create the cheese frico that lines the edges of a Detroit-style pizza. Cool for 15 minutes if continuing to topping and baking.

If making ahead, cool the parbaked dough completely on the rack. The dough is OK at room temperature for up to 4 hours. For longer storage, wrap completely in plastic wrap and refrigerate for up to 1 day or double wrap (with foil, another layer of plastic wrap, or in a bag) and freeze for up to 2 weeks.

CARAMELIZED ONION JAM

Makes 85 grams (⅓ cup)

PREFERENCES

Salt: kosher

150 grams finely diced white onion
45 grams unsalted butter
35 grams granulated sugar
4 grams kosher salt
60 grams water

1. Combine all of the ingredients in a small sauté pan. Set over medium-low heat and cook slowly, stirring occasionally as the liquid reduces and simmers. Continue to cook, adjusting the heat as needed to maintain a low simmer until the liquid has reduced almost completely and the onions have a jam-like texture, about 20 minutes more. (Cooking time can vary considerably depending on your burner setting.) If the liquid reduces too quickly and the sugar begins to caramelize too fast, add a splash of water to adjust the texture and slow down the cooking. The final jam should be golden brown and have the consistency of a chunky jam or chutney. Onion jam should be sweet and salty. Adjust the seasoning, if needed.

2. Remove from the heat and let cool to room temperature. The jam can be used at this point or refrigerated for up to 3 days. Let come to room temperature before using. To loosen, it can be gently reheated with a little bit of water.

GARLIC CREAM

Makes 105 grams (about ½ cup)

PREFERENCES

Italian herbs: blend of rosemary, thyme, basil and oregano
Salt: kosher

150 grams heavy cream
5 grams Roasted Garlic with Herbs (page 271)
1 gram crushed red pepper flakes
1 gram dried Italian herbs
Zest of quarter lemon
1 grams salt

1. Pour the heavy cream into a small saucepan. Add the garlic. Set over medium heat and stir continuously until the mixture comes to a boil. Lower the heat and simmer while still stirring until the mixture is reduced by one-third, about 10 minutes. Using an immersion blender, puree the garlic cream until smooth. The sauce should lightly coat the back of a metal spoon. If it is too thin, cook it a minute or two longer. Pour the mixture through a small chinois or strainer then stir in the red pepper flakes, herbs and lemon zest. Adjust as needed. Set aside in a warm spot while parbaking the crust or building the pizza.

WHITE PIE

Makes one 8-by-10-inch Detroit-style pie

PREFERENCES

Cheese: Grande 50-50 Blend, part-skim mozzarella and provolone

135 grams shredded part-skim block mozzarella and provolone cheese blend

12 Roasted Cherry Tomatoes (page 271), about 60 grams

90 grams Garlic Cream (see page 160), warmed as needed

40 grams Caramelized Onions (see page 160)

113 grams ricotta in a piping bag with a large opening

22 grams arugula

Small piece Parmigiano Reggiano cheese

14 grams Lemon Oil (page 270) or store bought

TO COMPLETE THE WHITE PIE

1. If the dough has been made in advance, position an oven rack in the center of the oven, preferably with a baking steel or stone and preheat to 525°F (or as hot as possible for your home oven) for at least 30 minutes.

2. Sprinkle the cheese over the top of the parbaked dough. Keeping in mind the pizza will be cut into 6 slices, arrange the tomatoes on top. Next, place the pan in the oven and bake, rotating the pan 180 degrees midway through baking, until the cheese is bubbling with some browning in spots and the crust is golden brown, 7 to 10 minutes.

3. Transfer to a cooling rack. Carefully, using a spatula, remove the pizza from the pan to the cooling rack or onto a pizza peel. Carefully, keeping the frico edges intact, move the pizza to a cutting board. Cut into 6 slices; one cut lengthwise and 2 cuts crosswise.

Watch Pete's video on piping and finishing a Detroit White Pie on page 158.

4. Ladle the warm garlic cream down each side lengthwise in two stripes. Make sure the top of the piping bag is twisted and secure. Pick up in your right hand (or dominant hand). Again keeping in mind six slices, hold the piping bag over the top of the pizza. Apply pressure with your right hand only and make a circle, stopping the pressure as soon as you finish while simultaneously twisting and lifting the bag away. Repeat 5 more times.

5. Using a small spoon, top with caramelized onions. Pile the arugula high down the middle of the pizza between the lines of ricotta circles. Grate Parmigiano-Reggiano over the top and then drizzle with lemon oil.

THOMAS "TOMMY" SCHNEIDER

OWNER, TOMMY'S PIZZERIA, WINNIPEG, MANITOBA

WPC MEMBER SINCE 2019

At just age 15, Tommy Schneider was already hungry for work, so he started making pizza at a small shop in Winnipeg, Manitoba, Canada. The friendly atmosphere of the place—plus seeing smiling guests happy to pick up their pizzas—spurred the dream of owning his own place one day.

"It's always been a fun business for me," Schneider says, "and I enjoy learning about it because I get better at it."

After three years at the University of Winnipeg, Schneider craved a true hands-on approach to business and pizza, and at only 19, he moved to Granbury, Texas, to become a Papa John's franchisee. A year later, he opened a second location in Weatherford, Texas, and ran both successfully for the next four years before returning to Winnipeg.

"I learned a lot about operations and marketing in the Papa John's system, things I could apply to my own place," he said. "But I wanted to be more creative with the menu and do a variety of stuff."

That quest brought him to San Francisco where he attended Tony Gemignani's International School of Pizza. His pizza perspective was never the same.

"There was a lot of art and science behind pizza making that I didn't know," Schneider says. "When you get around people who really know what they do, people who have such passion for something, you want to learn everything you can."

After Schneider partnered with a friend to open Timmy Tom's Pizzeria in 2017, he started "tagging along" with the World Pizza Champions to international contests. Not surprisingly, the camaraderie built with his pizza peers deepened his excitement for the craft.

"Those contests are intense, especially in Italy," he says of the World Pizza Championships. Encouraged to compete rather than merely assist, he traveled to competitions in Atlantic City and Las Vegas. At the latter, he placed third in the International division of the non-traditional category in 2018, and by 2019, when the WPC team headed to Parma, Italy, for the world championships, he was confident.

Schneider not only won Best Pizza Maker from Canada that year, he got the call to join the World Pizza Champions team.

"My goal was maybe getting on this team after 10 to 15 years," he says, laughing. "But when Tony presented me the (WPC) patch, I was speechless and honored."

In January of 2020, Schneider finally stepped out on his own with Tommy's Pizzeria in Winnipeg's little Italy neighborhood. True to his desire for menu diversity, the lineup goes beyond pizza to meatballs, subs and pasta dishes. Those items' titles are often infused with WPC members' names.

"The camaraderie on this team is the opposite of how operators treat each other in Canada, where everyone keeps to themselves," Schneider says. "You know how, as you get older, you stop playing team sports? This is like getting another chance to do that again, only it's on a pizza team."

Maple Bacon Pizza

What's more Canadian than maple syrup, eh? My winning entry for all of Canada at Le Pizza Week 2021 featuring maple syrup on the base and top, thick-cut bacon, apples poached in brown sugar, a special blended goat cheese, and candied walnuts.

POACHED APPLES

Makes 123 grams (about 1 cup)

250 grams warm water
40 grams brown sugar
½ cinnamon stick
1 gram vanilla syrup or pure vanilla extract
1 medium apple peeled, cored and cut into ⅛-inch slices

1. Combine the water, brown sugar, cinnamon and vanilla in a medium saucepan. Bring to a boil, stirring to dissolve the sugar. Add the apple slices and remove from the heat. Let the apples cool in the liquid at room temperature for at least 1½ hours for the flavors to infuse. If making ahead, transfer the apples in the liquid to a storage container and refrigerate for up to 3 days. Before using, remove the apples with a slotted spoon, blot dry on paper towels.

CANDIED WALNUTS

165 grams (about 1 cup)

84 grams walnuts, chopped coarsely
84 grams granulated sugar
3 grams water
0.5 grams finely ground cinnamon

1. Line a baking sheet with a silicone baking mat or a lightly oiled piece of parchment paper.

2. Combine sugar, water and cinnamon in a medium frying pan set over medium-high heat, swirling the mixture occasionally. When the mixture starts to bubble, lower the heat to medium and add the nuts to the pan to coat completely. Remove from the heat as needed to keep the sugar from burning. Once the mixture is a rich golden brown, remove from the heat and pour onto the lined baking sheet. Spread the nuts to prevent sticking and let cool to room temperature.

HERBED GOAT CHEESE

180 grams (about ⅔ cup)

125 grams chèvre
1 gram freshly squeezed lemon juice
1 gram finely chopped parsley
2 grams finely chopped oregano
0.5 gram finely chopped rosemary
0.5 gram minced garlic
Pinch of salt
Pinch of freshly ground black pepper
Heavy cream, 50 to 70 grams

1. Put half of the goat cheese in a bowl with the lemon juice and blend with a fork.

2. Put all of the herbs, garlic, salt and pepper on a cutting board. Chop together and then mash with the flat side of the knife to make a paste. Add the paste to the bowl with the remaining cheese. Mash the mixture together until well incorporated and smooth. Add the cream a little at a time until it has a pipable texture.

Video: Piping and finishing a Maple Bacon Pizza

3. Transfer to a piping bag with a medium tip or to a plastic bag with a finger-width hole cut in the bottom corner. * The herbed goat cheese is best made soon before making the pizza and kept at room temperature, but can be made in advance. If making ahead, refrigerate for up to 3 days, but bring to room temperature before using.

PAR-COOKED BACON

Yields 16 pieces par-cooked bacon

8 slices of bacon
   (about 175 grams)

1. Preheat the oven to 375°F. Line a baking sheet with parchment paper and prepare a plate with paper towels.

2. Cut bacon slices in half widthwise and place on the parchment paper.

3. Cook until the bacon starts to firm on the edges, but is not crunchy, about 7 minutes per side, depending on the thickness. Drain off bacon fat and transfer to paper towels to absorb additional fat.

MAPLE BACON PIZZA

Makes one 14-inch New York-style pizza

PREFERENCES

Mozzarella: Galbani

One 370 gram ball of Tony Gemignani's Master Dough (page 26)
80 grams maple syrup (70 g for baking and 10 grams for finishing)
150 grams shredded whole milk block mozzarella cheese
Par-Cooked Bacon
60 grams Poached Apples (see page 164)
90 grams Herbed Goat Cheese (see page 164)
15 grams walnuts or Candied Walnuts (see page 164)

1. Remove the dough from the refrigerator 1 to 2 hours before baking, but keep covered or in the container at room temperature (65°F to 68°F). The dough should come to room temperature before stretching and shaping, but should not be too warm. (Avoid setting the dough on any warm surfaces like the stovetop, which could parcook the dough.)

2. Position the oven racks in the upper and lower third of the oven with baking steels or stones on each. Preheat to 550°F (or as hot as possible for your home oven) for at least 30 minutes. Alternatively, you can use one steel or stone set on an oven rack positioned in the center of the oven.

3. Dust a smooth work surface with just enough flour to keep the dough from sticking, then dust the dough and a peel. Push and stretch the dough out to a 14-inch round **(watch Joe's demonstration on page 264)**, and slide onto the peel.

4. Drizzle the maple syrup over the dough, leaving a 1-inch border from the dough's edge. Cover the syrup with the mozzarella. Arrange the bacon slices and the apples on top.

5. Slide the pizza onto the top steel and bake for 5 to 7 minutes or until the crust is beginning to brown and the cheese has

melted, but isn't browning. Lift the pizza with the peel, rotate it 180 degrees and transfer to the bottom steel. Bake until the bottom crust is a rich golden brown and the cheese is bubbling with some browning in spots, 3 to 5 minutes. Alternatively, if baking on one steel or stone, bake for 8 to 12 minutes, rotating the pizza 180 degrees once during the baking. Baking time will vary depending on the max temperature of the oven.

6. Transfer the pizza to a cutting board.

Watch Tommy's video on piping and finishing a Maple Bacon Pizza on page 164.

7. Using a piping bag, squeeze small dollops of the herbed goat cheese onto each slice, keeping in mind there will be 8 wedges. Place a candied walnut on each dollop and sprinkle the rest across the pizza. Drizzle the remaining 10 grams of maple syrup onto the crust, then swirl towards the center. Cut into 8 wedges.

MICHAEL ANDROW

OWNER, E&D PIZZA COMPANY
AVON, CONNECTICUT

WPC MEMBER SINCE 2021

As a grandson of the owners of New London, Connecticut's legendary Downtown Bakery, Michael Androw's pizza journey began when he was very young.

"Every Italian bakery always had pizza, so it was no surprise that I loved pizza when I was very young," Androw says. Ironically, his first-ever job involved making pies at the local pizzeria in his hometown. "Pizza was my first love. It's what initially hooked me into the restaurant business." But before opening his own shop, he spent years exploring and learning every other facet of the restaurant industry, from casual and fine dining to nightclubs and bars. "I ventured out and learned every corner of the business and eventually returned to my first love."

In 2014, he opened E&D Pizza Company (named after his sons, Enzo & Dario) in Avon, Connecticut. Androw insisted on setting the bar of quality extremely high at E&D. The effort paid off. Within a year, the pizzeria had garnered top pizza honors from The Hartford Courant and Connecticut Magazine, an incredible feat in a state known for its legendary and iconic pizzerias.

"Then, one day, you get the call from Tony Gemignani telling you you're getting inducted to the World Pizza Champions. I was going to become a 'made' man in the business," he says with a laugh. "This is hands down the highest honor in our industry. Not only have I met several pizzaioli who share my passion for pizza but it's also given me the opportunity to educate others through writing and public speaking. Growing up in this industry, I could have never imagined anything like that being possible."

E&D Pizza Company has grown so much in a decade that Androw can now focus on different pursuits. He is a regular speaker at International Pizza Expo, writes frequently for Pizza Today, and has become a leader in his local community. "I feel as if some days we give away more pizza than we actually sell," he jokes. "We try to be the leaders in supporting our community's events, especially with the kids. Whether it be Little League, school sports, or other youth activities, we always want to be the first to lend our support and provide pizza."

What drives Androw? "Pizza. I'm driven by the love of pizza and loving this business and all the opportunities it provides for us to bring our neighbors and community together. Every day, I want to do right by everyone, my family, my staff, and the community."

The Positano

One of the unique and immensely popular pizzas on our menu is the Positano—a departure from the traditional red sauce pizza with assorted toppings. This pie brings together a plethora of complementary flavors that are a step away from the everyday norm. The combination of the creamiest of chèvre, black Mission figs and Mike's Hot Honey makes for a fantastic marriage of flavors. And we make a ton of this pizza at E&D Pizza Company!

Makes one 14-inch
New York style pizza

**Video: Oiling the top
of the dough**

One 366 gram ball of Tony
    Gemignani's Master Dough
    (page 26)
Extra-virgin olive oil
    (about 25 grams)
100 grams whole milk block
    mozzarella cheese, shredded
120 grams crumbled chèvre
130 grams dried black Mission figs
    stemmed and quartered
45 grams red onion, peeled, cut
    in half and sliced thinly on a
    mandoline or with a knife
Drizzle of Mike's Hot Honey

1. Remove the dough from the refrigerator 1 to 2 hours before baking, but keep covered or in the container at room temperature (65 to 68°F). The dough should come to room temperature before stretching and shaping, but should not be too warm. (Avoid setting the dough on any warm surfaces like the stovetop, which could parcook the dough.)

2. Position the oven racks in the upper and lower third of the oven with baking steels or stones on each. Preheat to 550°F (or as hot as possible for your home oven) for at least 30 minutes. Alternatively, you can use one steel or stone set on an oven rack positioned in the center of the oven.

3. Dust a smooth work surface with just enough flour to keep the dough from sticking, then dust the dough and a peel. Push and stretch the dough out to a 14-inch round **(watch Joe's demonstration on page 264)** and slide onto the peel.

4. **Watch Michael's video on oiling the top of the dough.**

Drizzle the olive oil, preferably using an oil can, in a spiral pattern over the dough, leaving a 1-inch border from the dough's edge. Then brush the oil across the entire surface of the dough.

5. Spread the mozzarella evenly across the dough followed by the chèvre, leaving a 1-inch border. Intersperse figs and red onion on top of the cheese.

6. Slide the pizza onto the top steel and bake for 5 to 7 minutes or until the crust is beginning to brown and the cheese has melted, but isn't browning. Lift the pizza with the peel, rotate it 180 degrees and transfer to the bottom steel. Bake until the bottom crust is a rich golden brown and the cheese is bubbling with some browning in spots, 3 to 5 minutes. Alternatively, if baking on one steel or stone, bake for 8 to 12 minutes, rotating the pizza 180 degrees once during baking. Baking time will vary depending on the max temperature of the oven.

7. Transfer the pizza to a cutting board and cut into 8 wedges. Drizzle with the hot honey.

FLORIANA PASTORE

OWNER, SIGNORA PIZZA
LAS VEGAS, NEVADA

WPC MEMBER SINCE 2022

Floriana Pastore always wanted to be in her grandmother Amalia's kitchen learning the traditional dishes of her hometown, Salerno, Italy. Not surprisingly, cooking became a lifelong passion that eventually hyper-focused on pizza. At age 21, she opened her first pizzeria, no small accomplishment in the homeland of such an iconic meal.

But five years later, she was on the move, relocating to Veneto, Italy, with her daughter Annamaria. Leaving home wasn't easy, she says, "but it was necessary for my professional growth. I was well aware of the obstacles I would face. But despite difficult times, I never gave up."

Along the way she stepped into competitive pizza making; she was a rarity in the male-dominated scene. Yet she racked up victories, including four championships in Italy from 2001 to 2004. A decade later, three other firsts would come at the International Pizza Challenge at the annual Pizza Expo in Las Vegas.

Her launch of Insonnia Café in Padua, Italy, in 2006 led to a profitable five-year run and an eventual sale that allowed her to travel and work globally in places such as London, Kerala, India, and Dubai, which was her base for six years while she worked as an executive chef. Some of those trips took her to Las Vegas to visit family. Turned out she liked the city and discussed moving there with her husband someday. That happened in 2020, when they created "our pizzeria on wheels, Signora Pizza."

The truck, designed and manufactured by family members in Italy, was created to capitalize on the U.S. mobile-food trend. Its inspiration, she says, was Neapolitan street food. "We decided to create the only pizza container truck in the world that merges fried and baked pizza in one place," she says. A brick-and-mortar location is in the works. "Our dream came to life by combining our family's skills in design and manufacturing."

Along the way, those three wins in Las Vegas attracted the attention of the World Pizza Champions. Wins were important, but she believes her dedication to the craft was what led to her invitation to join.

"I'm very proud to be a part of this group because we help each other and share a lot," she said. "The energy, the knowledge, the positive vibes and motivation from them—these are things everyone needs in life."

Pizza Rossana

This pizza means a lot to me because I created and dedicated it to my Aunt Rossana, who was my biggest fan and supporter. Pizza was her favorite food (and especially mine), and every single ingredient reflects her soul and her character. It is an explosion of tastes and colors from the first bite.

Video: Portioning, balling, and storing Neapolitan-style dough

PIZZA ROSSANA DOUGH

Makes 525 grams dough; enough for two 12-inch Neapolitan pizzas

PREFERENCES
Flour: Tipo 00 flour
Salt: fine sea salt

300 grams 00 flour
4 grams granulated sugar
1 gram instant yeast
200 grams water, at 65°F
10 grams salt
10 grams extra-virgin olive oil

1. In the bowl of a stand mixer fitted with the paddle attachment, mix the flour and sugar on the stir setting (speed 1) for 1 minute. With the mixer running, sprinkle in the yeast and then slowly add the water. This should take about 3 minutes. Once all of the water has been added, sprinkle in the salt, increase to low (speed 2), and mix for 5 minutes.

2. If the dough is sticking, scrape the bottom and sides and continue to mix to be sure all ingredients are evenly incorporated, and mix for 2 more minutes. With the mixer running, drizzle in the olive oil, increase to medium-low (speed 3 or 4) and mix until the dough is elastic, approximately 3 minutes more.

3. Remove the dough from the mixing bowl and place the dough in a large bowl, cover with plastic wrap, and let it rest at room temperature for 30 minutes, then refrigerate for 12 hours.

4. Remove the dough from the fridge and allow it to warm at room temperature (65°F to 68°F) for 1 to 2 hours (Avoid setting the dough on any warm surfaces like the stovetop, which could parcook the dough.)

5. Watch Floriana's video on portioning, balling, and storing Neapolitan-style dough.

Turn the dough out onto a clean work surface and, using a dough cutter/bench scraper, divide in half. Use the scraper and your hands to work the dough into a ball without adding extra flour. Lift the dough off of the work surface, gently folding it onto itself, turning and lifting with each fold. As the ball becomes more developed, the dough will become easier to work with. Once the dough is in a compact round, place your fingers on the sides and roll the sides to smooth and tighten even more. Repeat with the other piece of dough.

Lightly oil two round storage containers, ensuring they are large enough for the dough balls to double in size. Set a dough ball in each container and let them rise at room temperature until doubled, 4 to 6 hours.

If using a professional wood-fired or gas oven, start heating it early to ensure it is ready when you are. The temperature should be 800°F to 900°F. Bake, rotating 180 degrees midway through baking until the cheese is completely melted and browning in spots, and the crust is golden brown with some charring on the crust, about 90 seconds.

SEMI-DRIED CHERRY TOMATOES

Makes 120 grams (¾ cup)

240 grams cherry tomatoes, halved
10 grams extra-virgin olive oil
0.3 grams fine sea salt
10 grams granulated sugar
Pinch dried thyme
Pinch dried oregano

Preheat the oven to 275°F.

1. Toss all of the ingredients together on a small baking sheet. Roast in the oven until semi-dried, about 2 hours. The tomatoes should have lost a lot of their moisture, but should not be totally dried. Reserve at room temperature for the pizza. Remaining tomatoes can be refrigerated in a storage container for up to 3 days.

NOTE ON YELLOW DATTERINO TOMATOES

Yellow Datterino tomatoes are very low in acid and high in sweetness. They originated in Sicily and are available jarred and in cans, usually whole. For this recipe coarsely purée, preferably through a food mill or pulse in a food processor.

PIZZA ROSSANA

Makes one 12-inch Neapolitan pizza

One ball Pizza Rossana Dough (see page 174)
Semolina flour, for dusting
90 grams yellow Datterino tomatoes, pureed (See Note on yellow Datterino tomatoes, left of baking instructions.)
5 medium basil leaves
90 grams fior di latte, fresh mozzarella, torn into small pieces
25 grams Semi-Dried Cherry Tomatoes (see left)
Extra-virgin olive oil, for drizzling
125 grams burrata, cut thinly
20 grams microgreens, preferably a rainbow mix
15 small purple potato chips
Balsamic vinegar, preferably organic

1. Position the oven racks in the upper and lower third of the oven with baking steels or stones on each.). Preheat to 550°F (or as hot as possible for your home oven) for at least 30 minutes. Alternatively, you can use one steel or stone set on an oven rack positioned in the center of the oven.

2. Dust a smooth work surface with just enough semolina flour to keep the dough from sticking. Dust both sides of the dough as well as a peel. Push and stretch the dough from the center while simultaneously pressing the dough outward to a 12-inch round with a 1-inch rim (the puffy *cornicione*, which is consistent with authentic Neapolitan style pizza), while gently flattening the dough where the toppings will be added **(watch Thiago demonstrate on page 82).** Move onto the peel.

3. Using a large spoon, spread the yellow tomato purée evenly across the dough and then tear the basil leaves over the top. Arrange the fior di latte and the semi-dried cherry tomatoes evenly across the pizza. Drizzle with olive oil.

4. Slide the pizza onto the top steel and bake for 3 to 5 minutes or until the crust begins to brown and the cheese has melted, but isn't browning. Lift the pizza with the peel, rotate it 180 degrees and transfer to the bottom steel. Bake until the bottom crust is a rich golden brown and the cheese is bubbling with some browning in spots, 4 to 5 minutes more. Baking time may vary depending on the oven's maximum temperature. Alternatively, if baking on one steel or stone, bake for 6 to 10 minutes, rotating the pizza 180 degrees once during the baking.

5. Transfer the pizza to a cutting board and cut into 6 slices.

6. Using a spoon, lay the burrata slices in the center of each wedge, forming a circle atop the pizza. You can also lay one in the center. Top each slice with a small bundle of microgreens, and add a few drops of balsamic vinegar to the greens. Break the purple potato chips all around the pizza and lightly drizzle everything with extra-virgin olive oil.

Buon Appetito!!

SCOTT ANTHONY

OWNER, PUNXSY PIZZA
PUNXSUTAWNEY, PENNSYLVANIA

WPC MEMBER SINCE 2015

When Scott Anthony left college in 1983, one of many things he wanted was to be his own boss. His entrepreneurial bent led him to launch a janitorial service since there weren't many competitors clamoring to work in that space. Sexy as that endeavor wasn't, it helped Anthony learn business basics that would apply to whatever opportunity that followed.

And that was pizza. Be it a genetic tug from his Calabrian ancestors or "the fact that I just liked pizza," Anthony became an owner-operator in 1994, taking over an existing pizzeria. Pizza was its own animal and Anthony had to adapt quickly by reading trade publications and attending industry conferences. Through a lot of trial and error, success soon found him. Anthony's email marketing tactics gained him national attention and several awards.

"I always had a thirst to learn and grow personally," Anthony says. "So, in 2009, I attended Tony Gemignani's International School of Pizza, which was an eye opener."

A mind-opener as well. With nearly scripted irony, the Punxsutawney, Pa., resident's pizzeria experience had become a Groundhog Day existence—always the same rules and menu, which moved him to change.

"I took the step to full entrepreneurship in 2014, which really opened the way to creativity in the kitchen," Anthony says. "I felt I'd learned enough over the years operating the pizzeria I took over and that I could do things my way and succeed."

Having built many relationships with Punxsutawney customers, Punxsy Pizza did well from the start. Sooner than he'd imagined, not only was Anthony enjoying the freedom to create food his way, he was helping others inside and outside of the industry. As his pizzeria and restaurant consulting business flourished, he saw opportunities to help his community. Four times he's earned the Pennsylvania Restaurant & Lodging Association's Restaurant Neighbor award.

"I'm not from Punxsutawney, but I've always wanted to be a part of the community where I lived," Anthony says. "I think it's important to give back—whether it's your community or your industry—you help others, and especially those who've helped you. The WPC team has definitely helped me." Anthony's community event, 'Pizza and Prevention' has become famous in the industry.

Much to his surprise, Anthony was invited to join the World Pizza Champions in 2015, and he still jokes that he "might not really belong. These guys had so much notoriety and amazing skills, they were impressive. But they saw qualities in me that I never saw in myself, and they inspired me to reach for my full potential. I never felt like I was a superstar like many of these guys have become. I feel like a lot of people on this team: just lucky to be here."

The Caruso Summer Solstice Pizza

The recipe—which is easy and can be baked in any oven—was inspired by my industry experiences, my network of peers, my family and my travels to Italy. I am of Calabrian descent, so I incorporated Calabrian chili peppers in this pizza as a spicy note that offsets the sweetness of the strawberries I use in the sauce. You can taste the sweetness, but really can't put your finger on it. (I also chose strawberries because on my first trip to Italy, in the local markets, we got some of the best strawberries I have ever eaten.) I added Hawaiian black lava sea salt to this recipe because it makes an awesome purple hue in the crust.

Video: Checking bottom crust and topping the Summer Solstice pizza

THE CARUSO DOUGH

Makes 1283 grams; enough for two 12-by-12-inch Sicilian-style pizzas

POOLISH

71 grams Caputo Chef's Flour (for professionals the Metro)
2.5 grams active dry yeast
71 grams lukewarm water

DOUGH

4 grams active dry yeast
70 grams water, at 85°F
632 grams Caputo Chef's Flour (for professionals the Metro)
14 grams diastatic malt
352 grams ice-cold water, at 36°F (If time allows, weigh the water and refrigerate overnight. Or combine 176 grams of ice with 176 grams of tap water and let the ice melt.)
21 grams Hawaiian black lava sea salt
14 grams extra-virgin olive oil

TO MAKE THE POOLISH

1. Combine all of the ingredients in a small container with enough room to expand. (It will probably double in size). Blend well with a whisk, wooden spoon or rubber spatula, cover and refrigerate for 24 hours.

TO MAKE THE CARUSO DOUGH

1. Whisk the yeast and warm water together in a small bowl until the yeast has dissolved.

2. In a separate bowl, blend the flour and malt with your hands.

3. Set aside 2 tablespoons (about 30 grams) of the cold water aside. Pour the remaining cold water into the bowl of a stand mixer fitted with the dough hook attachment. Add the flour-malt to the bowl and start the mixer on the stir setting (speed 1) for 3 minutes. Cover and let rest for 20 minutes to ensure uniform water absorption.

4. Add the warm water yeast mixture to the mixer bowl and use the reserved cold water to rinse out any remaining yeast. Mix on medium (speed 3 or 4) for 5 minutes.

5. Add the poolish and mix on medium (speed 3 or 4) for 5 minutes. With the mixer running, sprinkle in the salt and mix for 2 minutes more. Lastly, with the mixer running, drizzle in the olive oil and mix until the dough takes on a smooth and satiny appearance, about 3 minutes.

6. Remove the dough from the bowl to the work surface. Using a dough cutter/bench scraper, divide the dough in half and trim to two 624-gram pieces. Form into balls **(see Mike demonstrate on page 26)**. Oil the dough balls lightly with olive oil and set on a clean baking sheet or container, cover and refrigerate for 24 to 36 hours.

TO PUSH OUT AND PARBAKE THE DOUGH

1. Remove the dough from the refrigerator 1 to 2 hours before baking, but keep covered or in the container at room temperature (65°F to 68°F). The dough should come to room temperature before stretching and shaping, but should not be too warm. (Avoid setting the dough on any warm surfaces like the stovetop, which could parcook the dough.)

2. Lightly coat a 12-by-12-inch Sicilian-style pan with olive oil.

3. Lift the dough from the baking sheet or storage container and place in the prepared pan. Gently stretch the dough evenly outward from the center. Using your fingertips, start to push the dough to the edges from top to bottom, turning the pan 90 degrees with each pass. Press the dough with your fingers one last time to ensure it is even. The dough will not reach the sides. Cover the top of the pan with its lid or plastic wrap.

I like to proof my dough in stages. Set the pan on a wire cooling rack and set near, but not on a heat source. Let sit in this warm spot for about 45 minutes.

4. At this point, the dough should be about 45 minutes from parbaking. Position a rack in the center of the oven, preferably with a baking steel or stone, and preheat the oven to 475°F. (If your oven allows, my preferred baking temperature is 480°F)

Repeat the pressing of the dough to reach the corners and move to a slightly warmer spot (near the preheating oven) and proof until the dough has doubled in size, about 45 minutes more. If the dough has come to the top, remove the cover very gently, so as not to tear the dough. Set the pan in the oven. Bake, rotating the pan 180 degrees midway through baking, until set with some golden color, 6 to 8 minutes.

Watch Scott's video on checking the bottom crust and topping the Summer Solstice pizza on page 180.

It can be a little hard to tell because of the color the black salt gives the dough, but the bottom crust will be golden brown.

5. Transfer to a cooling rack and using a large spatula carefully remove the parbaked dough from the pan. Cool for 15 minutes if continuing to topping and baking. If making ahead, cool the parbaked dough completely on the rack. The dough is okay at room temperature for up to 4 hours. For longer storage, wrap completely in plastic wrap and refrigerate for up to 1 day or double wrap (with foil, another layer of plastic wrap, or in a bag) and freeze for up to 2 weeks.

SUMMER SOLSTICE SAUCE

Makes 430 grams (1¾ cups)

397 grams drained San Marzano
 tomatoes
227 grams fully ripened
 strawberries, halved
30 grams extra-virgin olive oil
1 whole jarred Calabrian pepper
6 grams finely ground sea salt

1. Combine all of the ingredients
in a food processor, blender or
in a bowl with an immersion
blender. Pour into a saucepan
and bring to a simmer until
thickened and reduced a bit,
8 to 10 minutes.

2. Transfer to a storage container and cool to room temperature. Refrigerate overnight
before using for maximum
flavor. Bring to room temperature before using.

THE CARUSO SUMMER SOLSTICE PIZZA

Makes one 12-by-12-inch Sicilian-style pizza

114 grams Summer Solstice Sauce
90 grams pancetta, cut into a small
 dice
380 grams ciliegine mozzarella
 (cherry-sized fresh mozzarella
 balls), drained
12 medium-large basil leaves,
 chiffonade
54 grams shaved Parmigiano
 Reggiano cheese
29 grams Balsamic Glaze
 (page 270)
Extra-virgin olive oil
Finely ground sea salt
Finely ground black pepper

1. Position a rack in the center
of the oven, preferably with
a baking steel or stone and
preheat (or return the heat) to
475°F (480°F if you can).

2. Spread the sauce on the parbaked dough, leaving a ¼-inch
border. Top with the diced pancetta. Pinch half of the ciliegine
over the sauce, interspersing
with the pancetta.

3. Set the pan in the oven. Bake,
rotating the pan 180 degrees
midway through baking,
until the cheese is melted and
the crust is browned, 8 to 10
minutes.

4. Transfer to a cooling rack.
Carefully, using a large spatula,
remove the pizza from the pan
to the cooling rack or onto a
pizza peel. Check the bottom
of the crust. If needed, to crisp
the bottom, return to the steel,
stone, or directly to the oven
rack for 1 to 2 minutes more.

5. Transfer the pizza to the

cooling rack for 3 to 5 minutes
to cool slightly while keeping the
bottom crisp. While the pizza
cools, halve each remaining
ciliegine.

6. Slide pizza onto a cutting
board and cut into 9 pieces.
Sprinkle with the basil and
arrange the halved ciliegine on
top. Add the Parmigiano Reggiano shavings, drizzle with the
balsamic glaze and a little olive
oil, then season with salt and
pepper to taste.

SAMMY MANDELL

OWNER, GREENVILLE AVENUE PIZZA COMPANY
DALLAS, TEXAS

WPC MEMBER SINCE 2022

Seemingly everyone who's ever bar hopped into the wee hours has uttered the following: "Man, I wish I had some good pizza about now!"

One of those utterers was Sammy Mandell. But he didn't merely wish for late-night slices, he acted on that business opportunity. Though his restaurant work experience was negligible—a three-month run at Chili's which ended with his firing—he wasn't deterred.

"I was too young to know how little I knew," Mandell says, laughing. Things got serious, though, when he opened Greenville Avenue Pizza Company (GAPCo).

He used start-up capital accumulated from his off-premise ATM machine business to launch GAPCo. But when sales there didn't catch fire as he'd hoped, money quickly got tight. And then competitors arrived: pizza shops opening (and closing) in spots directly across the street from his. Still, Mandell didn't flinch.

"I told myself, 'I'm going to outwork them' and get better at controlling every detail of my business," Mandell says. "My mindset was that failure wasn't an option. I worked harder on the consistency and remodeled the interior and exterior to make GAPCo superior to others'."

The seemingly unending months of 90-hour work weeks were brutal, but his time invested improved him as a pizza pro and drove GAPCo's profits upward.

"I was newly married, heavily in debt and decided I couldn't work any less than I was," Mandell says. "But working that hard helped the restaurant grow in ways I couldn't have imagined."

Sixteen years later, GAPCo has two units, and Mandell had created the persona of the Pizza Slayer: a holster-wearing pizza-making badass. The over-the-shoulder holster holds a pizza cutter and a dough knife for speedy access.

Like many on the WPC team, Mandell met his future peers at the annual Pizza Expo in Las Vegas. Their shared professionalism and commitment to the craft was the connection that led to his invitation to join the team.

When co-founder Tony Gemignani told Mandell he wanted to talk, Mandell wondered why. When Gemignani later called him, he offered Mandell a spot on the team. The Pizza Slayer was floored.

"Here I am, a guy who had little to no restaurant background and worked as hard as I could to create a successful pizza restaurant, and now I'm asked to be part of the World Pizza Champions?" he said. "To be recognized in the industry by someone like him, that was a huge honor."

Crawfish Boil Pizza

Crawfish Boil Pizza is not only delicious, it's indicative of Greenville Avenue Pizza Company's creativity and commitment to differentiation.

PREFERENCES

Boil spices: Zatarain's boil spices often come bundled together, especially online.

Zatarain's Concentrated Shrimp & Crab Boil (liquid)

Zatarain's Crawfish, Shrimp & Crab Boil, for crawfish, potatoes, and finishing (dried)

Salt: kosher

BOILED RED POTATOES

Makes about 175 grams

- 1 medium red potato (about 200 grams), cut into ½ by ¼-inch pieces
- 3 grams white wine vinegar
- 11 grams Zatarain's Concentrated Shrimp & Crab Boil (liquid)
- 14 grams salt
- 2 grams Zatarain's Crawfish, Shrimp & Crab Boil (dried)

1. Put the pieces of potato in a small saucepan and cover by 2 inches with water. Add the vinegar, liquid crab boil and salt. Bring to a boil and then lower the heat to a simmer, cooking until the pieces are tender, but still firm, 5 to 10 minutes.

2. Drain and run potatoes under cold water for about 2 minutes to stop the cooking. Pat dry and toss with the crab boil spice. The potatoes can be cooked and refrigerated up to a day ahead, but should come to room temperature before using.

CREOLE MUSTARD CREAM SAUCE

Makes 115 grams (½ cup)

- 155 grams heavy cream
- 18 grams Creole mustard
- 3 grams Concentrated Shrimp & Crab Boil (liquid)
- 1 gram cayenne

1. In a small saucepan, bring the heavy cream to a slow boil over medium heat. Stir in the mustard, liquid shrimp & crab boil, and cayenne. Continue to cook, stirring often, at a low boil until thickened slightly, 5 to 10 minutes. Transfer to a storage container and cool at room temperature. Refrigerate until ready to use, up to 3 days.

Video: Rolling out the dough for Crawfish Boil Pizza

CRAWFISH BOIL PIZZA

Makes one 12-inch pizza

One 370 gram ball of Tony Gemignani's Master Dough (page 26)

10 grams olive oil

1 large link Andouille sausage (about 60 grams)

56 grams crawfish tails

2 grams Zatarain's Crawfish, Shrimp & Crab Boil (dried)

115 grams Creole Mustard Cream Sauce (see page 186)

170 grams whole milk block mozzarella, shredded

75 grams Boiled Red Potatoes (see page 186)

1 ear of corn

9 grams Roasted Garlic (page 271)

FOR FINISHING

4 grams Zatarain's Crawfish, Shrimp & Crab Boil (dried)

1 whole cooked crawfish, optional for garnish

1. Remove the dough from the refrigerator 1 to 2 hours before baking, but keep covered or in the container at room temperature (65°F to 68°F). The dough should come to room temperature before stretching and shaping, but should not be too warm. (Avoid setting the dough on any warm surfaces like the stovetop, which could parcook the dough.)

2. Position the oven racks in the upper and lower third of the oven with baking steels or stones on each. Preheat to 550°F (or as hot as possible for your home oven) for at least 30 minutes. Alternatively, you can use one steel or stone set on an oven rack positioned in the center of the oven.

3. Meanwhile, slice the sausage on the diagonal into 14 quarter-inch-thick slices. Heat the oil in a medium frying pan and brown the slices, a couple of minutes per side. The full link also can be browned and sliced afterward.

4. Toss the crawfish tails in the dry crab boil spice.

5. Dust a smooth work surface with just enough flour to keep the dough from sticking, then dust the dough and a peel.

Watch Sammy's video on rolling out the dough for the Crawfish Boil Pizza on page 186.

To roll the dough to a 12-inch round with a ¼-inch thickness, use a rolling pin starting in the center and rolling over the dough in a vertical motion. Add flour as needed to keep the dough from sticking to the rolling pin, then come back and roll the edges. Turn the dough and repeat the vertical rolling in the center followed by the edges to keep the dough at a consistent thickness. Return the rolling pin to the center and give it another roll out, then one on the left, and one on the right. Once you reach the desired 12-inch round, dust off the flour, and slide onto the peel.

6. With a spoon or spatula, spread the mustard cream sauce in an outward circular motion, leaving a ¼-inch border along the dough's edge. Sprinkle the mozzarella evenly over the sauce followed by the sausage and the potatoes. On a cutting board, carefully cut the corn so that the kernels stay attached in strips. Next, use your knife to lift each strip and place it onto the pizza. Pinch the roasted garlic into pieces and drop across the top. Lastly, add the crawfish.

7. Slide the pizza onto the top steel and bake for 5 to 7 minutes or until the crust is beginning to brown and the cheese has melted, but isn't browning. Lift the pizza with the peel, rotate it 180 degrees and transfer to the bottom steel. Bake until the bottom crust is a rich golden brown and the cheese is bubbling with some browning in spots, 2 to 5 minutes. If baking on one steel or stone, bake for 7 to 12 minutes, rotating the pizza 180 degrees once during the baking. Baking time will vary depending on the max temperature of your oven.

8. Transfer the pizza to a cutting board, sprinkle with boil spice and, if using, place the whole crawfish in the center of the pizza. Cut into 6 wedges.

MIKE BAUSCH

OWNER, ANDOLINI'S WORLDWIDE
TULSA, OKLAHOMA

WPC MEMBER SINCE 2009

"The fact that I love pizza does not make me special, but it does prove I have a soul," says Mike Bausch with a laugh. "If someone doesn't love pizza, I kind of don't trust them as a person." For Bausch, who is president of the World Pizza Champions, pizza is about community. "It's that one rare item that people gather around. They celebrate with it. They share it. It's truly a social food," he adds. This characteristic of family-style pizza has always been the source of his passion.

If you're a casual home chef, you might not have heard of Bausch. Maybe you've seen him on the Food Network or in a news appearance. But pizza-restaurant owners have undoubtedly crossed his path, whether by reading his articles or hearing him speak, especially at Pizza Expo, where he's held court for more than a decade. His book, *Unsliced: How to Stay Whole in the Pizzeria Industry*, has helped countless restaurateurs improve their businesses and communities. Much in line with Tony's original mission, Bausch believes that gatekeeping special industry knowledge is a detriment to the industry on the whole. He prefers to dynamite those gates.

He is not afraid to mess with tradition. Combining classic New York-style dough fermentation with California-style avant-garde toppings, Bausch then adds Shawnee Mills Flour, local to his home state of Oklahoma, to create what he calls "Tulsa-style pizza." It is an homage to the city where he lives and operates Andolini's Pizzeria, Bausch's first concept.

Created in 2004, Andolini's is not only a fan favorite, but it has received several local and national awards. He went on to develop the company Andolini's Worldwide, which now includes multiple pizzerias, standalone bagel, slice, sandwich and gelato shops, and a fine dining restaurant.

Scratch cooking matters to Bausch to the point of fanaticism: "If we can make it in-house ourselves, we will every time. It's not hard to do that, but it does mean more effort." Cooking from scratch isn't just a sales tactic to Bausch, but part of the purity of his love for the art form, one of the secrets to his success.

This kind of effort and dedication translates to his work in the larger pizza community, where he is dedicated to sharing knowledge, whether with restaurant owners or home cooks. Maybe that's because he comes from a Marine Corps family, which always held team and country over self. Then again, Bausch sees this kind of dedication in all of the World Pizza Champions, and believes that's what sets them apart.

Oktoberfest Pizza

I dig modifying popular elements of one cuisine and then applying them to pizza while staying true to the authentic ingredients. Then, the goal is to add our own twist to the execution. The Oktoberfest pizza is a perfect example, featuring unconventional toppings like bratwurst and pierogi. These flavors are potent but comfortable, and I love bringing them all together.

Video: Finishing an Octoberfest pizza

Video: Operational excellence with cutting a pizza evenly and readying for take-out or in-house dining

PIEROGIES
Makes 15 to 18

DOUGH

2 grams smoked paprika
2 grams of kosher salt
250 grams all-purpose or high-protein, high-gluten flour, plus additional as needed
60 grams unsalted butter at room temperature
110 grams egg (2 large eggs), lightly beaten
120 grams sour cream

POTATO-CHEESE FILLING

225 grams russet or Yukon gold potatoes, peeled and quartered
1 whole garlic clove, peeled
66 grams whole milk
8 grams unsalted butter
Salt
Freshly ground black pepper
60 grams shredded sharp cheddar cheese
3 grams smoked paprika
3 grams garlic powder
3 grams salt

FINISHING

60 grams unsalted butter
150 grams sliced shallots

TO MAKE THE PIEROGI DOUGH

1. Stir the paprika and salt into the flour in a large bowl. Stir in the butter, egg, and sour cream until the mixture comes together into a smooth dough. The dough should be sticky but not overly tacky. Add in a little more flour if needed.

2. Dust the work surface with flour and knead the dough, using additional flour as needed to keep from sticking, for about 5 minutes. Put in a clean container, cover and refrigerate at least 45 minutes while making the filling. The dough will firm as it chills.

TO MAKE THE FILLING

1. Put the potato and garlic in a medium saucepan with enough salted water to cover by about 1 inch. Bring to a boil, lower the heat to a simmer. Cook until the potatoes are tender and easily break apart with a fork, but not so much that they are water-logged, about 20 minutes. Drain and return the potatoes to the dry saucepan.

2. Towards the end of the potato cooking, heat the milk and butter in a saucepan until the butter is melted. Keep a watchful eye so the milk doesn't boil over.

3. Using a potato masher, mash the potatoes while slowly adding the warm milk-butter to incorporate. Mash until smooth and creamy, then season to taste with salt and pepper. Let the mixture cool before adding the cheese.

4. Stir in the cheese, paprika, garlic powder and salt.

TO ASSEMBLE THE PIEROGIS

1. Dust the work surface with flour. Roll out the dough until about 14-inches across and ⅛-inch thick.

2. Using a 3½-inch round cutter, a ravioli cutter (or even a ramekin with a paring knife), cut the dough into circles. The dough scraps can be pushed together once and rerolled for more circles.

3. Spoon 10 grams (about 2 teaspoons) of filling and place slightly off center onto each dough circle. Fold each circle edge to edge, then seal the rounded edges with the tines of a fork.

4. Bring a large saucepan of salted water to a low boil and place a cooling rack over a baking sheet. To avoid over-crowding the pan, cook pierogis in batches, until they float and are tender, 3 to 5 minutes. Gently stir occasionally to ensure the pierogis don't stick together. Transfer to the cooling rack.

TO FINISH THE PIEROGIS

1. Melt the butter in a large skillet over medium heat. Sauté the shallots over medium heat until beginning to look translucent, 3 to 4 minutes. Add the 7 pierogi needed for the pizza and continue to sauté until pierogies and shallots are browned, 3 to 4 minutes per side.

Pierogis can be refrigerated in a storage container until ready to use, up to 3 days. Bring to room temperature before using.

OKTOBERFEST PIZZA

Makes one 14-inch New York-style pizza

PREFERENCES

Flour: Shawnee Mills high-gluten flour

Mozzarella: low-moisture, made in California

One 370 gram ball Base Dough Recipe by Tony Gemignani (page 26)

1 link (about 50 grams) bratwurst

Extra-virgin olive oil

150 grams Roasted Garlic Purée (page 271)

241 grams part-skim block mozzarella cheese, shredded

7 pierogi (see page 192)

15 grams finely grated pecorino cheese

75 grams spicy mustard

150 grams sauerkraut, cold and drained

---

1. Remove the dough from the refrigerator 1 to 2 hours before baking, but keep covered or in the container at room temperature (65°F to 68°F). The dough should come to room temperature before stretching and shaping, but should not be too warm. (Avoid setting the dough on any warm surfaces like the stovetop, which could parcook the dough.)

2. Position the oven racks in the upper and lower third of the oven with baking steels or stones on each. Preheat to 550°F (or as hot as possible for your home oven) for at least 30 minutes. You also can use one steel or stone set on an oven rack positioned in the center of the oven.

3. Slice the bratwurst on the diagonal to make twelve 2 to 3-inch slices. Heat a film of oil in a medium frying pan and brown the slices, a couple of minutes per side. The full link also can be browned and sliced afterward.

4. Dust a smooth work surface with just enough flour to keep the dough from sticking, then dust the dough and a peel. Push and stretch the dough out to a 14-inch round **(watch Joe's demonstration on page 264)**, and slide onto the peel.

5. Watch Mike's video on finishing the Octoberfest pizza on page 192.

Drizzle the olive oil, preferably using an oil can, in a spiral pattern over the dough, leaving a 1-inch border from the dough's edge. Spread oil across the dough using your fingertips. With a spoon or spatula, spread the roasted garlic on top, followed by mozzarella. Arrange the bratwurst slices and pierogis with some of the shallots across the top.

6. Slide the pizza onto the top steel and bake for 5 to 7 minutes or until the crust is beginning to brown and the cheese has melted, but isn't browning. Lift the pizza with the peel, rotate it 180 degrees and transfer to the bottom steel. Bake until the bottom crust is a rich golden brown and the cheese is bubbling with some browning in spots, 4 to 5 minutes. If baking on one steel or stone, bake for 9 to 12 minutes, rotating the pizza 180 degrees once during baking. Baking time will vary depending on the max temperature of your oven.

7. Transfer the pizza to a cutting board, sprinkle with pecorino, spoon on mustard and add forkfuls of sauerkraut.

Watch Mike's video on operational excellence with cutting a pizza evenly and readying for take-out or in-house dining on page 192.

Cut into 8 equal slices.

SPENCER GLENN

EXECUTIVE CHEF, MANAGER OF OPERATIONS, FOOD AND BEVERAGE, PIZZA MY HEART
LOS GATOS, CALIFORNIA

WPC MEMBER SINCE 2015

An old-school psychoanalyst would get a lot of work from Spencer Glenn, given Glenn's long-term memory retention. The guy recalls the first time he ate pizza, at age 4. You read that correctly. The same analyst would likely say Glenn "bonded" to the site of that first experience since he has been working for that very company for 20 years now.

"That was Pizza My Heart's original location at Capitola Beach, California," Glenn recalls. "It was my favorite pizza growing up."

At age 15, he got his first pizza job at a small shop in Salinas, Calif., and he began moving across the state for work at six other pizzerias. His chance to work at Pizza My Heart came in 2003. He started as a delivery driver and worked his way up through every facet of the business until, four years later, he was promoted to general manager. That's when he began preparing for his first Pizza Expo in Las Vegas.

"That also was my first World Pizza Games and where my love and passion for pizza exploded," Glenn says. "I became a pizza geek with a borderline obsession to become the best pizzaiolo I could."

In 2009, the 6' 4" Glenn used his 6' 8" wingspan to take first place in the challenging but unsung category of largest dough stretch. To win again in 2015, he stretched a 18 ounce dough ball to a record-setting width of 45 inches. He won the fastest box folding challenge that same year, and began competing as a pizza baker in 2017. Victories in that category followed as well.

Around the same time, he was invited to join the World Pizza Champions, which he called a surprise.

"I certainly wasn't expecting it," Glenn says. "But I was getting to know all those guys by helping out at competitions. Being around them was inspiring because they helped other competitors to be as successful as possible, which never happens in other competitions. I wanted to be a part of that, and fortunately that's what happened."

Life is Gourd Pizza

This recipe won the grand prize and $10,000 at the Real California Pizza Contest in 2021. It highlights the produce of the fall season with creative flavors and visually beautiful ingredients. I searched farmers markets for ingredients and inspiration. I found some beautiful heirloom butternut squash and perfectly ripe pomegranates. That's when the recipe started to write itself.

SEASONED CREAM

Makes 167 grams (about ⅔ cup)

165 grams heavy cream
1 gram freshly grated nutmeg
.5 gram fine sea salt
.3 gram freshly grated pepper

1. Whisk all of the ingredients together and pour into a squeeze bottle or a liquid measuring cup (for controlled pouring).

2. Cover and refrigerate for at least 2 hours, but preferably overnight.

LIFE IS GOURD PIZZA

Makes one 14-inch
New York-style pizza

One 370 gram ball of Tony Gemignani's Master Dough (page 26)
One small butternut squash, about 500 grams
Clarified butter (page 270), about 90 grams
25 baby sage leaves
Fine sea salt
75 grams shredded toma or a semi-firm farmer's cheese
100 grams whole milk block mozzarella cheese, shredded
75 grams shaved Parmigiano Reggiano cheese
10 grams or so garlic oil, store bought or homemade (page 271)
60 grams unsalted pistachios
Freshly grated black pepper
Freshly grated nutmeg
45 grams pomegranate seeds

1. Remove the dough from the refrigerator 1 to 2 hours before baking, but keep covered or in the container at room temperature (65°F to 68°F). The dough should come to room temperature before stretching and shaping, but should not be too warm. (Avoid setting the dough on any warm surfaces like the stovetop, which could parcook the dough.)

2. Position an oven rack in the center of the oven with a baking steel or stone on top. Preheat to 500°F for at least 30 minutes.

Video: Applying sauce on top of the cheese

3. Meanwhile, prepare the butternut squash and the fried sage leaves. To prepare the butternut squash, trim, peel, and cut it in half, and remove the seeds. Set cut-side down and cut into ¼-inch-thick slices. Trim the slices into 1-inch-wide strips.

Working in batches as needed to not overlap, lay the slices in a steamer basket. Steam until tender, but still firm, about 5 minutes per patch. Transfer to a cooling rack or plate and let cool.

While the squash cools, prepare the fried sage leaves. Line a small baking sheet or plate with paper towels. Set near the stovetop.

Put 60 grams of clarified butter in a small saucepan. Heat the clarified butter to 350°F. (Ideally test with a thermometer, but it will be at temperature right when the butter begins to smoke.) Drop the sage leaves into the pan being careful because the butter will sputter and bubble up. Immediately turn off the heat and let fry in the hot butter, about 30 seconds. Using a spider or slotted spoon, transfer the fried sage leaves to the paper towels. Sprinkle leaves with salt.

* As long as it hasn't gotten too dark, the residual sage butter can be strained and used again.

Weigh 226 grams of the nicest squash slices to fry. Heat a large skillet over medium heat. Add 30 grams of the reserved sage butter or clarified butter and pan-fry the squash slices until browned on one side, 1 to 2 minutes. Return to the cooling rack or plate browned side up.

4. Dust a smooth work surface with just enough flour to keep the dough from sticking, then dust the dough and a peel. Push and stretch the dough out to a 14-inch round **(watch Joe's demonstration on page 264)**, and slide onto the peel.

5. Spread the toma, mozzarella, and half of the Parmigiano-Reggiano cheeses on the dough, leaving a 1-inch border from the dough's edge.

Watch Spencer's video on applying sauce on top of the cheese on page 198.

Starting at the edge of the dough on top of the cheese, squeeze or pour the cream sauce in a spiral pattern. Top with the pan-roasted butternut squash slices, browned-side up in a pinwheel pattern.

6. Slide the pizza onto the steel and bake until the crust is golden brown and the cheeses are bubbling, 10 to 12 minutes.

7. Transfer the pizza to a cutting board and brush the crust with the garlic olive oil. Add the remaining shaved Parmigiano Reggiano and the pistachios. Season with salt, black pepper, and nutmeg to taste. Sprinkle with the pomegranate seeds and place the fried sage leaves on top. Slice into 8 equal slices and serve.

KENNY BRYANT

KEN'S WOOD FIRED PIZZA CONSULTING
PALO CEDRO, CALIFORNIA

WPC CO-FOUNDING MEMBER SINCE 2004

As a teenager, Kenny Bryant wasn't looking for a job in a pizzeria, but that's where his high school sweetheart worked, and he wanted more time with her. Little did he know how profoundly pizza making and dough acrobatics would impact his life. (It also led to him marrying his sweetheart.)

Bryant worked at Pyzano's Pizzeria, the Castro Valley, California, restaurant owned by Frank and Tony Gemignani, and the unofficial birthplace of American pizza acrobatics. Like Tony, Bryant tossed dough for fun during breaks away from the pizza oven. Customers loved it, and Bryant wanted to equal his boss's skills.

"That became a friendly rivalry between us, and we'd stay after hours trying to best each other," Bryant said. Despite Gemignani's bag of tricks always being deeper, Bryant kept at it. "It didn't dissuade me from trying, it motivated me to practice more."

After Gemignani's back-to-back dough acrobatic wins in the World Pizza Games in 1995 and '96, Bryant joined the competition in 1997. Gemignani again captured the gold while Bryant earned a silver.

"No, I didn't let the boss win," Bryant said. "Tony threw blindfolded. That's hard to beat."

A talented acrobat in his own right, Bryant came back to win the World Pizza Games in 1998 and would spend the next few years spinning and tossing dough in private gigs and TV commercials, but he would leave the pizza business and competitive tossing altogether in 2000

to work as a police officer in Fremont. The hiatus didn't last long.

In 2004, Gemignani invited Bryant to be a founding member of the World Pizza Champions dough acrobat team. Using choreographed acro-routines set to movie theme songs, the five-man team raised the bar forever in team competition. At the 2005 World Pizza Championships in Salsomaggiore, Italy, the WPC earned scores of 9 and 10 from every judge except one. The Italian judge gave them a 6, which meant the Italian team won by a single point.

The team would return to dominate in 2006 and 2007, only to be told they couldn't compete in the team competition any longer at the World Pizza Championships.

"They said we'd won too many times," Bryant said. "We proved our point."

Though Bryant's competitive days ended in Italy, he has continued to help run pizza competitions at the annual Pizza Expo in Las Vegas alongside other WPC founding members. And just to scratch his pizza making itch, he started a wood-fired mobile pizza operation in 2014.

"The business is a lot of fun, and the WPC team members are fun people to be around," Bryant said. "I've done things with them for so long. Why not keep doing it?"

Pyzano's Breadsticks

Why a breadsticks recipe in a high-end pizza book? Because everyone loves them. And since I made about a million of these during my time at Pyzano's, I know they're really good! They're a delicious indulgence that's simple to make and hard to stop eating. Have some friends and family around so you don't eat them all yourself.

KENNY'S BASIC TOMATO SAUCE

Makes 550 grams of sauce; about 2 cups

Two 6-ounce (170 gram) cans tomato paste
160 grams water
7 grams table salt
22 grams granulated sugar
3 grams dried Italian oregano
8 grams dried basil
5 grams garlic powder or granulated garlic
0.5 gram crushed red pepper flakes
6 grams extra-virgin olive oil
7 grams Balsamic Glaze (see page 270)
2 to 3 large basil leaves

1. Combine the tomato paste and water in a medium bowl. Stir in the remaining ingredients except for the basil. When those ingredients are well blended, cut the basil into thin strips and add to the sauce. The sauce can be refrigerated in a storage container until ready to use, up to 3 days. Bring to room temperature before using.

Video: Pushing a dough into a round for breadsticks

PYZANO'S BREADSTICKS

Makes one batch; 10 to 12 breadsticks

One 300 gram ball of Tony Gemignani's Master Dough (page 26)
250 grams Kenny's Basic Tomato Sauce
150 grams part-skim or whole milk block mozzarella cheese, shredded
Granulated garlic, about 3 grams
Dried oregano, about 1 gram
Dried basil, about 1 gram
Salt, 1 to 2 grams

1. Remove the dough from the refrigerator 1 to 2 hours before baking, but keep covered or in the container at room temperature (65°F to 68°F). The dough should come to room temperature before stretching and shaping, but should not be too warm. (Avoid setting the dough on any warm surfaces like the stovetop, which could parcook the dough.)

2. Position an oven rack in the center with a pizza steel or stone on top. Preheat to 550°F (or as hot as possible for your home oven) for at least 30 minutes.

3. Watch Kenny's video on pushing a dough into a round for breadsticks.

Dust a smooth work surface with just enough flour to keep the dough from sticking, then dust both sides of the dough.

You want to be sure the dough moves freely as you shape it, but avoid adding too much and drying out the dough. (The dough can be dipped into a bowl of flour, but brush any excess flour back into the bowl.)

Using your fingertips, beginning at the center and working towards the edges, push out the dough keeping a ¼ to ½-inch border at the dough's edge. Lay your fingertips on the dough keeping them inside the border. Apply some pressure moving your hands away from each other to begin to stretch the dough. Avoid putting too much pressure directly on the center of the round. Once the dough has been stretched to about 10-inches, you can flip it back and forth on your open hands to stretch a bit more.

Next, rest the dough on top of loosely clenched fists. Slowly move your hands apart, continuing to stay within the border, rotating and stretching the dough, maintaining its circular shape as it stretches to 12 inches. Lay this fully stretched dough on a flat surface. (This is also the point where you can practice tossing the dough.)

4. Sprinkle mozzarella over the top of the dough leaving a ½ to 1-inch border for the crust. Shake the granulated garlic, dried basil, and dried oregano over the mozzarella.

5. Slide onto a lightly floured pizza peel. Transfer to the steel or stone in the oven. Bake, rotating 180 degrees midway through baking until the cheese is completely melted and browning in spots, and the crust is golden brown, 12 to 15 minutes. Baking time will vary depending on the max temperature of your oven set between 500°F to 550°F.

6. Remove to a cutting board. Using a pizza cutter or large, sharp chef's knife, cut the round in half. Turn the dough and cut into 1½-inch strips perpendicular to the original center cut.

7. Arrange on a serving platter with the dipping sauce.

If using a wood-fired oven, start heating your oven early to ensure it is ready when you are. The temperature of the baking surface should be about 750°F. Bake, rotating as necessary to ensure even browning of the crust. The cheese should be completely melted, browning in spots, and the crust is golden brown with some charring on the crust, 90 seconds to 2 minutes.

NICK BOGACZ

OWNER, CALIENTE PIZZA & DRAFT HOUSE
PITTSBURGH, PENNSYLVANIA

WPC MEMBER SINCE 2018

For years, Nick Bogacz worked five jobs, clocking 90 hours a week, chasing the dream to one day have his own pizzeria. Now, he runs an internationally recognized, multi-million dollar pizza empire. The first time he managed a pizza shop, he recalls being captivated by the collaboration required to make it happen. "It was a thing of beauty to me, and still is," Bogacz says. "Running a pizza shop takes the efforts of a synchronized team." Now he has more than 250 employees.

It all started when he was only 17, and took a job as a pizza delivery driver. His first night out, he wrecked his car—and borrowed his mom's so he could finish the shift.

By 22, Bogacz had become a family man. He knew he needed more income. Skeptics "urged me to get a real job," he says. Instead, he became a store manager, confident that the pizza industry was a good fit. But the need for more money forced him to take additional work, including as a courier for the post office, and a money counter at Pittsburgh Penguins games, and—plus as a delivery driver for three different pizza companies. "I was a father and a husband, and I did what I had to do," he recalls.

Though naysayers continued to doubt his dream of owning his own shop, he ignored them. "My ultimate goal was way off at that point, but I stayed dedicated to it." Bogacz worked through many levels of a major pizza chain to become a general manager (while still working full-time at the post office). Throughout, he learned corporate structures and procedures, and financial systems that would help him build his company fast.

In 2012, he opened Caliente Pizza & Draft House. It has since grown to 12 locations in the Greater Pittsburgh Area, which includes the homes of the Pittsburgh Penguins, Pittsburgh Pirates, Pittsburgh Steelers, Penn State Hockey and Penn State Football. His standing in the industry grew in step with his business. Publishing his book, *The Pizza Equation*, lifted him to a position of authority in the field, and led to the launching of his weekly podcast, *The Business Equation*. Before long, he was asked to lead seminars at the annual Pizza Expo in Las Vegas. And, of course, he received an invitation to join the World Pizza Champions.

"Being able to help others while being a part of a team of like-minded individuals is an incredible feeling," Bogacz says. "I feel lucky to be a part of it."

Smoked on the Seven Seas Pizza

I wanted to contribute a unique recipe to this book that combines two of my favorite backyard past times; pizza making and smoking. And, I absolutely love seafood! This pizza covers all of that and is a play on the traditional Italian Feast of the Seven Fishes. It is a hearty pizza, so be sure to gather hungry family and friends to enjoy it.

The hearty amount of toppings on the Smoked on the Seven Seas does well in a pan pizza too. I have made Detroit-style and Sicilian variations.

Video: Using backyard smoked ingredients on a pizza

BACKYARD-SMOKED SEAFOOD

450 grams Alaskan crab legs or snow crab cluster/legs

386 grams 21–25 count/size shrimp, peeled and deveined

226 grams large scallops, cut in half

232 grams tilapia, cut into 2 to 3-inch pieces

226 grams unsalted butter, cut into large chunks

84 grams minced garlic

TO SMOKE THE SEAFOOD

1. Heat a backyard smoker with the addition of cherry or apple wood to 225°F. Or, preheat an indirect grill (charcoal or gas) to 225°F with a smoker box filled with soaked cherry or apple wood. If you don't have a smoker box, put the soaked wood in a small disposable pan, cover the top with foil, and poke holes in it for the steam to escape. The final option is to do the smoking inside in the oven.

2. Combine all ingredients in a roasting pan where the seafood is in an even layer. Fill a separate pan with water. Set the pans next to each other in the smoker, on the indirect area of the grill, or in the oven. After 45 minutes, stir the seafood in the now melted butter. Cover the top of the pan with foil and continue to cook until the internal temperature of the seafood is 125°F to 130°F, 30 to 45 minutes more. (The seafood will cook further on the pizza.)

3. Remove the pan from the smoker and let sit at room temperature, 15 minutes. Using a slotted spoon, transfer seafood to a bowl, then strain the smoked butter from the pan into a separate bowl. Crack the crab, remove the meat and cut into pieces about the same size as the halved scallops.

SMOKED ON THE SEVEN SEAS PIZZA

Makes one 14-inch New York-style Pizza

One 567 gram ball of of Tony Gemignani's Master Dough (page 26)

Smoked Melted Butter (see step three on page 210)

Smoked Seafood

255 grams block mozzarella cheese, shredded

123 grams diced tomato

33 grams diced red onion

57 grams grated Parmigiano Reggiano cheese

1. Remove the dough from the refrigerator 1 to 2 hours before baking, but keep covered or in the container at room temperature (65°F to 68°F). The dough should come to room temperature before stretching and shaping, but should not be too warm. (Avoid setting the dough on any warm surfaces like the stovetop, which could parcook the dough.)

2. Position the oven racks in the center and the top of the oven with a baking steel or stone on top. Preheat to 500°F for at least 30 minutes. If using one steel or stone, set on an oven rack positioned in the center of the oven.

3. Dust a smooth work surface with just enough flour to keep the dough from sticking, then dust the dough and a peel. Push and stretch the dough out to a 14-inch round **(watch Joe's demonstration on page 264)**, and slide onto the peel.

4. Brush the smoked melted butter across the surface of the dough to its edges. Leaving a ½-inch border from the dough's edge, arrange the seafood uniformly as you work toward the center. Sprinkle the cheese over the seafood and then add the tomatoes and onion.

5. Slide the pizza onto the bottom steel and bake for 10 to 15 minutes or until the crust is a rich golden brown and the cheese is bubbling with some browning in spots. Lift the pizza with the peel, rotate it 180 degrees and transfer to the top steel for 1 to 2 minutes to brown the top even more. If baking on one steel or stone, bake for 10 to 17 minutes, rotating the pizza 180 degrees once during the baking.

6. Transfer the pizza to a cooling rack for 1 to 3 minutes to cool slightly while keeping the bottom crisp.

7. Slide onto a cutting board. Sprinkle with the Parmigiano Reggiano and cut into 8 equal wedges.

If using a wood-fired oven, start heating your oven early to ensure it is ready when you are. The temperature should be 650°F to 750°F. Bake, rotating 180 degrees midway through baking until the cheese is completely melted and browning in spots, and the crust is golden brown with some charring on the crust, 6 to 8 minutes.

JOHN GRISTINA

OWNER, PIZZA FENICE
PELHAM, NEW YORK

WPC MEMBER 2006-2009, RETURNED IN 2022

"I chose the name Fenice, the Italian word for phoenix, because I felt as if this was a rebirth for me," Gristina says of his restaurant. "Today, I am standing on my feet 12 hours a day with a smile on my face. If there's love and passion in your work, it comes through in the food."

Though John Gristina grew up watching his family work in and own pizzerias, he wasn't really drawn to the business. But after fulfilling a promise to his parents and himself to go to college, his job at a transplant immunology lab made him yearn for his pizza making days.

"I took a second job as a part-time pizza maker in Scarsdale, and that job became a full-time job as the manager," Gristina recalls. "Eventually that led to a partnership in the business and eventually into partnerships in multiple locations."

After joining the World Pizza Champions in 2006, he began competing and succeeding in pizza baking competitions. "I began learning more than I ever thought I would know about pizza and the pizza industry." But three years later, after his business partnership soured, he left pizza for work as a general manager of different restaurant concepts and work in institutional foodservice.

"For years I took up side gigs as a pizza maker because I felt I had more to do with pizza," says Gristina, who, during that time, graduated from Fordham University in 2015. "I guess deep down there was still something 'in the basement' that had to be dealt with sooner or later."

A stint as a food service director at a correctional facility appeared to end his food journey altogether, and he went back to the medical field. As an administrative supervisor for a hospital clinic, he considered getting a master's degree to keep climbing that ladder.

"But even though an old friend had helped me get the job, I was sad, hated every minute of it and completely stuck and stifled and bored out of my skull," Gristina says. To stave off the "soul crushing monotony, that same friend encouraged me as I started a mobile pizza catering business as a side hustle on the weekends. I loved every minute of it even though I should have been exhausted from all the extra work."

When moving from the Bronx to Pelham, a suburb of New York City, he noticed a small pizzeria located three blocks from his house. Feeling like it might be a second chance at resuming his first business love, he bought it. That became Fenice.

Despite his 13-year absence from the World Pizza Champions, cofounder Tony Gemignani asked Gristina if he wanted to return in 2022.

"I was blown away at how many people—old friends and new acquaintances—welcomed me back," he says. "I was honestly holding back tears at the induction ceremony—or re-induction in my case. It's great to be back with them."

Fenice Meatballs

Some time ago I decided to evaluate all the recipes I had for meatballs and came up with this recipe. It takes the best of the meatballs I grew up loving—my grandma's, of course—and includes touches from others. These come out tender and juicy as well as having a good balance between fluffy and firm with a nice bite. Note: They can be oven roasted or fried. Frying gives the meat a bit more of a caramelized crust and gives an added texture that is amazing.

This is a big batch of meatballs, but they can be refrigerated for up to 5 days or frozen for up to 1 month. Or if you prefer, the recipe can easily be cut in half. Lightly beat the eggs and weigh them too (84 grams for the smaller batch).

PREFERENCES
Crushed tomatoes: Mutti
Extra-virgin olive oil: Partanna

Video: Rolling meatballs

LIGHTLY ROASTED RED ONION

Makes about 180 grams of onion and 150 grams onion oil

1 medium red onion, 180 to 200 grams
Extra-virgin olive oil, about 200 grams
Fine sea salt
Freshly ground black pepper

Preheat the oven to 450°F.

1. Dice the onion and put in a small, oven-proof dish. Pour in enough oil to cover and season with a generous pinch of salt and black pepper.

2. Transfer to the oven and roast until the onions are translucent, but before the edges start to brown. Remove from the oven and let cool completely in the oil.

FENICE MEATBALLS

Makes twenty 113-gram meatballs

168 grams (3 large) eggs
95 grams heavy cream
80 grams Lightly Roasted Red Onion (see left)
35 grams Roasted Garlic (see page 271)
6 grams fresh basil leaves (10 to 12 leaves)
70 grams extra-virgin olive oil
5 grams granulated garlic
5 grams granulated onion
3 grams dried oregano
3 grams dried parsley
17 grams sea salt, finely ground
6 grams black pepper, finely ground
454 grams ground beef (80/20)
454 grams ground pork
454 grams ground veal
25 grams Pecorino Romano cheese, grated
25 grams grated Parmigiano Reggiano cheese
85 grams crushed tomatoes
30 grams dry Marsala wine
280 grams of panko breadcrumbs

1. Position the oven racks in the upper and lower third of the oven and preheat to 450°F.

2. In a medium bowl, beat the eggs and whisk in the heavy cream. In a high-powered blender or food processor, blend together the roasted onion, roasted garlic, basil and half (35 grams) of the olive oil. Blend only until it is a coarse mixture with no large pieces, but not a smooth puree.

3. In a small bowl, combine the granulated garlic, granulated onion, oregano, parsley, salt and pepper.

4. In a large bowl combine beef, pork and veal using your hands to keep some texture differentiation. Do not overmix. Fold the egg-cream mixture into the large bowl with the meat. Add the onion-garlic-basil mix, followed by the combined dry seasonings and grated cheeses. Combine well.

5. Add crushed tomatoes, Marsala, panko and remaining olive oil, then mix until evenly blended. Divide the meat into twenty even portions. For precise measurements, use a scale and an ice cream scoop, weigh out individual 113 gram portions and set on a baking sheet or the countertop.

6. Lightly oil two baking sheets for the formed meatballs. Blend a little oil and water in a small bowl to dip your fingertips into when rolling the meatballs. This will help to keep the meatball mixture from sticking as you roll.

7. Watch John's video on rolling meatballs on page 216.

How you roll your meatballs will differ depending on how you will serve them: finished and served in sauce or plated with the sauce. For both types, roll each meatball between your palms to form a sphere, but avoid rolling it too tightly. The more pressure you apply the tighter it will be. If too tight, it will be tough when it's cooked. Ultimately, rolling takes a little practice to perfect.

* If the meatballs are baked only (and sauced when serving), roll just until each meatball becomes a coarse sphere with some crags and crevices.

* If the meatballs are baked three-quarters done and then stewed in sauce, continue to roll until the spheres are smoother.

As you roll, set on the oiled baking sheets, spacing evenly. (The meatballs can also be fried, see Note on Frying Meatballs.)

8. Once all the meatballs are rolled, drizzle olive oil over the tops of the meatballs.

9. To prevent burning and sticking, add between ¼ and ½ a cup of water to each baking sheet and between the meatballs. If you are comfortable with moving the pans, pour the water in before it goes in the oven, or set the pans on the oven racks and then, using a spouted liquid measuring cup, carefully add the water.

10. Cook meatballs. For meatballs that will be finished in sauce, cook until the exteriors are browned but not completely cooked through, 12 to 15 minutes. For completely baked meatballs, cook until no longer pink in the center with an internal temperature of 165°F, 18 to 22 minutes.

11. Remove from the oven and let cool to room temperature. If making ahead, let the meatballs cool to room temperature. Ideally, the meatballs will be vacuum sealed, but an airtight container or storage bag will work as well if the meatballs are in an even layer. Refrigerate for up to 5 days or freeze for up to 1 month.

SUGGESTED PLATING FOR BAKED MEATBALLS

Spoon warmed tomato sauce onto a round plate or into a shallow bowl. Cut three meatballs in half and arrange on the sauce, leaving a space in the center of the plate. Spoon additional tomato sauce over the meatballs. Sprinkle the meatballs with grated Parmigiano Reggiano cheese and place a dollop of ricotta cheese in the center of the plate. Drizzle with olive oil and garnish with a basil chiffonade.

NOTE ON FRYING MEATBALLS

Set a cooling rack over a baking sheet. Pour enough oil to come one-third of the way up the sides in a large-frying pan. Heat the oil to 325°F. Working in batches as needed to not overcrowd, lower the meatballs into the oil using a slotted spoon. Adjusting the heat to maintain the temperature, fry the meatballs until a good crust forms and the internal temperature is 165°F, 2 to 3 minutes per side. Transfer to the rack to cool.

ANTHONY DESOUSA

OWNER, ANTONIO'S REAL NY PIZZA
ESTES PARK, COLORADO

WPC MEMBER SINCE 2021

When Anthony DeSousa and his family moved to Colorado, they couldn't find any pizza they loved. So he decided to start making pies himself.

"There was nothing close to the pizza we enjoyed in and around Massapequa, New York," he says. "So, I endeavored to learn to make Sicilian style, beginning in 2009."

Four years after elevating his home pizza game, DeSousa, then the owner of SummitView Coffee, saw an opportunity to sell his own pizza—from the coffee shop's drive-thru window. Armed with a well-used Amana combination microwave and convection oven that he bought from a Chinese food restaurant, he fashioned his own pizza stone and metal pan to fit the cramped oven cavity. It worked!

Turned out his pizza was really well received, and when the town of Estes Park's only wood-fired pizzeria closed its doors, its owners asked DeSousa to take it over. Having never run a restaurant, he wasn't confident enough to say yes, yet. And when his daughter endured a near-death experience and needed long-term medical care, he was sure he wouldn't accept the offer.

But, "Tracey, my wife, said, 'You can do it!'" he recalls. "She nurtured our daughter back to health while I learned to run a restaurant."

The business grew so successful that DeSousa moved Antonio's Real NY Pizza to a 6,000 square-foot location four years later. DeSousa credits some of that growth to multiple educational seminars he attended at pizza trade shows. He could make and sell pizza, but it was guidance from World Pizza Champions team members that helped move his pizza from good to great. DeSousa credits Tony Gemignani and John Arena with opening his eyes to techniques that only decades of experience could suggest.

"The words, 'I've found my tribe,' still ring loudly in my mind when I think about the day I met Tony Gemignani and Laura Meyer in their basic dough class back in 2015," DeSousa says of the two WPC board members. "This group has so much combined experience that it was like being called up to play in the World Series when they asked me to join the team."

When Gemignani called with the invitation, DeSousa engaged him with banter typical of their relationship.

"He said, 'We want you.' And I said, 'For what?'" DeSousa recalls. "When he told me he wanted me on the team, I said, 'What do I have to do?', jokingly, and he said, 'Stop it! Be serious. You've already done it. That's why I'm calling you.' Being chosen by your peers for inclusion in the World Pizza Champions is like being called up to the All Star game—it's an incredible feeling of accomplishment. What can I say? I was humbled, truly humbled, to be a part of this team."

Antonio's Italian Bread

This is a simple, rustic bread that's ideal for hot sandwiches like hoagies. Slice and toast for appetizer spreads or dip it in extra-virgin olive oil—use it as you like. During Covid shutdowns, we baked hundreds and hundreds of these each week and put them outside where people could come grab what they needed. Bread is life!

Makes 933 grams; enough for 3 small, 2 medium, or 1 large loaf

PREFERENCES

Flour: King Arthur bread flour
(If you choose a malted flour, eliminate the sugar or honey in the recipe.)
Salt: fine sea salt

Video: Shaping Italian bread

INGREDIENTS	Amounts	Baker's Percent
high-protein, high-gluten flour	516 grams	
semolina flour	90 grams	
TOTAL FLOUR	*606 grams*	*100%*
room temperature water, at 65°F	264 grams	
warm water, at 100°F	120 grams	
TOTAL WATER	*384 grams*	*62%*
active dry yeast	5 grams	0.825%
granulated sugar or honey	12 grams	2%
salt	12 grams	2%
unsalted butter	14 grams	2.5%
semolina flour, for dusting		
oil or cooking spray to coat bowl		
sesame seeds, for sprinkling (optional)		

NOTE ON INGREDIENTS

It is best to have all ingredients weighed out and ready to go before starting—except warm water, which should be measured when ready to start.

TO MAKE THE DOUGH

1. Whisk together warm water, yeast and 4 grams of sugar in a small bowl until yeast has dissolved. Use a non-metallic bowl so the water remains warm. It may cool quickly and stop the yeast from activating if you don't. (I like to use a plastic cup for optimal heat retention.) Set aside for 5 minutes.

2. In the bowl of a stand mixer fitted with the dough hook attachment, add the room temperature water, the yeast-water mixture and both flours. Mix on the stir setting (speed 1) for 1 minute, then increase to low (speed 2) and mix until well combined, 3 to 4 minutes. With the mixer running, add in the remaining sugar and mix for two minutes, then add the salt and mix for 3 minutes more. During this mix, melt the butter over low heat or in a microwave, until just liquid, making sure it is not too hot. Continue mixing while drizzling in the butter. Once all is added, increase to medium-low (speed 3 or 4) and mix for about 3 minutes more until the dough ball looks smooth, but no more than 5 minutes.

3. Using a storage container or bowl that is twice the size of your dough, add a little olive oil and smear by hand inside the container. Cooking spray also

works well. Transfer the dough to the container or to a baking sheet, cover and let rest at room temperature until the dough has doubled, 1 to 2 hours. Refrigerate for 24 to 48 hours. Remember, longer fermentation times equal greater flavor!

TO SHAPE INTO LOAVES AND BAKE

1. Remove the dough from the refrigerator for 1½ hours before baking, but keep covered or in the container at room temperature (65°F to 68°F). The dough should come to room temperature before dividing and shaping, but should not be too warm. (Avoid setting the dough on any warm surfaces like the stovetop, which could parcook the dough.)

2. Watch Anthony's video on shaping Italian bread on page 222.

Dust the work surface with semolina flour. Using a spatula, loosen the dough from the baking sheet and turn top-side down onto the floured work surface. If your dough is in a storage container or bowl, just invert the container and let the dough ease out and onto the flour. The dough can be shaped as one large loaf or using a dough cutter/bench scraper, divided in half for 14-inch loaves or into thirds for 12-inch loaves.

Working with one piece of dough at a time, lightly dust the top with semolina. Using your fingertips, dimple the top of the dough, then gently pull the corners to make a more rectangular shape, using additional flour as needed.

Grab the top corners and fold in

as if making a paper airplane, but leave a gap between them. Take the top piece of the dough and roll it over once and push it down to secure. Continue to roll, stretching as you roll just a bit to create some tension. Once you are about halfway down, push it down again to seal. Now with each roll as you work towards the bottom, push down to seal. On the last roll, move the dough to be seam-side up. Using your fingertips, pinch the edge with the seam together to keep from unrolling and to make points at both ends.

Position the dough seam-side down and roll to make a nicely shaped loaf with slightly tapered ends. If this is a full recipe, roll to about 15-inches; half recipe, roll to 13-inches; or a third recipe, roll to 11-inches. Repeat the full shaping process with the remaining piece(s) of dough, as needed.

Lightly dust a peel (if baking on a stone or steel) or a pan with semolina flour. Lay the loaf (loaves) on top, leaving a couple inches between them. Cover to let proof until dough expands about 1½ times in size. When pressed with a fingertip, the indentation should stay. If it springs back quickly it needs more time. This will take about an hour.

3. Meanwhile, position an oven rack in the center of the oven with a baking steel or stone on top and preheat to 425°F. See note below On Creating Steam in a Home Oven, optional.

4. Uncover the dough. If adding sesame seeds, very lightly brush the dough with water or an egg wash (1 egg lightly beaten with a

little water to loosen), and sprinkle with the seeds. Score the top with three parallel lines on the diagonal with a paring knife or similarly small, sharp blade.

5. If using the steel or stone, slide the loaves on top. If baking on the pan, set the pan in the oven. Bake until golden brown, 15 to 25 minutes, depending on the size of the loaf. An instant read thermometer inserted in the center should read 205°F to 210°F.

Transfer to a cooling rack and let cool for at least 15 minutes, but preferably completely before cutting. Enjoy!

NOTE ON CREATING STEAM IN A HOME OVEN

When setting up the oven, position one rack in the center with a baking steel or stone on top and another on the lowest rung. Set a cast iron skillet on the lowest rung as the oven preheats. Have a small bowl of ice cubes near the stove when ready to bake. Load the bread onto the steel or stone. Quickly and carefully with a gloved hand, pull the skillet out just enough to add the ice, slide it back in, and close the oven door.

NOTE ON FREEZING UNUSED DOUGH

If you have any leftover dough, shape into a ball, and lightly coat with oil. Wrap the ball in plastic wrap or a resealable plastic bag and place in the freezer. Be sure to date and use it within 90 days. Defrost in the refrigerator overnight before using. Set on a semolina dusted peel or baking sheet, cover and let proof before baking.

MELISSA RICKMAN

OWNER AND EXECUTIVE CHEF, WHOLLY STROMBOLI
FORT LUPTON, COLORADO

WPC MEMBER SINCE 2019

Growing up, Melissa Rickman knew she was destined to build her own restaurant. She set those wheels in motion at a very early age: While her friends watched cartoons, Melissa was watching and learning from Emeril Lagasse and other celebrity chefs.

That restaurant idea manifested itself in Wholly Stromboli 15 years ago, but the path toward restaurant ownership was long and unclear. During her years working in healthcare and auto finance, she got an unexpected nudge from an executive who requested she cater a luncheon for her coworkers.

"It was a meatball hero bar, and everybody loved it," Rickman says. Better still, the boss looked past the food and saw Rickman's passion. "He said, 'You've got a fire in your belly! You have something bigger to do with your life.' That caught my attention."

Equally unexpected was a layoff from that job, which triggered her career change. "I had recently remarried and had two children I'd always provided for. I didn't want to come home that night without a job," Rickman recalls. "I considered a number of opportunities with local bakeries and pizzerias, but they weren't the right fit for me."

Well aware of his wife's career dreams, her husband, Eric, reminded Melissa about her desire for a restaurant centered on her mother's stromboli recipe. "Eric said, 'If you want to do this, let's do it! I'll support you and we'll make it happen,'" Rickman recalls. "In retrospect, those other opportunities were the perfect non-fit because it eventually led me to build my own restaurant."

Like a lot of first-time restaurant operators without much capital, Rickman served as Wholly Stromboli's general contractor, interior designer and tile setter. "There wasn't any aspect of that buildout that I didn't have my hands in." Once opened, she cooked, tended bar, kept the books and did most everything else. And, as if she wasn't busy enough, she traveled to pizza tradeshows and competed in baking competitions too.

"I've met so many great pizza makers and friends through those competitions, and I've learned so much from those people," she said. On her first trip to Pizza Expo in 2008, "That's when I realized there was a World Pizza Champions team, and I was awestruck!"

She told her husband she wanted to be a WPC team member someday, but those hopes remained unrealized for a decade. Over that time she built a reputation as a top-level competitor and an authoritative writer and speaker about pizza and how to operate a successful business. Eventually, the call came.

"I can't explain the excitement and honor I felt that day," she said. "The day I received my WPC chef's coat is a day I'll never forget."

The Original Stromboli

This recipe is dedicated in loving memory to my mom, Margo Hart-Langley. Thank you for teaching me to never give up, and how to love with all of my heart. When I was a kid, she made what we called The Original Stromboli. I knew one day this would be the foundation of my life's work.

GARLIC BUTTER SAUCE

This makes much more than needed for two stromboli, but it will last in an airtight container in the refrigerator for up to 2 weeks. Use any excess on the garlic knots or for garlic bread.

Makes 110 grams (about ½ cup)

110 grams melted unsalted butter or liquid butter substitute
8 grams dried, chopped garlic
2.5 grams granulated garlic
5 grams kosher salt, plus additional to taste
2.5 grams chopped flat leaf parsley

1. In a medium bowl, whisk all of the ingredients together until completely homogenous. Season with additional salt, to taste. Ingredients will settle to the bottom of the bowl, so always stir the sauce before applying it.

THE ORIGINAL STROMBOLI

Makes two 10-inch stromboli

Two 227 gram dough balls, preferably Basic Direct Dough by Laura Meyer (page 34), refrigerated for 2 days (If using Laura's recipe there will be a little left over to tie up a few garlic knots [see the note on page 231].)
12 to 14 slices Genoa salami (about 3-inches in diameter)
8 slices smoked provolone cheese
12 to 14 slices deli-style pepperoni (about 3-inches in diameter)
8 slices Muenster cheese
Marinara sauce, for serving

1. Preheat the oven to 550°F (or as hot as possible for your home oven). Spray a baking sheet with nonstick spray or brush with oil.

2. Lightly dust the work surface and the dough with flour. Using a rolling pin or dough sheeter, roll each dough ball into a 10-by 6-inch rectangle, about ¹⁄₁₆-inch thick.

3. Watch Melissa's video on assembling a stromboli.

Lay the rectangle with a long end facing you. As you layer the slices of meat and cheese on the stretched dough, do so without overlapping, but it is OK if the slices extend over the edge facing you slightly. Begin with a layer of salami, forming two rows of 3 slices each. (If there is a rounded corner, add an extra piece.) Follow similarly with a

Video: Assembling a stromboli

layer of provolone, then a layer of pepperoni, and finishing with a layer of Muenster.

4. Beginning with the edge closest to you and starting with the meat and cheese extending over, roll the stromboli away from you creating a tight, smooth roll, finishing seam side down. Gently rock the dough back and forth to form a seal. Don't worry about pressing the seam together; the oozing cheese is crispy and delicious and is how the stromboli got its name.

5. Gently tuck the ends of the stromboli under the roll without pulling or stretching the dough out too far. Using a pizza wheel or sharp knife, cut the stromboli in half on the diagonal. Repeat with the other piece of dough

and the remaining meats and cheeses.

6. Set the strombolis 4 inches apart on the baking sheet. Spread the halves so there are 2-inches between. Bake, rotating the pan 180 degrees midway through baking until golden brown and crispy, 10 to 15 minutes.

7. Remove from the oven to a cooling rack, leaving the stromboli on the pans. While the stromboli are still hot, stir the garlic butter sauce well to suspend garlic and spices evenly. Brush the stromboli, ensuring that some garlic and parsley stay on top. Serve with marinara sauce on the side for dipping.

NOTE ON MAKING GARLIC KNOTS

You can make garlic knots with the leftover dough in this recipe or on their own with a larger piece of dough.

Lightly dust the work surface and the dough with flour. Roll the dough to a rectangle about ⅛-inch thick. Cut into 6 even strips. Tie each strip into a knot, dusting off any excess flour. Set on a small baking sheet and bake in a 550˚F oven (or as hot as your oven will go) until golden brown, 8 to 10 minutes. Right out of the oven, transfer to a bowl and toss with a generous amount of the garlic butter.

PAUL CATALDO

OWNER, ANTONIO'S ITALIAN RISTORANTE
ELKHART, INDIANA

WPC MEMBER SINCE 2008

Stop into Antonio's Italian Ristorante on any given night and you'll be fed by owner Paul Cataldo, at least three-six of his children, one of his sisters and a smattering of cousins. Such has been the staff makeup since Cataldo's father and brother—Antonio and Bruno, respectively—opened the northern Indiana spot in 1979, the same year Cataldo began working for them at age 15.

"My family immigrated from Italy to Elkhart in 1966," Cataldo says. "Though my dad and brother worked in the mobile home industry, sales in that industry were always up and down. Like a lot of immigrants, they wanted to determine their own destiny, and that led them to open up Bruno's Pizza in 1979."

In 1995 Paul acquired the pizzeria and renamed it Antonio's Italian Ristorante. Serving food that reflected Cataldo's Italian heritage, Antonio's became a beloved standard in the city of 53,000. It also became Paul Cataldo's business, one to which he gave his all to feed and support his family.

Ever in pursuit of evolving to meet customer demands, Cataldo traveled to pizza-centric trade shows for a knowledge boost. Witnessing those events' pizza baking contests, he viewed his pizza the equal of any competitor and soon joined the fray. Victories in those challenges saw him travel to the World Pizza Championships in Salsomaggiore, Italy, where the World Pizza Champions had just announced their formation in 2004.

"I gotta say that I was kinda star-struck when I saw those guys wearing chef coats and sunglasses," Cataldo says. "Back then, the team only did acrobatics, no cooking."

As the team grew, its founders moved to add cooking competitors, and Cataldo's invitation to join the WPC soon followed. What the team got was a proven winner with a slew of wins in the toughest American competitions.

"When they said they wanted to build the culinary side, I said, 'I'm in!'" Cataldo recalls. "I was honored to become part of that fraternity."

The accumulated years of competitions and those that followed as a WPC member broadened Cataldo's vision for Antonio's.

"All of this made me want to bring something to Elkhart that hadn't been seen before," he says, referring to new pizza styles added to the menu. New items often lead Cataldo to share stories behind each menu upgrade. "Customers ask about those competitions and they like to hear those stories. It's good for Antonio's reputation and it builds relationships with our customers."

Vegas Fortuna Pizza

Of all his winning pizzas, the Vegas Fortuna is his most highly awarded: three firsts and one second. But don't let this delicious Roman pizza's creds intimidate you. The recipe, though, detailed, is a manageable effort for anyone willing to follow its instructions. Smart pizzeria operators create such recipes for easy execution on a busy shift, so in other words, it doesn't have to be complicated to be great. The Vegas Fortuna proves that.

Video: Combining semolina and high-protein, high-gluten flour and pushing out a Romana dough

ROMAN DOUGH

Makes 1.2 kilograms; enough for 2 Roman-style pizzas

For best results, use an instant-read thermometer to take the temperature of the ingredients and the dough throughout the mixing process.

PREFERENCES

High-protein, high-gluten flour: Bay State Artisan Flour or All Trumps High Protein Flour
Refined semolina flour: King Midas Extra Fancy Durum Flour
Salt: fine sea salt

500 grams cold water (see Note on Water Temperature)
550 grams high-protein, high-gluten flour
130 grams refined semolina flour
2.5 grams instant yeast
13 grams salt
7 grams extra-virgin olive oil
Vegetable oil spray

NOTE ON WATER TEMPERATURE

When making my Roman Dough, the goal is to have the final dough at 75°F after all of the mixing. The best way to achieve this is to start with ingredients at 65°F. If the flour is at room temperature (65°F to 68°F), start with water that is at 40°F.

1. In the bowl of a stand mixer fitted with the dough hook attachment, combine the water, high-protein, high-gluten flour, semolina flour and yeast on the stir setting (speed 1), about 3 minutes. With the mixer running, still on the stir setting (speed 1) gradually add the salt. Increase to medium-low (speed 3 or 4) and very slowly stream in the olive oil, about 4 minutes. Transfer the dough to a clean work surface. Cover with plastic wrap and let rest for 15 minutes.

2. Uncover the dough. Gently pat the dough as needed until more rectangular in shape. Now do a "letter-style fold" by starting at the top, folding the dough one-third of the way down on itself, then folding the bottom up over the first fold as if folding a letter. Repeat the letter-style fold from left to right. Lightly spray the dough with vegetable oil, cover with plastic wrap, and let rest 15 minutes.

3. Uncover, repeat the folds, lightly spray, cover, and let rest 15 minutes more. Repeat the previous step for a total of three folds, then transfer the dough to a large bowl. Cover the top of the bowl with plastic wrap and refrigerate 24 hours.

4. Lightly spray two bowls (deep enough to allow the dough to double in size without reaching the top) or a baking sheet.

5. Using a dough cutter/bench

scraper divide the dough in half into two 550 gram portions. Form into balls **(see Mike demonstrate on page 26)** and set in the bowls or on a baking sheet. Cover and refrigerate for at least 24 hours or up to 4 days.

POMODORO SAUCE

Makes 380 grams (1½ cups)

15 grams extra-virgin olive oil
1 garlic clove, minced
350 grams San Marzano or pear tomato puree
50 grams grated Parmigiano Reggiano cheese
1 basil leaf, minced

1. Place the olive oil in a skillet and warm over medium heat. Add the garlic and cook until fragrant and lightly brown, about 1 minute. Stir in the tomato puree and cook for 1 minute, stirring occasionally to keep from splattering. Mix in the Parmigiano Reggiano and basil and remove from the heat. Season with salt to taste. Set aside to cool. The sauce can be made up to 3 days ahead and refrigerated. Bring to room temperature before using.

HOT HONEY SAUSAGE

200 grams spicy bulk sausage (not in the casing)
100 grams honey (for extra-spicy use Mike's Hot Honey)
Crushed red pepper flakes, optional

1. Mix the sausage and honey together. If more heat is desired, add a pinch or two of the red pepper flakes. The sausage is ready to use now or can be refrigerated for up to 3 days.

VEGAS FORTUNA PIZZA

Makes one 14-inch pizza

PREFERENCES

Sausage: Fontanini bulk sausage
Pepperoni: Hormel Cup N' Crisp

140 grams spicy or mild Italian link sausage
One Roman Dough ball (see page 234)
50 grams high-protein, high-gluten flour
50 grams refined semolina flour
125 grams Pomodoro Sauce (see left)
115 grams shredded block mozzarella cheese
175 grams of Hot Honey Sausage
65 grams cup-and-char pepperoni (skin on)
15 gram piece Parmigiano-Reggiano cheese
Salt, optional

TO COOK THE LINK SAUSAGE (AT LEAST 4 HOURS IN ADVANCE OF MAKING THE PIZZA)

1. Heat a gas grill to medium to medium-high heat. Alternatively, the sausage can be browned under the broiler or in a skillet. Grill the sausage, turning to char on all sides, about 3 minutes per side. Transfer to a small baking sheet or plate and refrigerate for at least 4 hours or up to overnight to firm up. Slice the sausage on the diagonal into ⅛-inch-thick rounds.

TO MAKE THE PIZZA

1. Remove the dough from the refrigerator 1 to 2 hours before baking, but keep covered or in the container at room temperature (65°F to 68°F). The dough should come to room temperature before stretching and shaping, but should not be too warm. (Avoid setting the dough on any warm surfaces like the stovetop, which could parcook the dough.)

2. Position the oven racks in the upper and lower third of the oven with baking steels or stones on each. If using one steel or stone set on an oven rack positioned in the center of the oven. Preheat to 550°F (or as hot as possible for your home oven) for at least 30 minutes.

3. Watch Paul's video on combining semolina and high-protein, high-gluten flour and pushing out a Romana dough on page 234.

Combine the high-protein, high-gluten flour and the semolina flour. Make a small mound of the mixture and spread it out to make a base for the dough. Dust a peel as well.

4. Set the dough on the mixture. Gently, without stretching, press the dough to push out around the edges. Keep pressing on the dough until it is 10 to 12-inches across. Lift onto the back of your hands, allowing any excess flour to fall off, and stretch on your hands until it is a 14-inch round.

5. Set the dough on the peel and slide the pizza onto the top stone and bake until there is some light browning on the dough, 3 to 4 minutes. Remove from the oven and keep the par-cooked dough on the peel. Pop any bubbles that are very large with a fork.

6. Starting in the middle of the dough, spoon on the pizza sauce and spread, leaving a ¾-inch border from the dough's edge. Using a brush will help to reach all of the crevices made after parbaking. Sprinkle the shredded mozzarella evenly over the sauce. Arrange the grilled sausage evenly over the top. Pinch penny-sized pieces of the hot honey sausage evenly around the sausage slices, and then add the pepperoni.

7. Return the pizza to the top steel or stone and bake 4 to 5 minutes more or until the crust is further browned and the cheese is melted, but not browning. Lift the pizza with the peel, rotate it 180 degrees and transfer to the bottom steel. Bake until the bottom crust is a rich golden brown and the cheese is bubbling with some browning in spots, 5 to 7 minutes. If baking on one steel or stone, bake for 9 to 12 minutes, rotating the pizza 180 degrees once during the baking. If the crust does not have the desired doneness, return to the top steel or stone and broil just to brown, keeping a watchful eye so as not to burn.

8. Transfer the pizza to a cooling rack for 30 seconds to 1 minute. Slide onto a cutting board. Grate the Parmigiano Reggiano over the pizza, and then cut into 8 wedges. Season with salt to taste, as needed.

CARMINE TESTA

OWNER, CARMINE'S PIZZA FACTORY, JERSEY CITY, NEW JERSEY
OWNER, JERSEY PIZZA BOYS, AVENEL, NEW JERSEY

WPC MEMBER SINCE 2015

Carmine Testa didn't consider a career in the pizza business when working at his father's pizzeria at age 13. But by the time he graduated high school, he was all in: pizza making full time.

"It's what I knew and what I enjoyed," Testa says.

After operating a Pizza Villa location for five years, Testa opened his first independent venture, Carmine's Pizza Factory, in Jersey City, N.J. Building a brand of his own didn't come easily, especially for a married father of three. To give his wife a break from their three kids, he'd bring sons Nicholas and Michael to the pizzeria on weekends. They performed simple chores and learned about pizza via dad's instruction to "taste this, smell that, touch that, kind of like I learned growing up."

When he noticed the boys trying to spin pizza dough, he bought them rubber analogues they could use anywhere and anytime. When he noticed Michael had a knack for tossing, "I made a grainy video of him doing it at home and then an iMovie of it. I asked him, 'What's your favorite song?' and he said Maroon 5's 'Moves Like Jagger.' Fortunately, it was perfectly in sync with his routine."

For fun, he posted it on the internet, and the response was off the charts. Sometime later, Nicholas joined his brother in the routine and network television programs from all over America began requesting appearances. What became his sons' globetrotting performances didn't hurt Carmine's either.

But nothing changed Testa's life like taking his sons to the World Pizza Games at the 2013 Pizza Expo in Las Vegas. When their proud papa wasn't watching them perform, he was eyeing the pizza making competitions and planning to enter the next year.

"I'm the type of person to challenge myself to see how my pizza compares to others'," Testa says. In his first competition, he finished fourth, but a year later, he finished twenty-seventh. "Flying home, I'm thinking, 'It's over. I'm done. I'm gonna be a carpenter.'"

The setback was short lived. He took second in a 2019 competition in Naples, Italy, and grabbed first in category three weeks later at the North American Caputo Cup in Atlantic City.

Awards are great, Testa said, but his love of the business is what drives him to improve.

"Being the owner in your restaurant, you're the captain of that ship, good or bad, and I put a lot of pressure on myself to be really good," he said. "I've always loved the atmosphere of the restaurant business, interacting with customers and being a staple in the community."

But nothing, he added, topped his invitation to join the World Pizza Champions in 2015.

"It was validation for all these years and all the struggles," he says. "I'm among my peers who are the best of the best in this industry. That they acknowledged that I belonged with them . . . I can't fully tell you what that means to me."

Carmine's Pizza

Carmine's Pizza: simply named and simply great. This pizza reflects those I've made all my life and it speaks to a combination that people love: tomato sauce, cheeses, pepperoni, sausage and basil. This also won the 2019 Caputo Cup in Atlantic City, N.J. I'm proud of that.

Makes one 14-inch
New York-style pizza

PREFERENCES
salt: fine sea salt

198 grams peeled ground
    tomatoes
Sea salt
Freshly ground black pepper
Semolina flour, for dusting
One 350 gram ball of Tony
    Gemignani's Master Dough
    (page 26)
226 grams shredded whole milk
    block mozzarella cheese
55 grams pepperoni
160 grams sweet Italian sausage,
    pinched into 1½-inch long
    pieces (about 20)
50 grams ricotta cheese in a piping
    bag with a medium opening
5 basil leaves, cut into chiffonade
One 30 gram piece Parmigiano
    Reggiano cheese

1. Remove the dough from the refrigerator 1 to 2 hours before baking, but keep covered or in the container at room temperature (65°F to 68°F). The dough should come to room temperature before stretching and shaping, but should not be too warm. (Avoid setting the dough on any warm surfaces like the stovetop, which could parcook the dough.)

2. Position the oven racks in the upper and lower third of the oven with baking steels or stones on each. If using one steel or stone, set it on an oven rack positioned in the center of the oven. Preheat to 550°F (or as hot as possible for your home oven) for at least 30 minutes.

3. Spray or oil a 14-inch pizza screen and keep nearby. (This step can be skipped if the screen is well-seasoned.)

4. Season the ground tomatoes with salt and pepper. Put in a squeeze bottle with a wide tip.

5. Dust a smooth work surface

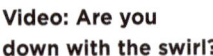

Video: Are you down with the swirl?

and the dough ball with just enough semolina to keep the dough from sticking. Push and stretch the dough out to a 14-inch round **(watch Joe's demonstration on page 264)**, and set on the pizza screen. Spread the mozzarella evenly across the dough.

Watch Carmine's video on page 240. Are you down with the swirl?

Starting in the center, squeeze the pizza sauce on top in a spiral pattern, stopping ½-inch from the dough's edge. Arrange the pepperoni equidistant on top and then pinch the sausage, putting it in the gaps between. (If your fingers stick to the sausage you can put them in a little olive oil.)

6. Slide the pizza onto the top steel and bake for 5 to 7 minutes or until the crust is beginning to brown and the cheese has melted, but isn't browning. Slide the pizza peel between the screen and the pizza, rotate it 180 degrees and transfer the pizza (off of the screen)to the bottom steel. Bake until the bottom crust is a rich golden brown and the cheese is bubbling with some browning in spots, 3 to 5 minutes. Baking time will vary depending on the max temperature of the oven. If baking on one steel or stone, bake for 8 to 12 minutes, rotating the pizza 180 degrees once during baking.

7. Transfer the pizza to a cutting board and cut into 8 wedges. Pipe four small dollops of ricotta onto each slice and sprinkle with the basil. Shave the Parmigiano Reggiano over the top.

ERIC VON HANSEN

DIRECTOR OF OPERATIONS, CALIENTE PIZZA & DRAFT HOUSE
PITTSBURGH, PENNSYLVANIA

WPC MEMBER SINCE 2018

Eric Von Hansen has made a name for himself by blending fine dining with humble pie. The hustling started at age 11, when he worked two jobs: After an afternoon paper route, he'd head to a pizzeria (where his mother made pasta, meatballs, bread and dough) to do odd jobs for the owner. The effort netted him $5 a week and a cheese pizza.

"I'd take that pizza and run to the woods and eat it all by myself," Von Hansen recalls. "I didn't know I'd become a chef, but I liked being around food and was eventually drawn to it."

He later earned a culinary arts degree at Community College of Allegheny County, and cooked in fine dining restaurants. He would log 25 years in that segment before his friend, WPC member Nick Bogacz, asked him to develop recipes for Caliente Pizza & Draft House. That opportunity grew into full-time employment as executive regional chef and director of operators for the seven-unit company.

Von Hansen and Bogacz forged a partnership to make Caliente an award winning pizzeria. Knowing—and wanting to maximize on—Von Hansen's chef skills, Bogacz nudged him toward pizza competitions. Without having ever entered a pizza contest before, Von Hansen signed up for the Pizza Expo Pan Pizza division in 2016—and won it.

"I thought that if I could get my grandmother's dough right and put my fine-dining flair into it, I'd have a shot," he says. "I was calling my mom and my Aunt Tootsie and asking, 'Do you know how Grandma did her dough?'"

Dubbed Quack Attack, Von Hansen's pizza used a Sicilian-style dough as the base for seared duck breast slices, a four-mushroom ragu, two cheeses, truffle oil and an arugula and cherry tomato garnish. It was awarded Best Pan Pizza at the 2016 International Pizza Challenge at Pizza Expo.

"I deconstructed a duck dish I'd done before and figured out how to use it on a pizza," he says, adding that a variation on that theme would pay off again at Pizza Expo 2018. "I won the best Non-Traditional division of that pizza using beer-braised hanger steak." Other titles followed, including a 2019 first place in the American Pizza division at the World Pizza Championships held in Parma, Italy.

Von Hansen credits WPC members for encouraging him to leverage his fine dining savvy to give his pizza a compelling uniqueness. "Being part of this team elevates your game," he says. "Everybody helps each other to get better at this. We're all family on this team."

The Quack Attack

You don't have to be a chef to execute the Quack Attack Pizza, but key to its success is having your ingredients prepared and organized. The pizza's prep is well detailed below, but knowing you're making—and then eating—a world champion pizza will motivate you to finish the job.

Video: Finishing a Quack Attack pizza

QUACK ATTACK DOUGH

Makes 1,272 grams; enough for two 12 by 12-inch Sicilian-style pizzas

PREFERENCES

Flour: All Trumps
Beer: a good IPA, but light beer will do
Salt: kosher salt

---

16 grams beer, at room temperature
4 grams active dry yeast
440 grams water, at 68°F
720 grams high-protein, high-gluten flour
10 grams salt
18 grams granulated sugar
28 grams olive oil, plus more for brushing

TO MAKE THE QUACK ATTACK DOUGH

1. In the bowl of a stand mixer whisk the beer and yeast together and let sit for 5 minutes.

2. Pour the water into the bowl and whisk again. Add the flour, salt and sugar, fit the mixer with the dough hook attachment, and mix on the stir setting (speed 1) until the dough comes together, 2 to 3 minutes. With the mixer running, slowly add the oil and mix 6 minutes more. If the dough is sticking to the sides of the bowl, stop the mixer and scrape dough from the sides of the bowl and continue mixing. Increase the speed to medium-low (speed 3 or 4) and mix until smooth, about 3 minutes more.

3. Transfer the dough to a clean bowl and brush the top of the dough with olive oil. Cover the bowl and let rest at room temperature for 10 minutes. Using a dough cutter/bench scraper divide the dough in half. Form into balls **(see Mike demonstrate on page 26)**. Transfer the balls to separate bowls or storage containers that will allow for them to double in size. Refrigerate for 24 hours.

TO PUSH OUT THE DOUGH

1. Remove from the refrigerator and allow the dough to warm to room temperature, approximately 1 hour. Lightly coat a 12-by-12-inch Sicilian-style pan with olive oil.

2. Lift the dough ball from the storage container and place in the prepared pan. Gently stretch the dough evenly outward from the center. Using your fingertips, start to push the dough to the edges of the pan. The dough will not reach the sides. It will probably fill the pan about two-thirds of the way before starting to shrink back. Cover the top of the pan and let rest for 30 minutes. Press the dough out to the edges. Cover the top of the pan and let proof at room temperature until about doubled in size, 1½ to 2 hours. While the dough is proofing, prepare the other ingredients.

MUSHROOM RAGU

Makes 335 grams (about 2 cups); enough for one 12-by-12-inch Sicilian-style pizza

- - - - - - - - - - - - - - - - - -

42 grams vegetable oil

28 grams minced shallot

14 grams minced garlic

112 grams sliced button mushrooms

112 grams sliced cremini mushrooms

112 grams sliced shiitake mushrooms

112 grams oyster mushrooms, chopped

5 grams kosher salt

3 grams finely ground black pepper

5 grams minced chives

3 grams roughly chopped thyme

10 grams black truffle oil, plus additional as needed

- - - - - - - - - - - - - - - - - -

1. In a large sauté pan or frying pan, heat the oil over medium-high to high heat until it is shimmering. Add the shallot and garlic, stirring frequently until softened and beginning to brown, 2 to 3 minutes. Add mushrooms and sauté, stirring occasionally until they release their water and begin to brown on the bottom, about 8 minutes. Continue cooking, scraping the bottom of the pan, and adjusting the heat as needed until the mushrooms are tender, a few minutes more. Season with the salt and pepper and transfer to a large mixing bowl to cool.

2. Mix in the chives, thyme and truffle oil. Let sit at room temperature until ready to use.

DUCK BREAST

Make one duck breast; enough for one 12-by-12-inch Sicilian-style pizza

- - - - - - - - - - - - - - - - - -

One duck breast, 225 to 300 grams

5 grams kosher salt

- - - - - - - - - - - - - - - - - -

1. Without cutting through to the meat, score the skin of the duck breast in a ½-inch cross-hatch pattern. This will help the fat to render and the skin to crisp. Pat the duck breast with paper towels to dry on all sides. Sprinkle generously on both sides with the salt and let sit at room temperature for 10 minutes.

2. Place the duck breast in the dry pan skin-side-down and set the pan over medium heat. (By not preheating the pan, the slow rising of the heat will maximize the fat rendering.) When the duck breast begins to cook, the skin at the top and bottom of the breast will contract, often leaving a small portion on the tail end that curls up and isn't in contact with the pan. Use tongs or a spatula to press down for 30 seconds to a minute for an even sear.

Adjusting the heat as needed, cook until the skin is golden brown, about 8 minutes in total on the skin side. Turn the breast over and reduce the heat to medium-low and cook on the second side until the duck breast reaches desired doneness, 3 to 4 minutes for medium-rare, 130°F to 135°F. Keep in mind that the duck breast will cook more on the pizza, so if you prefer, cook for less time to rare,

125°F. Another option is to cook the duck breast to your desired doneness and add the slices to the top of the pizza after it's baked. Transfer the duck breast to a plate and let rest for at least 10 minutes.

GARLIC BUTTER

Makes 45 grams (about 3 tablespoons)

- - - - - - - - - - - - - - - - - -

35 grams unsalted butter at room temperature

4 grams minced garlic

1.5 grams minced chives

1.5 grams minced parsley

1 grams onion powder

1 grams garlic powder

1 gram kosher salt

0.3 grams ground black pepper

- - - - - - - - - - - - - - - - - -

Blend all of the ingredients together and set aside at room temperature until ready to use.

THE QUACK ATTACK PIZZA

Makes one 12-by-12-inch Sicilian-style pizza

98 grams shredded Fontanella
  cow's milk cheese
98 grams shredded Parmesan
  cheese
Sliced Duck Breast (see page 248)
20 grams Garlic Butter, at room
  temperature (see page 248)
Mushroom Ragu (see page 248)
30 grams arugula
65 grams red and yellow grape
  tomatoes, cut into halves or
  quarters, depending on size
4 grams black truffle oil
28 gram piece Parmesan cheese

1. Position a rack in the center of the oven, preferably with a baking steel or stone and preheat to 500°F.

2. Combine the cheeses, then slice the duck breast thinly into 12 slices. Keep both nearby.

3. Lightly brush the dough with garlic butter covering completely, leaving no border. Spoon all of the mushroom ragu evenly over the dough. Arrange the duck breast slices over the ragu, and sprinkle the shredded cheese mixture over the top.

4. Set the pan in the oven. Bake, rotating the pan 180 degrees midway through baking, until the crust is crispy and golden brown and the center is cooked through, 20 to 25 minutes.

5. Transfer to a cooling rack and let sit for a few minutes for the cheese to set.

Carefully, using a large spatula, remove the pizza from the pan to a cutting board. Cut into 9 pieces.

6. Watch Eric's video on finishing the Quack Attack Pizza on page 246.

Top with the arugula and tomatoes, drizzle with the truffle oil, and grate the Parmesan cheese over the top.

DEREK SANCHEZ

OWNER, MIA MARCO'S PIZZA
SELMA, TEXAS

WPC MEMBER SINCE 2019

Derek Sanchez's pizza journey began like so many others inclined to love the craft: at the table of an Italian mother who fed him the classics of her homeland.

But that's also where his story's predictability ends. After decades of playing football, his desire to learn more about restoring damaged human bodies led him to earn a doctorate in physical therapy. Achieving the seven-year degree took a passion for research and a drive for evidence-based answers. He'd apply that combination of pragmatism and energy later to a pursuit of bread and pizza knowledge.

"My journey in pizza and bread science started 16 years ago after a visit to West Texas," Sanchez says. "Yeah, it's true: I had some of the best pizza I've ever had there. They do it really well there."

Sanchez's science-biased mind was drawn to the intricacies and chemistry behind dough making, and he read every article and egg-headed lab study he could to learn more. In addition to traveling to many pizzerias, he turned his home kitchen into a veritable lab for experiments. Those tests soon moved to his backyard and later to his garage, "where I got really serious," he says. Eventually, he turned pro with the launch of Mia Marco's Pizza food truck.

"I was driven by a passion to make the world's best pizza," he says. "We learned to serve customers from our food truck, and eventually that got us to a brick-and-mortar pizzeria."

Like so many looking for new ideas, Sanchez visited Pizza Expo in Las Vegas. When he caught a glimpse of its annual pizza battle, the longtime athlete felt his competitive juices flow again.

"I've been competing my whole life in sports . . . but this competition was different," he says. "I needed to have every scientific knowledge advantage I could to go against these incredible chefs."

His studies paid off with a Traditional division win at the 2017 North American Caputo Cup, and two firsts in 2019: the Caputo Cup Gluten Free-division and the Roman-Style Pizza division at Pizza Expo.

"After those wins, I was asked to join this great team of pizza masters, world-renowned and elite pizzaioli," Sanchez says of his World Pizza Champions invitation. Not ironically, part of Sanchez's appeal was his deep knowledge of dough making. "And now I'm teaching others dough science. It's an honor to do that."

Rita Bella

I thought it fitting to share the recipe to a world champion pizza, the Rita Bella. There's a lot of flavor going on in this sweet, spicy and savory pizza. The good news is it's easy to make and enjoy. I promise, it's worth making the time to do the apricot jam from scratch (recipe below). It's what makes this pizza one of a kind.

SPICY APRICOT JAM

Makes 585 grams (about 2 cups)

488 grams fresh apricots (If you can't find fresh, 400 grams of canned apricots [drained] is a suitable substitute.)

10 grams extra-virgin olive oil

350 grams granulated sugar

15 grams freshly squeezed-squeezed lime juice

1.5 grams crushed red pepper flakes

5 grams salted butter

1. Watch Derek's video on making apricot jam.

Peel and pit the apricots, then cut in half. Pour the oil, followed by the sugar in a heavy-bottomed, non-reactive saucepan and set over medium-high heat. Cook, stirring occasionally until the sugar liquifies and is clear, about 5 minutes. Add the apricots, and as the fruit begins to soften, use a potato masher to mash the fruit until the mixture is coarse and chunky. Continue to cook, adjusting the heat as needed, and stirring often until bubbly with a jam-like consistency, 15 to 20 minutes depending on the ripeness of the fruit.

2. Remove from the heat and stir in the lime juice, red pepper flakes, and butter (which stops the jam from foaming). Transfer to a storage container, preferably glass. (Dividing between two Mason Jars works well to have one for the pizza(s) and the other for another use.) Let cool completely at room temperature, then refrigerate for at least 24 hours or up to 1 week.

Video: Making apricot jam

RITA BELLA PIZZA

Makes one 14-inch New York-style pizza

One 370 gram ball of Tony Gemignani's Master Dough (page 26)

125 grams grated fontina cheese

75 grams fresh mozzarella, cut into cubes

4 strips peppered bacon, cut into 1-inch squares or 2-inch strips

Extra-virgin olive oil

4 canned apricots, optional

150 grams Spicy Apricot Jam (from page 252)

64 grams lightly toasted or candied pecans, coarsely chopped

3 grams grated Parmigiano-Reggiano cheese

6 basil leaves, chiffonade

10 grams arugula

1 lime

1. Remove the dough from the refrigerator 1 to 2 hours before baking, but keep covered or in the container at room temperature (65°F to 68°F). The dough should come to room temperature before stretching and shaping, but should not be too warm. (Avoid setting the dough on any warm surfaces like the stovetop, which could parcook the dough.)

2. Position the oven racks in the upper and lower third of the oven with baking steels or stones on each. Preheat to 525°F (or as hot as possible for your home oven) for at least 30 minutes. Alternatively, you can use one steel or stone set on an oven rack positioned in the center of the oven.

3. Dust a smooth work surface with just enough flour to keep the dough from sticking, then dust the dough and a peel. Push and stretch the dough out to a 14-inch round **(watch Joe's demonstration on page 264)**, and slide onto the peel.

4. Spread the fontina and mozzarella cheeses on the dough, leaving a 1-inch border from the dough's edge. Arrange the bacon evenly on top and drizzle with olive oil. Tear the apricots in half and place evenly on top.

5. Slide the pizza peel onto the top steel and bake for 5 to 7 minutes or until the crust is beginning to brown and the cheese has melted, but isn't browning. Lift the pizza with the peel, rotate it 180 degrees and transfer to the bottom steel. Bake until the bottom crust is a rich golden brown and the cheese is bubbling with some browning in spots, 3 to 5 minutes. If you prefer the bacon a bit more crisp, turn on the broiler for a minute or two, but keep a watchful eye so as not to burn. Alternatively, if baking on one steel or stone, bake for 8 to 12 minutes, rotating the pizza 180 degrees once during the baking. Baking time will vary depending on the max temperature of the oven.

6. While the pizza bakes, warm the apricot jam in a small saucepan or in a microwave-safe dish, until just warm to the touch. It should be thick, but spoonable. Add a little water if needed to loosen. (This is more jam than you will need, but especially if warming on the stovetop, it may be difficult to warm less easily.)

7. Remove the pizza from the oven to a cutting board or cooling rack. Spoon spicy apricot jam over the top, then sprinkle with pecans, Parmigiano-Reggiano, and basil. Arrange the arugula evenly on top and then grate the zest of half a lime over the top.

JEFFREY SMOKEVITCH

CO-FOUNDER AND CO-OWNER, BROWN DOG PIZZA AND
BLUE PAN PIZZA, TELLURIDE, DENVER AND GOLDEN, COLORADO

WPC MEMBER SINCE 2010

Jeffrey Smokevitch grew up eating Detroit-style pizza, the crispy, fluffy and chewy pan pizza standard named after the Motor City, his hometown. But that local delight wasn't enough to keep him there. After college, he headed to the San Juan Mountains to become a "professional ski bum" in Telluride, Colo., and funded his hobby-career on the slopes working nights at a local pizza shop. That job became an obsession with pizza that evolved into his first shop, Brown Dog Pizza, in 2004.

Figuring his pizza was good, but not as good as it could be, he enrolled at Tony Gemignani's International School of Pizza. There, he became fixated on perfecting the pizza of his youth.

"I'd been tirelessly testing different Detroit-style dough recipes for months," he says. When he rolled it onto the menu at Brown Dog, customers barely gave it a sniff. "The first day it was on the menu, I sold one."

When an opinionated customer suggested he spur sales by calling it Sicilian rather than Detroit, Smokevitch stood firm, declaring his hometown pride and its namesake product. Still, sales were slow.

Unable to convince customers to try it, Smokevitch sought to earn the Detroit pie some respect in pizza competitions. At the annual International Pizza Expo, the pie landed in second place overall— *by just 8/100ths of a point*. "Crushed" but believing "I had something good," he entered a second competition—and again finished second.

"This confirmed to me that the product was in place, but that I needed to execute better," Smokevitch says.

Finally, his pizza took first place in the pan division at Pizza Expo in 2013, and that hard-earned credibility got Brown Dog customers' buying it. When he backed that win with another at the World Pizza Championships in Parma, Italy (best pizza, North America category), Detroit-style became a strong seller in Telluride.

Unfortunately, its reputation didn't carry over to Blue Pan Pizza, a restaurant he co-founded in Denver in 2015. Being 6 hours from Telluride meant Smokevitch had to educate a new audience about Detroit-style pizza all over again.

"People made fun of Detroit, asking if we used motor oil instead of olive oil in our pans," he recalls. Smokevitch has since opened two more in Denver. "They'd also ask if we used bullets as toppings."

Undeterred, Smokevitch promoted the pizza with every victory, and more customers tried it. And like the judges at so many contests, Denver locals were highly impressed. Social media buzz helped attract shows such as "Diners, Drive-Ins and Dives" and "Barstool Pizza Review," which spurred Detroit-style sales to the point of running out. It was a problem he liked.

Smokevitch's professional success and dedication to Detroit-style pizza also caught the attention of the World Pizza Champions. Cooking and traveling with his peers has earned him lifelong friends.

"I regularly call them for advice, and they're the first people I seek out when I visit different cities," he says. "They have become the ultimate travel buddies and some of my best friends."

Campagna Detroit-Style Pizza

As an Italian by heritage and one of several pan-style pizza experts on the team, I created this Italian-American mashup dubbed Campagna. The toppings echo that sentiment, but from cheesy corner to cheesy corner, this is a great Detroit-style pizza that won first place, North America Division at the 2015 World Pizza Championships in Parma, Italy.

CAMPAGNA DOUGH

Makes 975 grams; enough for two 8-by-10-inch or one 10-by-14-inch Detroit-style pizza(s)

PREFERENCES

12% high-protein, high-gluten flour: King Arthur
14% high-protein, high-gluten flour: All Trumps
Salt: fine sea salt

PREFERMENT

75 grams 12% high-protein, high-gluten flour
51 grams water
0.3 grams instant yeast

DOUGH

500 grams 14% high-protein, high-gluten flour
1.5 grams instant yeast
10 grams low diastatic malt powder
320 grams water
9 grams sea salt
10 grams extra-virgin olive oil

MAKE THE PREFERMENT

1. Combine the bread flour and yeast in the bowl of a stand mixer fitted with the whisk attachment. Whisk thoroughly on the stir setting (speed 1). With the mixer running, still on the stir setting (speed 1) slowly add the water, and then mix for 3 minutes.

2. Remove from the mixer to a plastic container with a lid or cover with plastic and let ferment at room temperature 12 to 17 hours. After fermentation, you can store the preferment in the refrigerator for up to 5 days.

MAKE THE DOUGH

1. In the bowl of a stand mixer fitted with the dough hook attachment, combine the flour, yeast and malt on the stir setting (speed 1). Slowly, with the mixer running, add the water and mix for 3 minutes. With the mixer still running, add the preferment, then increase the speed to low (speed 2) and mix until combined, 3 to 4 minutes. Stream in the salt and mix 2 minutes more. Lastly, slowly add the oil and mix until incorporated, 2 to 3 minutes.

2. Remove the dough from the mixer and form into a large ball. Transfer the dough to a baking sheet or storage container that is twice the size of the dough. Cover and refrigerate for 24 to 48 hours.

Video: Pressing dough in the pan for a Detroit-style pizza

PARBAKE
CAMPAGNA DOUGH

5 grams vegetable shortening
30 grams aged white cheddar,
  shredded

PUSH OUT AND
PARBAKE DOUGH

1. Position a rack in the center of the oven, preferably with a baking steel or stone and preheat to 450°F.

2. Watch Jeff's video on pressing dough in the pan for a Detroit-style pizza on page 258.

Using a paper towel or a brush, coat the sides and bottom of an 8-by-10-inch Detroit-style pizza pan with the shortening. Lift the cold dough from the baking sheet or storage container and place top-side up on the work surface, maintaining the dough's rectangular shape. Lay into the pan and press lightly. Cover and let rest for 20 minutes.

3. Grab the top corners of the dough and stretch the dough and press into the corners with your thumbs. Repeat with the bottom corners of the dough, pressing them into the bottom corners of the pan. Lightly press the edges of the dough so that it reaches the side walls of the pan. Gently press over the surface of the dough to make sure the dough is even in the pan. Cover and let proof until it has doubled in size, 1 to 2 hours.

4. Meanwhile, position a rack in the center of the oven, preferably with a baking steel or stone and preheat to 450°F (or as hot as possible for your home oven) for at least 30 minutes.

5. Spread the shredded white cheddar around the edges, sidewalls and corners of the pan. Set the pan in the oven and bake, rotating the pan 180 degrees midway through baking, until golden brown, 9 to 11 minutes.

6. Transfer to a cooling rack. Cool for 15 minutes if continuing to topping and baking.

If making ahead, cool the parbaked dough completely on the rack. The dough is OK at room temperature for up to 4 hours. For longer storage, wrap completely in plastic wrap and refrigerate for up to 1 day or double wrap (with foil, another layer of plastic wrap, or in a bag) and freeze for up to 2 weeks.

CAMPAGNA GARLIC
CREAM SAUCE

Makes 142 grams (about ⅔ cup)

28 grams unsalted butter
85 grams cream cheese
43 grams dry white wine
0.3 gram dried oregano
0.3 gram granulated garlic

1. In a medium saucepan, melt the butter and cream cheese over medium-low heat, while whisking continuously. Increase the heat to medium and add the wine, oregano, and granulated garlic. Continue to cook until the mixture is combined and smooth, about 3 minutes. Remove from the heat and let sit at room temperature to cool. It can be refrigerated to cool down more quickly.

CAMPAGNA PIZZA

Makes one 8-by-10-inch Detroit-style pizza

30 grams Campagna Garlic Cream Sauce (see page 260)

100 grams shredded whole milk block mozzarella

40 grams shredded brick cheese

8 slices cooked thick-cut applewood smoked bacon, broken in half

70 grams Roasted Cherry Tomatoes (page 271)

30 grams sun-dried tomatoes

20 grams arugula

Extra-virgin olive oil

½ lemon

Salt

5 grams shaved Parmigiano Reggiano cheese

16 grams fior di latte (fresh mozzarella) cut into ¼-inch cubes

5 grams Balsamic Glaze (page 270)

1. If the dough has been made in advance, position an oven rack in the center of the oven, preferably with a baking steel or stone and preheat to 550°F (or as hot as possible for your home oven) for at least 30 minutes.

2. Spread the sauce over the top of the parbaked dough, leaving a ½-inch border from the dough's edge. Combine the cheeses. Spread about 60 percent of the cheese blend around the side-walls and corners of the pan, and then use the remaining cheese to spread evenly across the remainder of the dough. Arrange the bacon on top.

3. Set the pan in the oven. Bake until the cheese is bubbling, about 6 minutes, then remove from the oven. Add roasted cherry tomatoes and sun dried tomatoes. Return the pizza to the oven until the cheese on top is evenly browned, 6 to 8 minutes.

4. Transfer to a cooling rack. Carefully, using a large spatula, scrape the browned cheese edges from the sides of the pan. Remove the pizza from the pan to the cooling rack or onto a pizza peel. Check the bottom of the crust. If needed, to crisp the bottom, return to the steel, stone or directly to the oven rack for 1 to 2 minutes more. Transfer the pizza to a cooling rack for 3 to 5 minutes to cool slightly while keeping the bottom crisp.

5. Move the pizza to a cutting board and cut into 4 slices. Next, toss the arugula with a drizzle of olive oil and lemon juice, and season with a pinch of salt. Arrange evenly on the slices and then sprinkle with the Parmigiano Reggiano. Place the mozzarella cubes across the top and drizzle the balsamic glaze in a zig-zag pattern over the top.

JOE CARLUCCI

OWNER, VALENTINA'S PIZZERIA & WINE BAR
MADISON, ALABAMA

WPC CO-FOUNDING MEMBER SINCE 2004

Joe Carlucci's love of Italian food began at age 7, while watching his grandmother make her homemade tomato sauce. Eight years later, he found himself working in the dish room of his brother-in-law's pizzeria.

"That's how my career started: doing dishes, which was glamorous, right?" says Carlucci, a Bronx, New York, native who was raised in nearby Carmel. He did not stay on dishes long. As Carlucci says, "Anybody who knows me knows I like to talk. So, trust me when I say I enjoyed the move to the front counter. That's where I could see people and talk."

After graduating high school, Carlucci gave college a try before figuring out the quiet confines of the classroom wasn't for him. That is when he signed on to help a restaurateur open a new restaurant, where he was assigned to the sauté station. Instantly, he knew he was in the right spot. "I have ADHD, so needing to do nine things at once was attractive to me," Carlucci says. "I liked the energy of the kitchen, the pace. I like to work, and you work in a kitchen."

At age 23, he opened his first pizzeria, Carlucci's, nearby in Connecticut. Running his own place was pressure packed but, he says, "I felt like I was doing what I was supposed to be doing." Still, he needed help, and he began reaching out to more experienced operators for advice. That search led him to Tony Gemignani. The two met in 2000 at the US Pizza Trials in Ohio. It was a brief meeting, but one that made a lasting impression.

"Tony wasn't as well known as he'd become later, but I could tell he was knowledgeable, and he was generous with his time," Carlucci recalls. "Some time after, I called him with a question about dough, and he remembered exactly who I was. I knew he was busy, but he was so helpful. Trust me, he's not normal; he's unusual in that way."

As the relationship grew, Gemignani encouraged Carlucci to begin competing as a pizza maker and a dough acrobat. Even though he'd done neither. "I liked competition. I liked putting my food out there against the other guys'. And like most pizza guys, I already liked tossing and spinning dough," says Carlucci. This love for pizza would eventually turn into the co-founding of the World Pizza Champions.

Fast forward a few years later to 2004, when Carlucci recalls the group making a "Here we are!" splash witnessed around the industry. "I'm sure people thought we were just out for the show as pizza acrobats, but we knew we'd eventually start competing in baking," he says. "We believed our pizzas were as good as others in the world and we proved it."

Carlucci and the other founders are still growing their own craft, but have now also turned their focus to mentoring their peers and growing the industry even more. "I'm always learning about the craft, and my passion is to raise my personal bar," Carlucci says. "But I really enjoy helping others be as good as me—if not better—in the craft. It's really what this team is about."

The Award Winner

The name of this pizza says it all: a winner! This pizza reflects my journey of competing and of really understanding what the judges want. I have learned that sometimes less is more. Do not overcomplicate things. When you use fewer ingredients, but you prepare them perfectly, it creates an amazing pizza. This pizza is simple, but it is packed full of flavor and is delicious.

NEW YORK-STYLE DOUGH BY JOE CARLUCCI

Makes 825 grams dough; enough for 2 New York-style pizzas

PREFERENCES

Salt: kosher

POOLISH

125 grams water
0.1 grams active dry yeast
125 grams high-protein, high-gluten flour

DOUGH

0.4 grams active dry yeast
175 grams water
325 grams high-protein, high-gluten flour
50 grams Caputo Nuvola Super Flour
15 grams salt
10 grams extra-virgin olive oil

TO MAKE THE POOLISH

1. The night before making the dough, pour the water into a small airtight storage container. Stir in the yeast until dissolved. Add the flour and mix with your fingers until combined. Cover and let sit at room temperature for 12 hours.

TO MAKE THE DOUGH

1. Add water and poolish to the stand mixer fitted with the dough hook attachment. Make sure to scrape the bottom and sides of the poolish container to get any mixture that might be stuck. Use your fingertips to break up the poolish in the water. Mix on stir (speed 1) until the mixture is combined.

2. Once combined add all flours and the yeast to the mixer and mix on low (speed 2) until combined, roughly 2 minutes. Cover the top of the bowl and let rest for 30 minutes.

3. After resting, add the salt to the bowl and mix on low (speed 2) for 2 minutes. Stop the mixer and pull the dough away from the hook, leaving a 1-inch space around the hook where there is no dough. Pour the olive oil into that gap. Mix on low (speed 2) until smooth, about 3 minutes.

4. Transfer the dough to the work surface and using a dough cutter/bench scraper, divide in half, scaling to two 400 gram pieces or the weights needed for the desired recipe. Form into balls **(see Mike demonstrate on page 26)** and set in a large storage container that will allow the dough to expand or on a lightly oiled baking sheet. Cover and refrigerate for at least 24 hours and up to 3 days.

If making your own pizza, remove the containers from the refrigerator, keeping the dough covered. Let warm at room temperature (65 to 68°F) for 1 to 2 hours. (Avoid setting the dough on any warm surfaces like the stovetop, which could parcook the dough.)

Video: Pushing out a dough into a round for a New York-style pizza

JOE'S PIZZA SAUCE

Makes 720 grams (about 3 cups)

....

PREFERENCES

Tomatoes: Cento
Salt: kosher

....

One 14-ounce (411-grams) can
  whole, peeled tomatoes,
  preferably San Marzano
One 14-ounce (411-grams) can
  ground or crushed tomatoes
2 grams minced garlic
1 gram chiffonade basil
5 grams grated Parmigiano
  Reggiano cheese
2 to 8 grams granulated sugar
0.7 grams salt
0.7 grams freshly ground black
  pepper

....

1. Mill the tomatoes in a food
mill fitted with a medium-large
die. Alternatively, the tomatoes can be crushed by hand or
pulsed in a food processor. Stir
in the remaining ingredients,
starting with the smallest
amount of sugar. Add additional
sugar to reach desired sweetness. Transfer to a storage
container and refrigerate until
ready to use, up to 1 week. Bring
to room temperature before
using.

THE AWARD WINNER

Makes one 14-inch New York-style pizza

One 400 gram ball New York-Style Dough by Joe Carlucci (page 264)

113 grams Joe's Pizza Sauce (see page 266)

142 grams shredded part-skim or whole milk block mozzarella

57 grams sweet Italian sausage, pinched into penny-sized pieces

57 grams peppadew peppers (if whole, cut or torn into pieces)

142 grams fior di latte, pinched into thumb-sized pieces

10 grams grated Grana Padano cheese

1. Remove the dough from the refrigerator 1 to 2 hours before baking, but keep covered or in the container at room temperature (65°F to 68°F). The dough should come to room temperature before stretching and shaping, but should not be too warm. (Avoid setting the dough on any warm surfaces like the stovetop, which could parcook the dough.)

2. Position the oven racks in the upper and lower third of the oven with baking steels or stones on each. If using one steel or stone, set on an oven rack positioned in the center of the oven. Preheat to 550°F (or as hot as possible for your home oven) for at least 30 minutes.

3. Watch Joe's video on pushing out a dough into a round for a New York-style pizza on page 264.

Dust a smooth work surface with just enough flour to keep the dough from sticking, then dust the dough and a peel. Turn the dough over, lightly dusting on both sides, gently flatten the dough into a disc. Place your left hand (or reverse to right if you are left handed) against the dough's edge. Lay your other hand on the top of the dough, about ½-inch from the edge. Use your fingers to press the dough towards the other hand, creating a walled edge, while turning the disc. Once you have done this all the way around the dough round, there will be a cylindrical edge around the full disc.

Flip the dough over and repeat the same pressing and rotating to create a cylinder on that side. Using the fingertips of both hands, press across the center of the dough outward, stopping short of the edges to flatten slightly.

Pick up the dough with both hands, maintaining the cylindrical edge. To begin to stretch, pull the dough up with your right hand as it moves through the fingers of the left, working your way around the circle.

Now, let the dough drape over loosely clenched fists. Slowly rotate the dough on your fists, maintaining the edge until it is stretched to a 14-inch diameter. Lay dough on the work surface and sprinkle the underside with flour as needed.

4. Starting in the middle of the dough, spoon on the pizza sauce and spread to the inside of the raised edge. Sprinkle the shredded mozzarella evenly over the sauce. Arrange the sausage and peppers evenly over the top, followed by the *fior di latte*. Slide onto the peel.

5. Slide the pizza onto the top steel and bake for 5 to 7 minutes or until the crust is beginning to brown and the cheese has melted, but isn't browning. Lift the pizza with the peel, rotate it 180 degrees and transfer to the bottom steel. Bake until the bottom crust is a rich golden brown and the cheese is bubbling with some browning in spots, 3 to 5 minutes. If baking on one steel or stone, bake for 8 to 12 minutes, rotating the pizza 180 degrees once during baking. Baking time will vary depending on the max temperature of the oven.

6. Transfer the pizza to a cooling rack to cool for 30 seconds to 1 minute. Slide onto a cutting board, add the Grana Padano and cut into 8 wedges.

SHARED
RECIPES

In our effort to streamline and standardize this book, our pizza makers shared specific recipes that can be used on a wide range of recipes featured in these pages. Following is a collection of those shared recipes.

CLARIFIED BUTTER

140 grams (¾ cup)

- -

225 grams unsalted butter, cut into
    pieces

- -

Put the butter in a small saucepan and melt over low heat,
without stirring. Skim off the
foam that has risen to the top
and discard. Carefully pour the
clear yellow liquid into a container leaving the milky white
layer behind.

Store in a covered container
in the refrigerator for up to 2
weeks or refrigerate for up to 1
month.

BALSAMIC GLAZE

Makes 95 to 126 grams
(¼ to ⅓ cup)

Balsamic glaze can quickly turn
from sweet and syrupy to burnt
and sticky, so keep a watchful eye.
If you have a simmer burner on
your stove and/or a diffuser that
will help

- -

255 grams (1 cup) balsamic
    vinegar

- -

Pour the vinegar into a small,
heavy saucepan and set over
medium heat. As soon as there
is steam rising, reduce the heat
to the lowest setting, keeping
the vinegar just below a simmer.
Cook until it has reduced and
thickened, about 10 minutes.
(Cooking time can vary considerably depending on the heat
level.)

Remove from the heat and let
cool. Store in a covered container at room temperature for
up to 1 month.

LEMON OIL

Makes 110 grams (½ cup)

Be sure the lemon is clean and
scrubbed well before peeling
the strips.

- -

Strips of lemon zest from half
    lemon, about 10 g
110 grams extra-virgin olive oil

- -

Put the lemon zest strips and
the oil in a small saucepan.

Set over medium heat and
cook until warm, but with no
bubbling, adjusting the heat as
needed for 10 minutes. Remove from the heat and let the
lemon zest strips cool at room
temperature the oil to infuse.
Discard the lemon zest strips,
letting any oil drip off and
remain in the pan. Transfer to a
clean jar or storage container.

Refrigerate for up to 1 week.
Before using, remove from
refrigerator and allow to warm
to room temperature.

ROASTED GARLIC AND GARLIC OIL

Makes about 50 grams of roasted garlic and 275 grams (1¼ cups) garlic oil

50 grams of whole garlic cloves, peeled
Extra-virgin olive oil, about 300 grams

METHOD ONE

Put the garlic cloves in a saucepan and add enough oil to cover. Set over medium heat and heat just until the oil simmers. Adjust the heat as needed to maintain. Continue to cook just until the cloves are tender and begin to brown, about 20 minutes.

Remove from heat and let the cloves cool at room temperature in the oil. Refrigerate for up to 1 week. Let come to room temperature before using.

Note on Roasted Garlic and Garlic Oil with Herbs for Pete Tolman: For 50 grams of garlic cloves, add 5 grams each dried thyme and rosemary to the oil and simmer until the garlic cloves are soft and spreadable with the back of a spoon.

METHOD TWO

Preheat the oven to 350°F.

Put the garlic in a small, but deep baking dish. Add enough oil to cover. Cover the top with foil. Make a small hole for oil to escape from. Roast in the oven until the cloves are tender, about 45 minutes. Let the cloves cool in the oil for at least 30 minutes before using.

NOTE ON ROASTED GARLIC FOR SAMMY MANDELL

Sprinkle the garlic and oil with salt and pepper before covering and roasting.

TO MAKE GARLIC PURÉE (FOR EITHER METHOD)

Simply mash the roasted garlic cloves until completely smooth. If making a large batch this can be done in a food processor.

ROASTED CHERRY TOMATOES

Makes 100 grams (about ¾ cup)

184 grams cherry tomatoes
56 grams olive oil
Finely ground salt and pepper to taste
Dried oregano, optional

Preheat the oven to 400°F.

Toss tomatoes in olive oil, season with salt and pepper and spread on a small baking sheet. Roast in the oven until tomato skins begin to brown and split, about 20 minutes. If using the oregano, toss in for the final 5 minutes of roasting. Remove from the oven and cool.

The roasted cherry tomatoes can be refrigerated for up to 3 days.

A WORLD RECORD PIZZA PARTY

On the chilly morning of January 21, 2023, Andolini's Pizzeria was abuzz at the unusual hour of 8:30 a.m.—30 minutes before staff arrived to start prepping and almost three hours before opening to customers. The dining room of the Tulsa, Okla., pizzeria was that morning's meeting space for two dozen members of the World Pizza Champions (WPC) preparing to create a pizza party that afternoon.

But not just any pizza party. This effort would see the team create and coordinate the world's largest pizza party and make the Guinness World Book of Records, an effort months in the making. The team's president, Mike Bausch, was describing the day ahead but barely skimming the details of all that had to happen to make the record theirs.

"This is a logistical nightmare, and we have a lot—*a lot*—to do," Bausch said in a friendly but forceful tone. "The good news is, so far, planning has gone scarily well, and I think we're in good shape."

What lay before the team was the daunting challenge of making roughly 1,000 pizzas: 850 for the Guinness effort, and 150 more for a post-event party.

For the record attempt, a mix of cheese, sausage and pepperoni pizzas had to be baked, sliced, boxed, delivered and handed out to 3,400 people—*in less than two hours*. Accomplishing such a feat required a skilled pizza team that could make and bake such a great number of pizzas at multiple sites then bring them to a single point of distribution.

"So, pay attention to your WhatsApp today," Bausch admonished the group. "There are a lot of moving parts and a lot of people involved, and we need everyone to work together."

Just days before, Bausch learned that a similar world record attempt conducted in Los Angeles fell short of the current record of 1,046, set in 2019 by a group of Italian pizza makers. Bausch acknowledged that the WPC's goal of more than tripling the record was "ambitious and a little crazy," but he saw it as "doable. We have the professionals and we have Tulsa," he said. Since the idea was shared with Tulsans months before, feedback had been positive, giving Bausch confidence that locals would cooperate with the rules, which state:

Participants in the record attempt must eat two regular-sized slices of pizza and drink a small bottle of water in 15 minutes or less. That quarter hour would begin at 5:45 p.m. and end at exactly 6 p.m. Any portions left unfinished at 6 p.m. would be disqualified from the total, and if unfinished portions amounted to 10 percent of the total number of participants, the record attempt also would be DQ'd.

Just getting 3,400 people inside the Reynolds Center (home to Tulsa University's Golden Hurricane basketball teams) and seated by 5:30 p.m. would be no mean feat, Bausch said. "We also had to keep them from eating the pizza before the official start time."

Ensuring no one violated that rule, each of 68 volunteer proctors would closely monitor groups of 50 participants. If the pizza police caught anyone cracking the pizza tin or breaking the seal on a water bottle before allowed, he or she was out.

"Guinness is serious about its rules," Bausch stressed. "A lot of things could go wrong in this attempt, and that was a big concern for us."

HELPED BY A HUB-AND-SPOKE SYSTEM

Andolini's Pizza shops are part of Andolini's Worldwide, a multi-concept restaurant company created and operated by Bausch and his brother, Jim Bausch. The hub of their restaurant system is a production commissary where large-batch products such as dough, sauce and gelato are made fresh and distributed to its restaurants. (Commissary production reduces store-level labor costs while boosting quality and consistency across a system of restaurants.) Among the wide array of large-scale production machines, there are multiple high-volume pizza ovens. Logically, most of the pizza would be produced at the commissary while other units in the Andolini's system would share the load.

"That Mike and Jim let the team use their facilities was ideal," said Scott Anthony, WPC member and board treasurer. "A large pizza chain could utilize multiple stores in a single market to make that many pizzas at once, but whether they could get them all to the location, organize and follow the rules of a contest like this is another matter."

Each tin of pizza was marked with a C, P or S to designate that the slices within bore cheese, pepperoni or sausage. Stashed in hot bags, all were delivered to the arena by 5 p.m. When the doors opened, the participant queue stretched about 20 yards from the arena. Ten minutes later, the line's end extended beyond the portico and out of sight.

Inside, WPC members, spouses, friends and local volunteers hurried to hand participants boxes of pizza, bottled water and instruction sheets to read and follow once seated. The frenetic process resembled a disaster-relief operation.

Over the arena's PA system came a steady stream of reminders on how to follow the rules and avoid disqualification. Team members entertained the crowd with acrobatic dough tossing as music thumped in the background. When at the mic, Bausch talked about the contest's big goal of raising funds for the Make-A-Wish Foundation's Tulsa chapter and interviewed previous wish recipients. Later, Scott Anthony, a WPC member and board treasurer, talked about the team's partnership with Make-A-Wish.

"In 2021, we decided to partner with an organization for which we could be a benefactor" across multiple markets, Anthony said. Of the group's choice to support Make-A-Wish, he added, "Kids love pizza, pizza makers love sharing their craft and making food for people, and we raise funds in the process, which is good for everyone."

As the minutes wound down toward the pizza party's start, event sponsors stepped up to make check presentations: $5,000 from distributor Roma Performance Foodservice and $10,000 from Hormel Foods, a food products manufacturer. Participants seated in the arena also made on-the-spot donations to Make-A-Wish Tulsa using a QR code on their instruction sheets. Their spontaneous generosity came to $6,045.

Upstairs at the front entrance, stragglers dashed inside, grabbed their pizza and water and rushed toward any open seats. As Bausch called out, "Two minutes left until we start!" a father, holding his toddler daughter under one arm, nabbed his goodies, looked hurriedly left and right before spying an empty seat near the floor. At 5:45, when Bausch gave the signal to eat and drink, mass mastication ensued and the near-deafening din softened temporarily.

Bausch ticked off the remaining minutes to eat before calling a hard stop 15 minutes later. Proctors instructed participants to hold up their empty pizza tins and water bottles, counted participants in each row, then gave directions to attend a post-event pizza feast. There, the success or failure announcement would be made. As participants left they heard the surprise news that Tulsa University was doubling all donations.

"We set a goal to raise $15,000, so we were surprised to eventually hit $40,000," Anthony said. The final total, including on-the-spot donations, was $42,090. "In the 20 years I've worked with Make-A-Wish, I'd never seen things fall into place like that."

Still, the big question remained: Would Guinness approve the attempt as a record? Bausch admitted fretting over multiple ways the goal could have been thwarted.

"Bad weather could have thrown a wrench in this if people didn't show up," he began. "And what if too many didn't listen to the rules or not enough proctors showed up? I know

it's only two pieces of pizza, but what if a kid couldn't complete his on time?"

Eventually, Michael Empric, an adjudicator with Guinness World Records, worked his way through the dense throng at the post-event party. Grabbing Bausch and positioning him before three TV news camera crews, Empric began his announcement: "You had a total of . . . (dramatic pause) 3,357! It's the new Guinness World record!"

Amid the flurry of hugs, handshakes and high-fives, some toasted the record with water, others with beer and soft drinks. Later that night, the Bausch brothers invited the team to Prossimo, their Italian fine dining restaurant, for the real party.

Several days after the event, Bausch was asked why world record pizza party attempts in major restaurant towns such as Chicago and New York failed to beat the Italian mark or even come close to the WPC's bar. He pointed to an unexpected intangible that allowed it to work at such a scale.

"The answer is Tulsa, this town, these people," Bausch said. "Chicago, New York and L.A. all failed with people."

He explained that a city the size of Tulsa (population 412,000) sees something like the Guinness record as an opportunity to do something together. People in larger cities probably don't regard such an event or a fundraiser with similar importance.

"Here we are, little ol' Tulsa, Tulsa U, the little pizza team that could and Andolini's coming together to do this," Bausch said. "A city of this size gets into it, and the next thing you know, we've tripled the previous record, and we're funding eight kids' Make-A-Wishes."

Not surprisingly, he's most proud that two dozen WPC members were able to participate. That typically meant pitching in either by staying after their photoshoots for this book or by arriving well before their turns before the camera. Just more evidence of people making sacrifices to ensure it all comes together, he said.

"Something should have gone wrong that day, but by late in the afternoon when it hadn't, I was basically freaking out," Bausch said. "That's this team at work. We have a group of people who are so good at what they do that they can pull off events at this high a level and make it look easy. They are amazing people."

ACKNOWLEDGMENTS

The World Pizza Champions wants to acknowledge and thank our sponsors and so many others who helped move this book from concept to reality. They include but are not limited to:

Roma and Performance Food Group (namely Joe Davi, Fred Dallas, Fred Sanelli, Karen Marshall, Linda Bott, Giulio Binetti, Mark Duffy, Susan Highly, Tim Horton, Mike Bennett, Toby Bronson and Spencer Irons), for providing food for our photo shoot.

Lloyd Pans, especially Tracy Rennaker, for providing tools we needed for our photo shoot.

Palazzolo Cheese Hog (namely Scott Fahey and Dana Palazzolo) for providing such a quality machine that makes this industry more manageable and cost-effective.

Gi.Metal (namely Silvia Bartolini, Francesca Fedi, Irene Matteini and Francesca Cristini), which provided tools for our photo shoot.

Larry Nicholson and his fantastic Pizza Master ovens, which we used in many of our recipes.

Ooni Ovens (namely Ed Choi, Ana Diaz and Arthur Bovino) for providing multiple outdoor, home-use ovens used to demonstrate wood- and gas-fired pizza baking.

Hormel Foods (namely Anthony Panichelli and Colby Strilaeff) for providing food for our photo shoot and being such a generous donor to our Make-A-Wish fundraiser.

Perfect Crust (namely Eric Bam and Nick Hedlund) for supporting the World Pizza Champions for so many years.

Allen Kieny from Roto-Flex Ovens, whose high-volume ovens were essential to the production of so many pizzas for the Guinness event.

The team at Pizza Today magazine and Pizza Expo, the tradeshow that brings us together every year. Special thanks to Pete Lachapelle, Bill Oakley, Jeremy White, Josh Keown, and Denise Greer.

A massive thank you to our incredible food photographer, Valerie Wei-Haas, whose eye for photography is unparalleled. Additionally, the food styling of Lisa Riley and their prowess as a team to capture the essence of the Champion's creations. Their talent is what made this book what it is.

The book team and everyone at Brilliant Media including Derek George, Mary Horn, Sam McCracken, and Meghan McCracken, who helped get this book across the finish line.

Recipe tester Amy Volger and WPC board member, Laura Meyer, for making and checking every recipe in this book—a massive undertaking.

Steve Coomes, for all his work piecing together the interviews and recipes.

Jane Borden for her acumen and professionalism to help in this process

The University of Tulsa and Rumbledrum, for their support and documentation of The

Guinness Book record win. That event wouldn't have been possible without their cooperation.

Everyone at sixPR, including Samantha Powell, Marni Fernandez, and Sheila Moore along with Jennifer Riddle of Stinabee, who promoted the Guinness event. Danny Boy O'Connor and the team at the Outsiders Museum who welcomed and hosted the WPC team while in Tulsa. All of the good people of KMOD and Iheart Radio of Tulsa who pulled out all the stops to make sure everyone in Tulsa knew about the Guinness event, Corbin Pierce, Michael Berger, Genny Cram, Lindsey Adank and DC.

The many staff members at Andolini's Pizzeria and Prossimo Ristorante who helped immensely in the execution of the Guinness event. Just as importantly, they patiently accommodated our pizza team, photographers, and food stylists as we invaded their working spaces for a week-long photo shoot.

The Make-A-Wish® Foundation, a longtime charitable partner of the World Pizza Champions. A special thanks to Jane Rohweder, Erin Nantois, Lacy Bair, and Sheila Marcello Victor for allowing us to help enrich the lives of children through our passion for pizza.

The Pursuit of Pizza
Recipes from the World Pizza Champions
First Edition

Photography by Valerie Wei-Haas
Book Design by Derek George

ISBN
PB: 978-1-962341-99-8
HC: 978-1-962341-98-1
PREMIUM PB: 978-1-962341-31-8
PREMIUM HC: 978-1-962341-24-0
EBOOK: 978-1-962341-26-4